"A compassionate and practical work. Margo Requarth's counsel is sound, wise, and sensitive. Anyone who works with grieving children—especially those grieving a suicide—needs this book."

—**Kenneth J. Doka, Ph.D.,** Professor, The College of New Rochelle
Senior Consultant, The Hospice Foundation of America

* * * * *

"An extraordinary, beautifully written resource that provides effective and appropriate interventions to empower children and help them heal."

—**Doreen Cammarata, M.S., L.M.H.C.**
Author, *Someone I Love Died by Suicide:*
A Story for Child Survivors and Those Who Care for Them

* * * * *

"Anyone who knows a child whose parent has died by suicide, or anyone with a loved one who has experience with suicide, will find this remarkable book of great comfort. I wish it had been available for those around me when my own mother attempted suicide (unsuccessfully) when I was seventeen. Using the most powerful and compelling medium possible—the voices of children themselves—Requarth brings this crucial issue to the fore, courageously battling the stigma that adds to the suffering of those who are already deeply wounded. This book should be required reading for mental health professionals."

—**Lori Hope,** Managing Editor, Bay Area Business Woman News
Author, *Help Me Live: 20 Things People with Cancer*
Want You to Know

* * * * *

"A comprehensive guide and resource, written with compassion, understanding and expertise."

—**Richard Lieberman, M.A., N.C.S.P.**
Coordinator, Los Angeles Unified School District
Suicide Prevention Unit

"Writing from her 'survivor's heart,' Margo Requarth makes a significant contribution to the difficult and often misunderstood task of guiding child survivors through the minefield of suicide grief. I recommend this book for parents, caregivers, support group facilitators, educators, clergy, friends and mental health professionals."
—Mary Pat McMahon
Chair, National Survivor Council—American Foundation
for Suicide Prevention
AFSP National Board of Directors

* * * * *

"*After a Parent's Suicide* is a sensitive and insightful blueprint for surviving the suicide of a parent with the least amount of damage. It describes everything I wish had been done for me after my mom's suicide."
—Dara Berger
Filmmaker, *A Secret Best Not Kept*

* * * * *

"Literate and wise—this book offers beautifully organized answers to the haunting questions that nobody ever wanted to hear."
—Eve R. Meyer, M.S.W., M.H.S.A.
Executive Director, San Francisco Suicide Prevention

AFTER A PARENT'S SUICIDE

Helping Children Heal

───────────────◆───────────────

AFTER A PARENT'S SUICIDE

Helping Children Heal

◆

MARGO REQUARTH, M.A., M.F.T.

HEALING HEARTS PRESS • SEBASTOPOL CA

The names and identifying characteristics of some of the people whose
stories are told in this book have been changed to protect their privacy.

The ideas, suggestions, and opinions presented in this book are not intended
to replace the direct services of a trained health-care professional. All matters
regarding your health require medical supervision. Neither the author nor
the publisher can be held responsible for any adverse effects resulting directly
or indirectly from information contained in this book.

Grateful acknowledgement is made for permission to print:
"I Need to Move Real Slow Right Now" by Sharon Lukert.

Second Edition
Designed by Laurie Binder, Schmidt Creative

Cover painting "Me and Daddy Holding Hands Looking at the Sky"
by Emily Rose Horstman, age 5

Library of Congress Cataloging-in-Publication Data
Requarth, Margo.
After a parent's suicide : helping children heal / by Margo Requarth.
p. cm.
Includes bibliographical references.
ISBN 0-9777468-0-1
LCCN 2006920803
1. Children and death–Psychological aspects. 2. Suicide.
3. Suicide victims–Family relationships. 4. Bereavement in children.
5. Bereavement in adolescence. 6. Grief in children. 7. Grief in adolescence.
8. Children–Counseling of. 9. Teenagers–Counseling of.
I. Title.
BF723.D3R47 2006
155.937
CIP

HEALING HEARTS PRESS

PO Box 1843, Sebastopol, CA 95473 • www.HealingHeartsPress.com

This book is dedicated
to my mothers...

Dolores
who couldn't stay

Jane
who raised me

Mary Elizabeth
who believed in me

and

to my husband,
Mike
who cherishes me

Acknowledgments

Writing this book has been a profoundly meaningful experience. As part of my research, I have spent time over the past five years with nearly two hundred children, teens, and adults who have been deeply impacted by the suicide of a loved one. I am grateful to them for their willingness to share their stories of love and loss. They have been my greatest teachers, and they continue to inspire me.

I would also like to thank my editor, Andrew Hidas, whose guidance has been invaluable. I have very much appreciated his skill, encouragement, and sense of humor.

Thanks also to my colleagues and friends in the mental health field who have shared their wisdom and expertise, particularly psychiatrist Dr. Brent Cox, who reviewed the chapter on depression and bipolar illness in children. I am grateful for his generosity and reassurance that the medical information I have included is accurate.

I would also like to thank my dear friends and family members who read parts of the book and encouraged me every step of the way.

A special thank you to my husband, Mike, for his love, patience and continued support. He always said I would write a children's book, although he thought it would be a storybook for young children. Little did either of us know that this book would emerge.

Finally, an appreciation for the experience of writing the book itself, which has been the most challenging endeavor I have ever taken on (other than raising two sons!). The research, writing and reflecting has allowed me to heal another corner of my heart, honor the memory of my mother, and more deeply appreciate the simple fact of being alive.

"In the midst of winter,
I finally learned that there was in me an invincible summer."
—Albert Camus, *Summer*

This book is for anyone wishing to support a child who has lost a parent to suicide. While I have written it primarily for parents whose partners have died by suicide, other adults—family members, friends, teachers and mental health professionals may also find it of use.

Although I was very young when my mother took her life, I remember the anguish and confusion that followed her death. My world turned upside down. I learned that relationships are impermanent and can end at any time. I became more acquainted with uncertainty and isolation. But I also learned over time that I had courage and grit, the ability not only to survive, but also to flourish. I discovered that healing is a process—gradual and slow, with bouts of sadness, anxiety and anger. I learned about the resilience of the human spirit and the strength of my own.

I have been a psychotherapist working with families for over thirty years. As a bereavement counselor for children and teens, I have learned much about the specific concerns and feelings that young people experience around the deaths of special people in their lives. And as a group facilitator for adult survivors of suicide, I have also accompanied many parents who must confront the monumental task of coping with their own grief while trying to support their children at the same time. For all of you, I have written this book.

Losing a loved one to suicide is a life-changing event that will necessitate grief work over the long haul. There are no shortcuts. But there are pathways through the despair, confusion and fear that follow. Your children will be impacted, but you need not fear irreparable damage. If given love, support and guidance, most children who have suffered such a trauma can become compassionate, successful adults.

In the following chapters I offer information to help you support your children and take care of yourself during this difficult time. Here, you will read stories of children at various ages who experienced the suicide of a parent, as well as adults who look back on their experience as children. Their perspectives allow us to understand in more intimate detail what goes on in the hearts and minds of child survivors.

For our purposes here, I define "child" as anyone from infancy through eighteen. Because every child is unique, I want to emphasize that each child's response—emotional, cognitive, physical, behavioral and spiritual—will be different. Our task is to acknowledge each individual spirit and personality. While we have learned there are general guidelines that can assist us in helping young people survive emotionally through this tumultuous time, we must remember to let each bereaved child teach us what grief is like for him or her—and to respond accordingly.

In addition to interviewing child and adult survivors of parental suicide, I have also included information from surviving spouses. Death by suicide has a profound impact on the entire family constellation, including a surviving spouse who may have been estranged or divorced from the parent who dies.

Finding the energy to sort through the myriad feelings that result from the suicide of a co-parent or partner is extremely difficult. Often, surviving parents feel beleaguered by the overwhelming task of supporting their children while they are grieving themselves. This book includes concrete suggestions to help you care for your children as you find your way through the labyrinth of suicide grief.

I wish you well. I know the journey will be difficult and fraught with questions, worries and doubt. You will be faced with the responsibility of being a single parent. You are likely to encounter despair and anger in the days ahead, but you will also come to experience joy and closeness. You will discover the unique spirit and creative coping mechanisms that we all have within us. Your faith will be tested and, hopefully, you will learn about asking for help and taking care of yourself.

It is important to remember that all children experience adversity as they grow up. Not every bump in the road that they encounter will be related to the trauma of a parent's suicide. As parents, we can't explain why bad things happen to good people. We don't know why some people languish as they try to cope with life events while others thrive. What we can offer our children is the support and love they will need to eventually come to terms with their loss. We can decide to give them every opportunity to have their grief acknowledged, along with the encouragement to express their feelings. We can try to be there for them in whatever way they need, within the limitations of our own personality and situation, and we can learn to step back when they have to go it on their own. Even though the way through this grieving journey looks arduous, the resilience of the human spirit is truly incredible. Please know and take comfort in the thought that you and your children will find your way.

CONTENTS

CHAPTER ONE

My Story

"The world breaks everyone and
afterwards many are stronger at the broken places."
—Ernest Hemingway, *A Farewell to Arms*

When I was nine months old, my mother, six months pregnant with my brother, contracted a rare mystery illness. Characterized by severe headaches and frequent vomiting, it was finally diagnosed as "Valley Fever," a type of dust-borne meningitis. Though not fatal, it was terribly debilitating. When my brother was born, my mother was draped in sterile dressing and not allowed to touch him. Nearly three years later, worn down by her illness, two young children, and a husband who did not know how to support her, she gave up. Or at least that is what I have surmised these many years later. She may also have suffered from depression. In 1951, the year she died, not much was known about treating clinical depression, but I remember she was often in bed, wan and dispirited.

Her name was Dolores. She lived in the corner bedroom, a pale yellow room with white shades, which were often drawn. The room always felt infused with sunlight, a kind of golden hue that was comforting to me, not dark or fearful. I remember her sitting up in bed, dark hair softly curling at her shoulders, cheeks flushed, her long, gentle fingers resting on the quilted comforter. She wore an ivory-colored nightgown, ruffled at the neck with long sleeves. To me she looked beautiful, but somehow fragile, engulfed in the bedcovers, propped up against the antique mahogany headboard. With my straight chin-length hair, dark bangs, and solemn face, I would hold my teddy bear and stand hesitantly in the doorway, watching her. Sometimes I would climb in bed with her to snuggle.

On July 24, 1951—two months before I turned four—she shot herself. I was later told that she survived for nearly two more weeks, but I was never to see my mother again after that fateful day. According to the memorial book I have from her funeral, she died on August 7, at the age of thirty-seven years, nine months and three days. I don't remember it happening: I wasn't there at the time. It wasn't until years later that I discovered she had taken her own life.

My maternal grandmother told me that my mother was a fighter—stubborn and tenacious when her mind was set on a goal. The morning she died she told my grandma that she was going to fight the depression she felt. She wasn't going to let her illness get the best of her. By the afternoon she must have changed her mind.

She drove her car to her good friend's home. The neighbors later recalled a pretty, dark-haired woman pacing on the front steps, knocking on the door, apparently agitated that no one was home. They said she sat on the porch, smoked several cigarettes and seemed to be having a serious conversation with herself. Supposedly, my mother didn't smoke, but maybe in those moments before taking her life she reverted to an old habit, or maybe she was a closet smoker. Whatever the case, several stubbed-out cigarettes were found in the flowerbed below that porch.

She then went to a motel owned by friends of hers. She knew a gun was kept in the drawer under the cash register. When she arrived they were tending to some errands in the back office. She removed the gun and shot herself in the head, right there in the motel lobby.

I later learned that during the two weeks my mother survived before succumbing to her injuries, she asked incessantly for those around her to turn on the lights, not knowing she had blinded herself. She didn't know who she was or why the world was so dark. My father, lost soul that he was, told her angrily that there was light all around and that all of the rest of those in the room could see. She was bewildered until she died.

Of course, metaphorically speaking, we all felt enveloped by darkness during that time, and I knew that the uncertainty I had lived with during her illness was sure to continue. No one knew how to explain to a four-year-old that her mommy had chosen to leave her, so I was told that she had gone on vacation. All of her personal belongings, all pictures of her, were put away. She just disappeared.

I remember some months later hearing my dad on the phone talking about taking my younger brother and me on a vacation to Lake Tahoe. I was terrified, thinking of vacation as a place you went to and never came back.

Eventually I realized she had died. I don't remember the moment that I figured this out or was told, but somehow I got the impression a terminal illness had claimed her. Even her obituary, which began, "Dolores Montgomery, age 37, died after a lengthy illness...." implied she had succumbed to illness rather than by her own hand.

The months following her death are a blur. I remember Mrs. Henderson, a big, buxom woman who cared for us while my father was working. He was a highway patrolman and kept odd hours. Sometimes he would wake up my brother and me in the middle of the night to talk with us when he got home from work. He would sit us on the counter and we'd have cereal together. Did we talk about missing Mommy? I don't remember, but I don't think so—talking about the hard stuff was not my father's forte. Fifty years ago people believed talking to children about the subject of death, and particularly suicide, should be avoided. My brother and I soon learned not to ask questions.

But we were angry and confused. I remember taking scissors to the plastic shower curtain and trying to make paper dolls. We drew with crayons on the white walls of our bedroom. My brother cried at night, bouncing his head on his pillow, calling "Mama" over and over. This routine became a source of self-comfort as he put himself to sleep in the years following her death.

I have been told that after she died I would often imitate my mother's illness, which was characterized by sudden waves of nausea and quick trips to the bathroom. Apparently, I would announce I had to "bop," my word for vomit, and run to the bathroom, bend over the toilet and try to be sick. Years later when I was pregnant with my first child and incessantly nauseous, I saw a surgeon trained in hypnosis to try and control the morning sickness that plagued me all times of the day. During my one session with him I remembered those childhood attempts to throw up, and realized that for many years I had carried with me a sense of being somehow responsible for her death. If only I had been a better little girl, if only I didn't fight with my brother, if only I hadn't played that game where if you "step on a crack, you'll break your mother's back" that summer day on the sidewalk. Responsibility for our loved one's suicide runs deep, often below the surface of our logic, in a place we cannot reach. It is a place we must eventually visit to forgive ourselves for somehow not being enough to make our parent want to stay with us, to make her want to continue living.

About eighteen months after my mother died, my father remarried. Jane, a widow with children aged thirteen and eighteen, moved into our tiny tract home, a big adjustment for all of us. My brother and I didn't understand the notion of having a stepmother, stepbrother or stepsister, equating the idea to the story of Cinderella. We wondered what was in store for us. We were shy about having a new mother, and we didn't know what to call her. In the beginning she was Jane, and then at some later point she became Mom.

Jane was a good mother who did right by us, took care of our basic needs for food, shelter and clothing, made sure I took ballet and joined a Girl Scout troop. In some ways, she was more comfortable with children than my father, since her kids were older and she had raised them alone for five years following the death of her husband. She wasn't as protective as my dad, often going to bat for me and convincing him to give me more freedom. Unfortunately, she developed an alcohol problem, and so did my dad. By the time I was twelve I felt that I was often parenting them, acting as a mediator during their many alcohol-induced arguments. They eventually divorced when I was in my early twenties. Jane had tried her best to care for me, and for that I will always be grateful. But we were never close in the way I envisioned mothers and daughters to be. I don't remember sitting in her lap as a little girl and being comforted. I missed that. I missed hearing stories from my mother about her earlier life, about my own birth and infancy. Every child loves those moments. Instead, I was left with vague feelings of longing for a mother who couldn't stay.

Everything was so secretive in those years that I learned not to ask questions. I thus felt isolated and alone, disconnected from other members of my family. The price of this isolation was high, as I was estranged from my brother for many years. Only recently have we begun to repair our relationship. Perhaps we could have depended on each other at the time, but we didn't know how. I had learned that I must comfort myself and find my own answers.

I had so many questions. I remember the green closet in my father's and stepmother's bedroom. High above the closet were cabinets, containing my mother's things that I was told I was too young to see. Much later I learned that her china and silverware were stored there, but I would often sneak in that room as a young child and gaze up at those cupboards, wondering if she was behind those cabinet doors. I had been to the mausoleum where she was buried. My brother and I had wandered around, listening to our voices echo in the marble building. I was fascinated by the flower arrangements in their silver vases, attached to the smooth stone walls. High up on the wall of flowers was a plaque with her name on it. How could she fit behind that wall? Where was she really?

I didn't find out the truth of my mother's death until I was eighteen, during an argument between my father and stepmother. I was shocked by this revelation, hurt and angry. I had always felt a little different from the other kids. I didn't know anyone else whose mother had died, but I had seemingly adjusted, appearing successful on the outside, even though I felt separate and uncertain on the inside. Although I had considerable needs for control and predictability, I had also developed keen powers of observation and a strong sense of independence.

Because of the stigma of suicide and the needs of the adults in my circle to protect me (and ultimately, themselves) from the trauma of her death, no one ever talked about my mother. That is the part of her death, other than the fact that she killed herself, that has impacted me the most. I never really knew who she was. Did she love nature like I do? Was she a reader or a writer? What did she want to be "when she grew up?" I tried at various points in my life to piece together bits of information about her, but I never got to ask her the questions many of us have as we are growing up. I wanted to know her perspective about girl stuff—periods and babies and falling in love. As I grew older and began to look inward, I wondered how she felt about God and what her belief systems were. And, always: What did she think and feel about me? Finally, the key question: Why? Why did she leave me?

A child who loses a parent grieves over time. For me, there have been milestones and significant life events—birthdays, graduations, marriage, motherhood, and coping with the death of someone else dear to me—when I have found myself longing for my mother. My task has become learning over time to dig deep and find my own inner resources. This has been no simple task, but a lifelong journey, complete with moments of profound anguish as well as great self-discovery.

Like many suicide survivors, there were times when I defined myself by my loss, feeling incomplete and disconnected. In my twenties I entered individual psychotherapy and began to acknowledge the deep hole I felt inside. I found myself confronting obstacles like doubt and the inability to trust others and myself. I was often cautious, armoring myself against feeling so vulnerable again. While I didn't take excessive risks like some survivors, I struggled with self-esteem issues as I tried to come to terms with my loss. I discovered that other forces had shaped me as well. Growing up in a family with an alcoholic father and an alcoholic stepmother had taken its toll. As I explored who I was, I found myself drawn towards psychology as a career path, and I eventually became a psychotherapist myself.

I am blessed with a curious personality and a resilient core. I have also been blessed by having a loving primary relationship with a man who has given me lots of emotional space, encouraged my self-exploration, and stood by me through my struggles with learning to love myself. We have raised two sons and have a good life. I remember the doubt I felt as I wondered if I would ever see the other side of abandonment. But here I am.

I have learned that there are no short cuts to grief, that in order to grow into ourselves and develop to our fullest, we have to give grief its rein. In the case of a parent's suicide, we must be supported as children and given love, information and positive role models who express grief appropriately. We also need encouragement to feel our feelings. While this was not my experience growing up, I have been able to find my way as an adult. At fifty-eight, I can now say that I no longer define myself as the little child whose mother killed herself, but as a resilient adult with my own unique essence.

I believe that each of us has the potential to transcend our despair and fear. Poets, philosophers, and healers have long said that the pathway is love. Who am I to argue?

Every day that we live after a loss or traumatic experience, there is the possibility of growing stronger inside. We have the opportunity to open ourselves to love—loving others, loving animals, loving life, loving whatever activity or belief system brings us joy. Being committed to something big or small, serving others and, despite the difficulties we all encounter, choosing to view the universe as a friendly place—that is both the challenge and the reward.

That is my story. Your children will develop their own. With your love and support, they will embark on their own healing journeys. May they grow in wisdom and compassion as they come to terms with their loss. May they become "stronger at those broken places."

CHAPTER TWO

How Could This Happen?

"Perhaps what finally makes him kill himself is not the firmness of his resolve, but the unbearable quality of his anguish."
—A. ALVAREZ, *THE SAVAGE GOD: A STUDY OF SUICIDE*

Every sixteen minutes someone in the United States dies by suicide. This translates to more than thirty thousand deaths every year. According to the American Foundation for Suicide Prevention (AFSP), women dominate the half million or more Americans who attempt suicide, but men, by a four-to-one margin, are more likely to end their lives.

Men aged twenty-five to sixty-five account for more than half the suicide deaths in our country. For women, the rate of suicide peaks between the ages of forty and fifty-four, declining after age sixty.

These statistics are probably understated, since some people are able to make their deaths look like accidents, and sometimes those left behind prefer to believe their loved ones died accidentally. Medical and law enforcement agencies may also under-report or cite other causes of death in an attempt to spare surviving families the embarrassment and shame of a stigmatized death.

According to AFSP, every suicide dramatically affects at least six other people in the victim's intimate circle. These people are often referred to as "suicide survivors," a term used for someone who is grieving the suicide of a loved one. (It does not mean someone who has attempted suicide and survived.)

Although statisticians have not been able to determine the number of survivors who are children and teens, we know that many young people face the anguish of this painful loss every year.

Suicide is not just an American problem. The United Nations

World Health Organization's (WHO) most recent estimates suggest that the annual number of suicides worldwide is about one million, more than deaths by war and homicide combined.

Why?

The "Why?" question haunts survivors. This death does not make sense. Those who are grieving a loved one's suicide have an unrelenting need to reconstruct every detail prior to the death. Inevitably, every such reconstruction returns again and again to "Why?" The notion of choice and the ostensible purposefulness of the act are always in the shadows, contributing another layer of grief and confusion to the raw pain felt by those left behind.

It is impossible for anyone to completely understand the suicide victim's thought process. We have learned enough in recent decades, however, to surmise that he probably wasn't choosing death as much as choosing an end to what he perceived as unbearable pain, a pain that reduced his world to a solitary alternative. He no longer believed that he could improve his life situation or be happy and loved. He may have felt that his presence was such a burden for his family that ending his life would actually help them. He probably experienced a sort of psychic pain or soul sadness that was excruciating, constant, and endless.

This torment inside the suicidal brain is not something we can fully understand. As William Styron explains in his work, *Darkness Visible: A Memoir of Madness*, "Incomprehension has usually been due not to a failure of sympathy but to the basic inability of healthy people to imagine a form of torment so alien to everyday experience." He goes on to say, "For myself, the pain is most closely connected to drowning or suffocation—but even these images are off the mark."

While we don't know exactly what makes a person lose hope or believe he has run out of options, we are learning from neuroscience and genetic research that the brain is an organ, just like the heart or lungs, and it can become diseased or impaired. Research on suicide over the last thirty years indicates that there are measurable chemical imbalances and changes in the brain chemistry of people who attempt and/or carry out suicide. While a tendency toward suicide doesn't appear to be inherited, many researchers believe that people can inherit a genetic predisposition to certain illnesses or mood disorders such as major depression, bipolar illness or schizophrenia, just as they do to heart disease or diabetes. If not effectively treated, these disorders can in turn make a person vulnerable to suicide—particularly when combined with other factors such as an impulsive personality, loss of economic stability, legal troubles, deep shame, or physical illness.

Risk factors for suicide also include substance or alcohol abuse, a family history of mental illness, relationship upheavals, access to firearms, previous suicide attempts, exposure to the suicidal behavior of others, and a family history of violence, including sexual abuse.

Over sixty percent of people who die by suicide suffer from major depression. If one includes alcoholics who are depressed, the figure rises to over seventy-five percent. Depression affects more than nineteen million Americans over the age of eighteen every year, and about fifteen percent of the population will suffer from clinical depression at some point during their lifetime. While most people who suffer from depression do not take their lives, thirty percent of all clinically depressed patients attempt suicide, and half of them ultimately prevail.[1]

Coping with the anguish and sadness following the suicide of a loved one is always challenging, even when we think the suicide can be "understood." My friend Sandra's ninety-two-year-old father-in-law took his life after his home was destroyed by the 2004 Florida hurricane. He was in failing health and fearful that a stroke might render him helpless. He missed his wife who had died nine years earlier. Despite Sandra and her husband's sincere wish that he move in with them, he decided to end his life. Somehow, even though we deeply grieve a death like this and regret that anyone would suffer such despair, many of us might say we understand his feelings.

In the state of Oregon, voters decided in 1997 that a terminally ill person with less than six months to live can choose to end his life legally if certain conditions apply. Reasonable people may differ on the law, but the specter of terminal illness at least provides a context for our understanding of the person's motivation. It is far more difficult, however, to comprehend how a parent with young children and no terminal illness would "choose" to die.

Is Suicide a Choice?

Based on my years of experience in the field, I am inclined to believe that the word "choice" trivializes death by suicide.

It is not uncommon to hear people refer to suicide as a "cowardly" or even a "courageous" act. Such judgments largely miss the point, reinforcing the notion that a person who ends his life feels he has a choice. Most people who end their lives are not brave, cowardly, hostile, amoral, selfish or mean, but simply lost, desperately alone, and without hope. In most situations, they are suffering from incapacitating mental illness. While choice may be a factor in circumstances involving a terminal illness, applying it to all suicides perpetuates the stigma that still surrounds the act, adversely impacting survivors and creating an environment that makes it difficult for those suffering from biochemical illnesses to receive help.

For this reason I use the phrases "died by suicide" or "carried out suicide" rather than "committed suicide." The word "commit" implies a rational "choice" that modern knowledge tells us is frequently absent in suicides. In addition, I have learned that many people feel further stigmatized by negative associations of the word "commit," as if their loved one has "committed" a crime. While history shows us that the Massachusetts Puritans and other early American colonists did view those who killed themselves as criminals and sinners, fortunately today's thinking has shifted as scientists continue to study the human brain.

Confronting the Stigma

Having a parent die is extremely stressful for a child, regardless of the nature of the death, but death by suicide complicates grieving. Survivors are faced with a sudden, often violent, and in most cases unexpected death, a death that may be viewed as the ultimate abandonment. As you support your children, you are also likely to face the stigma of suicide death yourself, a death that our culture often judges, sensationalizes, or ignores.

Researchers have concluded that people who lose a loved one to suicide experience more psychological distress following a suicide than from death by natural causes.[2] They are more often blamed and avoided than those whose loved ones die in other circumstances. They are also more likely to feel guilt. Because the stigma of suicide makes talking about their feelings more difficult, they experience more isolation than those grieving most other deaths. This complicates the grieving process. Children are often caught in this backlash, confused by what has happened, and fearful that peers will judge them or their families.

Since most of us, adults as well as children, are mystified by suicide and confused by the element of choice, coming to terms with the suicide death of a parent becomes a journey we experience and explore over time. With guidance and support, we come to learn that our loved one didn't rationally "choose" to leave us, but was seeking a way to end unimaginable pain and anguish. Although we may not be able to understand such suffering and hopelessness, at some point we may come to recognize that we needn't be ashamed. As our culture becomes more educated about mental illness and brain chemistry, we can hope that suicide will be seen as the result of an illness, rather than the choice of a rational mind.

Depression and Mental Illness

For some people, simply getting out of bed in the morning is a struggle. According to the National Alliance for the Mentally Ill (NAMI), the symptoms of major depression include: profoundly sad or irritable mood; pronounced changes in sleep, appetite and energy; difficulty thinking, concentrating, and remembering; lack of interest in or pleasure from activities that were once enjoyed; feelings of guilt, worthlessness, hopelessness, and emptiness; recurrent thoughts of death or suicide; and persistent physical symptoms—such as headaches, digestive disorders and chronic pain—that do not respond to treatment.

Major depression can occur at any age—including childhood and the teenage years. It strikes men, women, adolescents and children of all races, economic and education levels. I remember watching an interview several years ago with CBS News *60 Minutes* correspondent Mike Wallace, who spoke about his depression. He discussed the stigma of his illness, his initial fear of being labeled a "nut case," and the reality that "you cannot snap out of it." He reported that during his struggles, he would say to himself, "Come on, Mike, don't pamper yourself, you've got the blues, but you've had the blues before, get out of it." Then he went on to say, "But it isn't the blues. It's something much deeper than that, and...the worst thing you can do is to feel ashamed of it. You wouldn't be ashamed if you had scarlet fever or if you had a cold or if your appendix burst. Truly, this is simply an illness."

Depression isn't something you can talk yourself out of or a weakness to be conquered solely by will. Despite the entreaties of those who believe otherwise, a person suffering from clinical depression may have very little control over how he thinks or feels. "Life inside the suicidal mind is tortured," relates Susan Blauner in her enlightening book, *How I Stayed Alive When My Brain Was Trying to Kill Me.* "Telling a depressed person not to feel sad is like asking a color-blind person to find you a red shirt."

What many fail to understand and appreciate is that between eighty and ninety percent of those suffering from major depression or other mood disorders can be effectively treated and return to their normal daily activities and feelings. If untreated, depressive episodes commonly last anywhere from six months to a year, and severe depression can lead to suicide. Unfortunately, a depressed person is not always able to ask for help, due to the stigma or because of the illness itself. And sometimes it takes several tries with different medications to find the one that helps lift the dark cloud from the victim's psyche. But depression and other mental illnesses are treatable, and many lives can be saved when support systems are put in place and medication is properly prescribed.

The Challenge of Surviving

As you and your children do the work of mourning, you will continue to wonder why, but the answer will likely remain elusive. Carla Fine, in her book, *No Time to Say Goodbye*, states, "The challenge of surviving is to mourn without understanding; with pain and grief, yes, but with the awareness that we will never know why we have been left by those we have loved." Perhaps nine-year-old Danielle, a child in one of my support groups whose father shot himself, said it best. "You know, all we have is our best guess, and our best guess might be wrong."

Your job will be to help your child find her own answers. This means providing her with information, support and love, and encouraging her to explore her own thoughts and feelings about life and death. It will be important to recognize that her physical, intellectual, spiritual, and emotional development is specific to her, shaped by many forces. Like you, she has her own strengths and resources that need to be built upon as she does the lifelong work of mourning.

As caring adults, we are called upon to listen to what children and teens have to say, and to learn from them what their grief is like. It's not up to us to tell them how they should be feeling or what to think about their experience. If we are patient and observant, they will let us know what is in their hearts and minds, what they need and what will empower them. In the end, what is important is continuing to love and support your children, and talking with them about the suicide rather than avoiding it, even though you don't have all the answers and never will.

At some point, years down the road for most of us, the "Why?" becomes less important as we do the work of mourning, allowing ourselves to grieve while going on with the responsibilities of daily life. Among those responsibilities, most assuredly, is creating a context where each of us can feel renewed joy in life, even as we never "forget" our loved one and the tragic circumstance of his or her death.

In her book, *My Son, My Son*, Iris Bolton, often considered one of the architects responsible for creating support groups for survivors, writes: *"I don't know why./ I'll never know why./ I don't have to know why./ I don't like it./ What I have to do is make a choice about my living."*

CHAPTER THREE

Telling Your Child

*"Having to tell my nine-year-old daughter that her father
had killed himself is the hardest thing I have ever had to do."*
—THERESA

Telling your child about the death of her parent may seem like an impossible task, especially because you may be so undone yourself that you wonder if you can even get the words out. Maybe there is a part of you that clings to the hope that the death was an accident. You may wonder if you should even say the word suicide, or if there is a "right" way to tell your child.

Many surviving parents worry about expressing their grief in front of their children, feeling that tears will further upset them. While uncontrollable sobbing may frighten a young child, sharing rather than hiding grief allows for children to learn about feelings. Dad explaining that he is "very, very sad about Mommy dying, and when we are sad, we cry," gives children words to describe what is happening. Given that children often mimic the behavior of others, if they are able to observe healthy grieving responses, they often respond similarly and are able to learn important lessons about expressing themselves. They can also learn that death is a part of life, and that the feelings we have around the loss of someone special can be expressed and managed.

First Steps

If possible, take time for yourself before talking with your child. Give yourself the opportunity to talk with someone who understands the dynamics of suicide and who can help you sort out what you want to say to your child. You may want to ask a trusted family member, friend, or professional mental health counselor to be with you as you tell your child. That person can support both of you as you try to cope with the initial response to this traumatic news.

Children who experience the suicide death of a loved one do best when they get honest information about what has happened—in doses suitable for their age. Telling a child about his parent's death is best done by his surviving parent or someone else he trusts, in language he can understand, in an environment that is familiar and comforting. (In some tragic situations, however, a child may discover the body, necessitating immediate crisis support. This is a profoundly traumatic experience that may cause emotional and behavioral problems as well as post-traumatic stress disorder. See Chapter Sixteen – *Complicated Suicides,* for more information.)

A Truthful Explanation

Finding the words to impart the grim news of a parent's death is very hard. You may be tempted to "protect" your child from such traumatic information by telling her "white lies" or half-truths. You may hope if you explain the death "later," when she is "older," she will be more able to understand. However, without a truthful account, children tend to make up their own stories. Such self-explanations can create even more confusion, fear, and isolation. Your honesty is also critical because a parent's suicide leaves a child feeling betrayed and vulnerable. While shielding a child from the truth may seem like a kindly act, deception may interfere with the trust bond.

When you are ready to talk with your youngster about the death, place her on your lap (or next to you) and start with a simple statement that "Mommy (or Daddy) has died." This will be very hard, and it is O.K. if you cry. If your child is very young, you may need to explain in concrete terms what "died" means by using examples a child this age can understand. ("When a person dies, his body stops working. His heart stops beating and he no longer breathes. He can't eat or talk or move. He can't hear or see anymore because he no longer alive. He is dead.") Avoid using euphemisms such as "passed away," "expired," or the new-age term "transitioned." Such explanations, while intended to help, often only confuse children, who know something terrible has happened.

A young child who has had a pet die or who has experienced the death of a grandparent may have some idea of what "dead" means, but since the notion of suicide will not be in his realm of understanding, you will not want to include that piece in the initial statement. Most young children will not ask how, but may ask "Why?" or "What will happen?" Questions like "Who will take care of me?" or "Are you going to die, too?" are also common, and they need to be addressed in a straightforward manner. You can reply to your child's concerns about this by saying, "No, I am not going to die for a long, long time, but if I did, which is very unlikely, Grandma and Uncle Dave would take care of you." (You may have had a guardianship plan in order before your partner's death, but if not, do so as soon as you are able.)

If a child asks a direct question, such as, "How did he die?" answer it simply. "Daddy died by suicide, which means he killed himself." This will be confusing to a young child, and your continued dialogue will depend on her response to that statement. She may just say, "Oh," and change the subject. If she asks why (older children who have more understanding of death and suicide will want more information) you can tell her you aren't sure yet, but that he was probably suffering from an illness in his brain that made him confused, and he didn't know he could get help.

A young child's concerns are most likely going to revolve around her own safety and care. She will be less concerned with how Daddy died and more focused on his absence and how you are responding to what has happened. She may also be unable to comprehend the permanence of death and ask, "When is Daddy coming back from being dead?" While this may be upsetting to a newly bereaved parent, such questions are normal. You or someone close to her can remind her that Daddy is dead and when a person dies, he can't come back. You may need to reiterate this point again in the days ahead because sometimes it takes time for children to really understand what it means to be dead.

While it is preferable for a surviving parent to be the one to relay the news, you simply may not be able to do so initially. Another member of your family or a trusted friend who is also close to your child can be enlisted to talk with him and explain what has happened. "Mommy is in the bedroom because she's very sad and upset. Your Daddy has died. She is crying right now and Aunt Janet is helping her. Mommy will still be able to take care of you, and I am going to help her. And your grandma and Uncle Dave are going to be here, too. We are all going to help each other during this very sad time."

Most children will want to see their surviving parent at this point because they will be feeling frightened and confused. While seeing the collapse of a parent can be upsetting, not being able to see either parent is equally worrisome. If possible, allow your child to sit on your lap or lay on a bed with you as you grieve. Physical contact with you is comforting. Even though you may be upset and crying, she can see you are still alive. Hugging each other and cuddling is a way to reassure each other of your connection and love.

I will always remember a telephone call I received from Jan, a young mother who told me that two law enforcement officers were in her living room, having just told her that her ex-husband had taken his life. They had suggested she call her sister who lived nearby and ask her to come to the house to be with her. Her sister had told her to call me for help with how to tell her children. Five-year-old Helena was due to awaken from her nap soon and twelve-year-old Brian would be home from school any minute.

On the phone, Jan and I quickly rehearsed what she could say to the children. Her sister arrived as we were talking. I later learned that moments after the police had left, Helena, hearing the front door shut, sleepily wandered into the living room. She settled into her mother's lap, initially unaware of her mom's tears. As she woke up more and sensed her mother's emotional state, she began asking, "What's the matter? Why are you crying?" Brian arrived minutes later, and Jan sat him down on the couch, putting her arm around him as she cradled Helena. As we had discussed, she told them, "Something very, very, sad has happened. Daddy has died." Helena didn't say anything, just put her thumb in her mouth and looked at her mother, bewildered. But

Brian began asking a barrage of questions. "What do you mean? When did he die? What happened? Who told you?"

Jan, in tears herself, told the children, "Two policeman came to tell me a little while ago. They said that Daddy had died by suicide, which means he killed himself."

Brian was stunned: "Well, he wouldn't do that. He couldn't do that." Then: "Why would he do that?" He got up from the couch and began pacing. Jan proceeded to tell the children that she didn't know why, that sometimes people have terrible emotional pain or a sickness in their brain and that maybe that is what had happened with their dad. She remembered to say, "It isn't anyone's fault. Daddy loved you and I love you, but something inside of Daddy got mixed up and he didn't know how to get help for the pain he was feeling."

Jan later shared with me the extreme pain of watching her children try to comprehend this news. Helena appeared to be most worried about her mother's tears, and she kept telling her mom not to cry. Jan's sister intervened, saying, "Mommy is sad about your daddy dying. When people are sad they cry," at which point Helena started crying, too. Brian continued to pace, repeating, "This couldn't have happened. He wouldn't do this," and then stopped suddenly, asking his mother. "How did he do it?" Jan said this was the hardest part for her, and that her voice shook when she told the children, "The police said he drank a lot of alcohol and then shot himself." At this point Brian sat down and stared at her, then looked away and started to cry.

It's Not Your Fault

In addition to a truthful explanation geared to their age and developmental level, children need reassurance that the suicide was not their fault, and that they could not have done anything to prevent it. Like adults, children wrestle with concerns that their thoughts or behaviors may have contributed to the death. Because children often have unrealistic views of themselves as being all-powerful and able to control situations or other people through wishes or rituals, they may feel they did not behave well enough or had unkind thoughts, and therefore, "caused" the death.

Your child may believe he is responsible for the death in some way. If so, hear him out as he attempts to explain how his actions or thoughts contributed to the suicide. Listen without interrupting, and then gently go over his beliefs with him. This is a conversation you may need to have many times. Let him know that sometimes mental illnesses occur which change the chemistry of people's brains. These illnesses can cloud a person's judgment and cause them to feel hopeless and unable to improve their lives. Educate your child that brain illnesses, just like other severe illnesses such as heart disease or cancer, can cause some people to die. In many situations, people who have these serious medical conditions can get treatment and medicine that helps, but sometimes attempted remedies do not work.

Children must also be reassured that they are not responsible for adult decisions.

I remember when eight-year-old Eddie announced in a support group I was leading, "My mom killed herself because me and my sisters made her do it." I asked Eddie to tell us more about how that happened, and he said with conviction, "She said our fighting was driving her crazy and she couldn't stand it anymore." We talked more about this notion and then I asked the group, "How many of you have had a parent tell you that you were driving them crazy by some sort of behavior?" The entire group of kids raised their hands. I then said, "I used to say that from time to time to my boys as well. Parents just say things like that sometimes when they are frustrated, but it doesn't mean they want to die because their children are misbehaving." We talked about how some people have diseased hearts or kidneys, and how Eddie's mom had a diseased brain that caused her to be confused, and resulted in her ending her life. Eddie's dad had told him this already, but Eddie needed continued reassurance from him that kids don't cause suicide, but that the illness his mom had could, and did. Eventually Eddie was able to introduce himself to new kids in the group and explain that his mom had an illness in her brain called "major depression" that contributed to her suicide.

Coming to terms with those feelings of responsibility and regret takes time. Often, regardless of the words and reassurance we receive as children, we internalize this sense of being responsible, and we may remain unaware of its presence until we are older. As a parent, you may have to reassure your child again as he matures, and his perception of how and why the suicide occurred changes. This theme of responsibility is likely to resurface.

Helping Your Child Respond to Others

Children and teens often need help learning how to answer questions and respond to comments that may come their way following a parent's suicide. Unfortunately, in our media-driven culture that frequently seems to thrive on gossip and sensationalized incidents, many people have come to believe it is their right to know details, and that asking intimate and intrusive questions is acceptable.

Many adult survivors report being taken aback by such encounters. They experience conflicting emotions: anger and hurt towards those who seem insensitive to their pain, and uneasiness with others whose motives they question. Children, who may be less able to discern the intentions of others and feel uncertain about what to share, may experience awkward or distressing moments with those who do not know how to support a youngster grieving this type of death (or any death). While some people feel it is better to remain silent and act as if nothing has happened, others are curious and ask for details. Both responses can leave a child feeling anxious and upset.

Because questions and comments from curious family members, friends, or acquaintances can be intimidating, it is important to prepare your child for these inevitable encounters. Let him know it is up to him to decide with whom he wishes to talk about his experience, and what information he wishes to share. You may want to practice having "pretend" conversations with your children. They will very likely hear comments like, "I understand your father died. I am very sorry." Let them know that a simple "thank you" is enough response unless they choose to say more. Sometimes, well-meaning adults will try to engage a bereaved child in further discussion, but if he doesn't want to continue the conversation, let him know it is O.K. to say, "I'm too sad (or too uncomfortable, or don't want) to talk about this right now." He also needs to know it is perfectly acceptable to refer an inquisitive person to another adult. ("I don't want to talk about what happened—maybe you can talk to my mom.") Sharing information or expressing feelings is not required just because an adult (or anyone) asks.

If your child would like to respond, it helps to have an answer ready. Depending on his comfort level, he might say, "My dad had an illness in his brain that caused him to end his life. The medicines he tried couldn't help him." He could also say, "My dad died from complications of depression."

Some children report difficulty with peers at school or in their neighborhood. While most children will not deliberately set out to hurt another child, they are naturally curious and no less likely than adults to talk among themselves and ask questions when they hear about the death of a classmate's parent. The notion of suicide is very scary, and when children are frightened they can make cruel or upsetting comments.

Responding in the moment to thoughtless remarks or intrusive questioning is hard. Most children have difficulty letting peers know their feelings are hurt, or that they are feeling overwhelmed. If you hear from your child that she is experiencing difficulty with peers at school, let her teacher know— don't be afraid to ask for help.

When Destiny's mother heard from her eight-year-old daughter that two boys at school were asking her a lot of questions about the gun her dad used to end his life, and teasing her because she didn't have a dad anymore, she was furious. "I wanted to drive right down to the school myself and tell those bullies off, but I knew I needed to calm myself down." She told Destiny she was angry about those comments, but she also comforted her daughter by saying, "I am so sorry that happened, but I'm glad you told me about it. I will talk with your teacher and we will work on a plan for you to feel more comfortable at school. I think those two boys must not feel very good inside about themselves. I know that sometimes when kids tease other kids it is because they have some trouble in their own lives, and they think they will feel better if they bother someone else. It isn't your fault that Daddy died, and you don't have to answer their questions unless you want to. We will talk with your teacher and figure out a way to let those boys know that their comments and questions are hurtful, and that this sort of behavior is not O.K."

Teachers can be enlisted as allies for children who may be encountering difficulties at school. Without being overly protective or solicitous, a teacher can be attentive to how children are dealing with information about a suicide death. They can become a valuable means of education and support. (See Chapter Nine – *Back to School: What Your Children's Teachers Need to Know*.)

Some children will reject any discussion or attempts to prepare a response. You will have to take your cue from your child, being aware not to pressure him. He may not be ready to talk. Most children will either tune out words they aren't ready to hear or be obstinate in some way. A brief monologue may be helpful: "If someone came up to you at school and said something that hurt your feelings or asked you a question about Daddy, you could always say, 'I don't want to talk about that because I am too sad,' or just walk away and talk to your teacher, or ask if you can call home."

The primary message we want to convey to children who have experienced this trauma is to trust their instincts, and to respond accordingly. In addition to encouraging them to ask for help from a trustworthy adult if they feel confused or overwhelmed, we must let them know it's O.K. to say no to questions or requests that do not feel safe.

Suicide Notes

Sometimes a person who takes his life will leave a suicide note. While the majority of those who carry out suicide do not leave notes, survivors report that those who do often leave messages that are rambling and unclear. Some who end their lives express hopelessness, and request that survivors not blame themselves. Some ask for forgiveness, while others assign blame. In the absence of a suicide note, you may wish you had one in the hope that words from your loved one will give you and your children insight or comfort you in some way. However, many people who do find a note report that it doesn't make their anguish any easier. While a note may initially seem to shed light on the "Why" question, survivors discover the answer is still incomplete.

If your child's parent does leave a note, it will be up to you to decide when to share it with her. Your feelings about this may change over time, so even if you feel so inclined, try to resist any temptation to destroy the note in order to help you and your child "get on with life." Better to put the note away for safekeeping, because as your children mature, it may well become a critical link to their deceased parent, providing solace, clarity or necessary information as they try to come to terms with the death from an adult perspective.

*   *   *   *   *

It is important to help a child understand that no one lives a life without emotional pain. We all experience anxiety, sadness and conflict, but there are ways to cope with life's difficult times. We need to communicate to our children that talking with others is a way of dealing with painful situations. Sharing our worries and concerns helps us feel better and may allow us to find a solution. Often, we learn that time changes our perspective or our situation. Again, we can remind our children that suicide is a permanent solution to a temporary problem, and the product of a mind that is confused.

CHAPTER FOUR

How Young Children Grieve

A Father
A father should be a good guy
A father should be tall and strong
With laughter in his eyes
I know the kind of man
A father ought to be
A shining knight that fights for good
And wins it just for me
—CAROLINE, AGE 12
WRITTEN AFTER HER FATHER'S SUICIDE

How a child grieves and understands death will depend on his personality, age, intellectual development, cultural traditions, previous experiences with death, and the emotional environment in which he lives.

As we support children in their grief, we need to keep in mind that they grieve differently than adults. While some youngsters may initially respond with tears, angry outbursts, regressive behavior or anxiety, others appear to be lost in play or unfazed by the news of a death. Children tend to grieve sporadically, in doses, going in and out from grief to play. They are often more capable than adults of putting grief aside. Such responses are not indicative of a child's love for his lost parent, nor the depth of his grief. Rather, they reflect his limited maturity.

Helping children learn to cope and heal following a traumatic death means we need to encourage them to express their grief—the sadness, anger, hurt, guilt and confusion they feel inside. By gently talking with them about the death and *listening* to what they say, while also observing their actions, we can discover what they may or may not know, and whether they have misconceptions, worries, or fears. By allowing them to express how they feel or what they think, we can provide comfort and understanding as well as information.

While some children are comfortable talking about what has happened, many do not have the words or the inclination to verbally express what is going on inside themselves. They may prefer drawing or play activities as a way to express their grief. They must not be rushed or coerced to talk. Patience, love, limits, and support are required at this time. The important thing for parents to remember is that there is no one "right" way to grieve.

The Myth of Stages

What we must also remember as we try to support our children is that the mourning process does not move in an orderly, predictable manner. Noted grief pioneer Elisabeth Kübler-Ross, in her 1969 book, *On Death and Dying*, described five stages of grief: denial, anger, bargaining, depression and acceptance. Many people accepted her model as the "proper" way to grieve, but it has been much misunderstood over the years. Kübler-Ross developed her model as a way to describe what she had observed in her work with dying people. She noted that those going through the dying process often experienced these phases. We now know that she did not intend for this sequential stage theory to be applied literally to the bereaved as well, although many who are grieving find themselves experiencing some of those stages. However, most people move back and forth between these phases, which often overlap in time, with one or the other stage perhaps absent altogether. What we need to remember about our own grief and the grief of our children is that each of us is unique, with our own way of expression and our own pace of recovery.

In this chapter we will look at how children of different ages and developmental levels may understand death. While age and developmental level are important and often indicate how children will generally perceive death, not all children think alike or have the same emotional orientation toward grief. You may find it helpful to read about each developmental level since there is often significant overlap. At the end of each section is a story about a particular child's experience following the suicide death of his or her parent.

Birth to Three

The lives of babies and very young children revolve around the relationships they have with those who care for them. They are focused on the comings and goings of their mothers and fathers, and often have difficulty separating from them. Universal games like "peek-a-boo" or modified hide 'n seek are early indicators of children learning to cope with losing sight of their loved ones and re-discovering them. In addition to providing entertainment, such games also help them learn that Mommy and Daddy and other important people disappear, but also return.

When this foundation is disrupted by the death of a parent, infants and toddlers have immediate physical, emotional, and behavioral responses to the loss that can best be met by providing love, comfort, and consistent care. Since their experience is primarily physical, the most important mode of comfort is human touch in large doses. This is not a time to worry about "spoiling." Hugs, holding, cuddling, rocking, gentle words and soft singing are all appropriate and necessary ways to support an infant or toddler who feels the separation, but is unable to comprehend what has happened.

Infants

Most infants develop a special bond with their mothers and fathers during their first year, an attachment that is very powerful for both parent and child. If a mother has been breast-feeding, the baby's bond with her is even more compelling. When a parent dies, an infant's world changes. She knows someone special is missing, but because she lacks language to express her feelings, her behavior will indicate her anguish.

You may see decreased or increased sleep with more episodes of awakening, increased crying, and changes in eating and elimination patterns. If she is nursing and her mother disappears, she is likely to protest a bottle, will turn away or act irritable. She will be tuned into the parent caring for her and will sense that parent's anguish at a physical level. Holding her, loving her, and taking care of her basic needs are essential at this time, and will continue to be important as she and those around her adjust to the absence of her parent.

For those of you who are coping with a partner's death, comforting your baby may feel like a respite from the reality of what has happened. Holding your infant close may soothe you as you struggle with your own feelings. But, ultimately, your baby will get fussy or demanding. Sometimes babies are simply inconsolable, even without major traumas. In those moments, nothing may work to comfort an infant's cries of distress. After ruling out hunger or a dirty diaper, try rocking, walking her around, gently massaging her, putting her in a front pack or sling, and talking or singing to her if you have the energy. You may find your grief simply too overwhelming to soothe her for very long, but she will eventually settle down and go to sleep. *Ask for help.* As you and others provide love, comfort, and care following the loss of her parent, her grief will subside, and she will learn that *someone* will always be there for her, even though her mother or father is no longer available.

Toddlers

Following the death of a parent, toddlers are likely to experience regression, returning to developmental behaviors that at one time brought them comfort. They may go back to sucking their thumbs or talking baby talk. They often lose toilet-training skills. Sleep patterns may be disrupted and they might awaken in the night, agitated and anxious. They may not feel like eating much and will often show resistance to change. Temper outbursts are typical, as is an unwillingness to be separated from loved ones or parted from special blankets or toys. Some of these behaviors are normal and expected, but your toddler may demonstrate them more often and more ferociously as a result of his or her loss.

Searching behaviors may also be demonstrated by a toddler attempting to "find" the absent parent in familiar places, under a blanket or in a favorite chair. Some young children mimic familiar behaviors or words of the absent parent in an attempt to bring that missing person back. Verbal toddlers may frequently repeat words, phrases or questions like "Where's Mommy?" "Daddy, home?" as they attempt to come to terms with the reality of their loss.

Following her father's death, twenty-one-month-old Eliza would run to the front door when she heard a car drive up, thumb in her mouth, tattered yellow blanket trailing. Eyes glued to the doorknob, she would wait for her father to open the door, pick her up and twirl her around like he always had. Her distraught mother, a client of mine, had told her several times that Daddy wasn't coming home because he died. Each time Eliza headed for the door her mom would cry, heartbroken herself, and worried that she hadn't explained things correctly to her daughter. When Eliza's eyes would fill with tears, her mother would pick her up and hug her, saying, "Oh, we are so sad that Daddy isn't coming home anymore because he died." Eliza continued this searching behavior intermittently for several weeks after her father's death.

Needs of Bereaved Infants and Toddlers

In addition to lots of physical touching and comforting, infants and toddlers need consistent and reliable care. The suicide of a parent obviously disrupts most attempts at trying to maintain any semblance of normalcy, but regular naps, bathing, and eating schedules need to be maintained as closely as possible, as should any rituals associated with these routines.

Minimizing other changes is also important. Maintaining ongoing relationships with familiar people, sleeping in the same place, attending already formed playgroups or childcare will help a child cope with the loss of his parent. This is not the time to start a child with a new daycare provider unless you have no alternative. Try to keep a young child's life as predictable as possible for the time being. Avoid weaning him from the breast or bottle, potty training, or moving him into a "big boy bed." He needs loving structure and continuity right now as he learns to cope with his loss.

Infants and toddlers are tuned into their environment and will reflect the feelings of those who care for them. When a parent dies, a child in essence may lose two parents, one to death and one to mourning. While most parents want to take care of their children during this time, they may initially be unable to do so, given the intensity of their own grief. If you find yourself in this situation, try to have physical contact with your child whenever possible. She needs to see you. Other family members or friends who are familiar to your child can help with household tasks and routines as well as provide physical comfort, but an infant or toddler needs to have visual and physical contact with her surviving parent whenever possible.

Young children will teach us what they need to know about death. Although they may not be able to tell us directly, we can assume that at this developmental stage they are most concerned with questions that have to do with them: "Did I cause this to happen? Who will take care of me? Is anyone else going to leave me?" And since they are egocentric, toddlers need to be reassured that they did not cause the death, and that the feelings expressed by their surviving parent are a response to loss and not a result of any thoughts, actions, or words the child has expressed.

Addressing these concerns and providing lots of physical touching and comfort will go a long way in helping infants and toddlers begin to cope with the death of a parent.

*   *   *   *   *

In the following story, fourteen-year-old Parker, a recent middle school graduate, shares his thoughts about his father's death and his own newly diagnosed bipolar illness. Because Parker's mother has been active in the field of suicide prevention and has involved her children in her work, Parker has learned to speak freely about his dad's suicide. He is determined to triumph over the illness that contributed to the suicide deaths of his father, grandfather and aunt.

PARKER'S STORY

"In my dad's family suicide was swept under the rug and he didn't believe he could get help for his illness."

I don't have many memories of my dad because I was only two and a half when he died. But I do remember playing with him in our basement playroom. I slid down the toy slide into his lap and he was crying. I also remember walking down the stairs and seeing a big, black hole in the door and feeling scared. I didn't know at the time that he had punched the hole in the door during a rage, but I knew something wasn't right. Those memories must have made an impression on me, I guess, because they stayed with me.

I know from my mom and grandparents that my dad was a good person who worked hard to provide for us. He suffered from bipolar illness, a brain disorder that is treatable, but he worried that he would lose his job if his employer found out about his problem. I have learned how his illness prevented him from getting the help he needed. That makes me sad, but I have learned not to be ashamed of him or how he died. He was a good man and a lot of people loved him. He never wanted to hurt us, but I guess because of his illness, he felt hopeless and believed we would be better off without him.

I really miss my dad. He did what he did and that cannot be changed, but my mom has taught my sister and me that what can be changed is how we deal with his death. We have learned to be open about our feelings and how he died. We also know it is important to be educated about depression and other mood disorders that can contribute to suicide. I have learned that brain disorders aren't anything to be ashamed of and that there are things that can be done to help someone who is thinking about suicide. I wish my dad had known that, too, but people didn't talk openly about suicide when he was young. There was too much stigma and they didn't understand about brain disorders. My mom is working to change that pattern in our family. She believes honesty is the best policy, and that even though we have had this terrible loss that we can work together to have a good life. I think she's right.

My mom tells me I am a little like my dad in subtle ways. She says I have similar hand and facial gestures. He also liked the Minnesota Vikings, and they are my favorite football team, too, even though I can't remember watching football with him. So far I don't think I am as hard of a worker as he was—maybe I am a little bit of a slacker—but I do O.K. in school. I guess the biggest difference between me and my dad is that I can talk about my bipolar disorder and I know I can get help. In my dad's family suicide was swept under the rug and he didn't believe he could get help for his illness.

What I miss most about not having my dad here is just talking to him about guy things. I live with my mom and sister and they are more into stuff like cooking and sewing. I want someone interested in sports and watching violent movies, stuff that men like. I can talk to my mom about girls somewhat, but it is a little awkward. You need a dad for that.

A couple of years ago I was involved in volunteering with my mom in an organization working to help prevent suicide. I talked at some big rallies about how important it is for everyone to work together to change the way people think about brain disorders and suicide in this country. I still believe there is more work to be done so that some day maybe fewer people will die by suicide, but I don't do as much of this sort of volunteer work now. I have to focus more on school and I would rather hang out with my friends, but volunteering was a way to honor my dad's memory, and I'm glad I did it. I think I made a difference, and that experience helped me learn how to talk about my dad's suicide. We still talk about my dad a lot and on his birthday, every August 24, our family always does something special and my mom tells us stories about him.

I have had my own struggles with bipolar illness. At first we didn't know anything was really wrong, but I felt depressed a lot. My sister was having problems and I was starting middle school. My mom thought maybe I was just being a teenager, but she knew because of studying mood disorders that something might be wrong. I saw a psychiatrist and started on medication for depression, but it took a while to find the right medicine for me. During this time I was cutting myself, but no one knew because I cut high on my arm and on my leg, where it wasn't obvious.

My mom caught me doing the cutting and she and my psychiatrist had me hospitalized for three days. That was actually an O.K. experience because I was in some therapy groups where we talked about coping skills and I learned other ways to deal with stress. My doctor realized that I was bipolar rather than depressed, and my medication got changed. That was three months ago, and I have felt really good since then. But I don't enjoy having this illness. My mom told my sister and me that we might have it some day, but I didn't want to have it. It's scary knowing I have an illness that killed so many people in my family, but the medication helps me not feel so worried.

I take medication twice a day, and it's extremely helpful. Most of the time I remember to take it on my own, although sometimes my mom reminds me. I don't have those major highs and lows anymore. I am kind of stuck in the middle, but it's O.K. I feel comfortable, not tranquilized, and I like not feeling so worried about stuff. I was kind of more on the depressed end of bipolar, but I have learned to divert my attention to something positive when I feel down. I like to write poems and stories, and I like to do physical stuff, too—skateboarding and soccer. I'll go outside and kick the soccer ball into the goal or do tricks on my skateboard.

I wish my dad could know about all those little accomplishments that are big to me, like when I did an "ollie" on my skateboard for the first time. That's when you pop the tail down on your board, slide your foot up and you go up in the air. Sounds complicated, but staying on the board is basic physics.

I think my dad would like my friends. I am going with my best friend and his family to Uruguay this summer for two months, which is pretty cool. I am going to learn Spanish, I hope. I like hanging out with my friends, playing video games, and doing sports. I am pretty open with them, and really most anyone, about my dad's death. I don't go into the details with everyone, but I don't mind saying he died by suicide.

I do have a good life and I am excited about my future. I want to be an adult, go to college and become a writer or a journalist. I would like to write for CNN. I don't really worry about my future. I guess I have challenges ahead like staying focused on my goals, but I am pretty confident I can have a good life. My experience around my dad's death and this disorder I have has helped define who I am. I like who I am. I have been through a lot, but I am doing great. As horrible as all of this has been, it does help you grow as a person.

I guess if I had any advice for adults it would be to grieve as a family and be open about what has happened. Be willing to talk to your kids and try to have a positive attitude about life. My mom has told us ever since I was really young that no matter what problem we face, we can choose to expect the best and work to find a solution. That message helps me when I get down or when I am struggling. I know life isn't always easy, but I do feel like I am learning ways to work things out.

*   *   *   *   *

Three to Six

Generally, children from three to six years old are unable to conceptualize the permanence of death. Even though they may freely use the word "dead," they don't grasp death as a normal and final process, believing instead that death is akin to sleep or going on a long journey. To them a dead person may still be seen as someone who breathes, eats, thinks, and who will, at some point in the future, "come back or wake up."

Addressing the issue of suicide with this age group comes with its own challenges. Most adults feel intimidated about explaining suicide to such a young child. How do you explain what has happened to her missing parent when it is likely she won't yet understand the permanence of death or the concept of taking one's own life?

Children are perceptive. They readily pick up when something is amiss. For a child to feel secure, he needs to be able to trust the adults who care for him. While it is not advisable to give detailed information about the suicide to a young child, if he asks a direct question, do not respond with a deceptive story or false and misleading information. A simple statement of what has happened to his missing parent is best. (For more information refer to Chapter Three – *Telling Your Child*.)

Where Has Daddy Gone?

Young children have learned since infancy that important people "go"—to work, the store, school or on vacation—but they always come back. When a death occurs, trying to explain where the person has gone and why he or she is not coming back is difficult, given a child's limited frame of reference. A child this age will often place the deceased in heaven and want to visit, write, or call her absent parent.

Jenny, age four, explained to me while coloring intently that, "My daddy died." When I responded with a simple, "Oh?" she went on to say, matter-of-factly, "When he comes back, he's bringing me a Barbie." She had been told he died, but she was unable to comprehend the reality of death. We talked about how when someone dies his body stops working. We discussed how Daddy couldn't talk anymore or eat or sleep or go to the toy store, and that she wouldn't be able to see him again or be with him because he was dead. She looked sad and perplexed, and nodded solemnly. Several weeks later her mom heard her discussing her dad's death with her seven-year-old cousin. "Daddy's in heaven and he can't go potty or eat anymore, but when Mommy and me fly in the airplane to visit Grandma we are going to jump on the clouds and visit him." As adults we often work at encouraging kids to use their imaginations, but a parent's death is one circumstance where it is best not to encourage fantasy thinking.

Jenny's understanding of death is typical for this developmental level and not cause for concern. As she matures she will be able to grasp the concept of death. Jenny's mother is learning to use these conversations to allow Jenny to express her confusion and her feelings, by responding with comments like, "Oh, Jenny, remember how when someone dies we can't visit them. Their bodies don't work anymore and they are no longer alive. You really miss Daddy and wish we could see him again, but we can't because he is dead. That makes me sad, and I know you feel sad, too."

Sad and Mad

Because a young child does not understand the finality of death, he may also react to a parent's absence with intense anger, subjecting his surviving parent to a comment like, "I wish you died instead of Mommy!" Of course, this is upsetting to any parent, but it is not a personal rejection. A child is expressing his grief, not attacking you personally. This anger is a healthy form of protest, but in those moments when you are feeling vulnerable and abandoned yourself, such comments can be wounding. You might find yourself feeling angry or at a loss for words. If you can remember that your child is bewildered, angry, and frightened, you might be able to respond by saying something like, "Yes, I know you really miss Mommy and don't want her to be dead. You want her here, and so do I."

Young children often have faith in their own omnipotence, feeling that they can make things happen or not by simply wishing it so. To a young child whose concept of death includes impermanence and reversibility, "I want you dead!" is more likely to be a reaction to discipline or disappointment, rather than a wish to be fulfilled. This sense of omnipotence, which we sometimes call "magical thinking," can contribute to a child feeling responsible for what befalls his loved ones. If his mother "disappears" (dies) after he has had an angry outburst, punctuated by a wish for Mommy's demise, a young child is likely to feel quite troubled. Even games or rhymes that include parental catastrophes are unsettling in the wake of a parent's absence. I remember wondering if playing the game "Step on a crack, break your mother's back" on the sidewalk in front of my house had anything to do with my mother's sudden disappearance.

Trying to Integrate the Death

Pre-schoolers often incessantly repeat information they have gathered, or ask the same questions over and over. When they do this after a parent's suicide, it isn't necessarily a reflection on a surviving parent or other caregiver's ability to explain what has happened. This is how they integrate their experiences.

They are also likely to announce that "Mommy (or Daddy) died" to strangers in line at the grocery store or to other parents picking up their children at pre-school. These statements often make adults feel uncomfortable and concerned about how to respond. A simple acknowledgement like, "Oh, I'm sorry. I feel sad about that," validates a child's attempts to communicate an event that has shaken her world.

Because young children lack experience with death and may not know how to express what they are experiencing, they need words to help them describe what they may be feeling (sad, lonely, angry) inside. Sharing your own feelings can be helpful. Some youngsters play out their feelings and experiences, re-enacting funeral services or what they imagine the death was like. While this may be unsettling or seem irreverent to adults, such "death play" is normal.

Play is a child's way to come to terms with what has happened, her way to work through feelings and explore her experiences. While this will be very difficult for her surviving parent, other adults who are comfortable with the idea can even enter into the play and offer gentle support and guidance as a child tries to make sense of her loss. With support and appropriate channels for mourning, bereaved children are less likely to become depressed or act out their unacknowledged pain through destructive behaviors.

However, adults should be watchful if children are engaged in death play. Shortly after his mother's partner hung herself, four-year-old Jeremy was observed putting a rope around his playmate's neck as they played "horsey." His pre-school teacher stepped in gently and redirected the play, talking about how ropes around necks could cause serious injury or even death. Jeremy nodded solemnly, but said nothing about the death.

Short-term regressive behaviors are also normal. Your child may demonstrate increased clinginess or revert to thumb sucking or baby talk. Soiling or wetting may occur as well as increased separation anxiety. This is not a time to be punitive or demanding, but to understand that children often regress in times of profound anxiety. By offering your child support and comfort, these behaviors will usually go away on their own once he or she feels more secure.

•   •   •   •   •

In the following story Cody, a kind, thoughtful fourth-grader shares his memories of his dad. He was the youngest of four children when his dad died. His mother has since remarried, and Cody has a good relationship with his stepfather.

CODY'S STORY

"I wondered if we were ever going to be O.K. again."

I'm ten now, but I was five when my dad died. I still have lots of memories of him. My dad was tall and a very good football player. He was a great dad, a very loving dad, and a good soccer player, too. He was my coach for my "Under six" team and always encouraged me. I used to go to work with him at his mortgage broker office. He would let me play on his computer and copy stuff on his copy machine. We used to go to my grandparents' house together in his Honda Prelude.

I will never forget the day I found out that he had died. I was playing PlayStation with my brother when a policeman came to the door and asked for my mom. They talked quietly for a few minutes. When my mom came back into the room, she had a scared and shocked look on her face. She told me to shut off PlayStation, but she couldn't really talk at first. Then she said, "Dad has died," and we started crying for a very long time. Then my mom's friend, Dana, came over and tried to help make us feel better.

I remember just sitting there on the couch in our living room, crying. People kept coming over. I didn't know what to say. I kept wondering where he was and what was going to happen. I wondered if we were ever going to be O.K. again. I didn't really know how he died, just that he was gone and I was very, very sad. My mom comforted me, but I was probably too young to really understand what was going on.

Even now I feel confused about exactly what happened. My mom had to explain it to me again recently because I couldn't remember the details. I knew he had chosen to die, but I didn't really remember how. I remember coming home from school every day and wondering where he was. Seems like I wondered about that for a long time.

I also remember the memorial service. There were a lot of chairs and we all sat in the first row. People got up and said stuff about my dad, and sometimes I cried when they talked about him. I liked hearing all that good stuff, and it made me sad, too.

My teacher told the kids that my dad had died and they made a book for me. Everyone drew pictures and wrote stories. I had forgotten about those pictures until a little while ago, but remembering about all my friends doing this for me makes me feel good. My mom has a box of stuff she saved, and that book is in there. I am going to look at those pictures again. I have a scrapbook my grandma made of my dad when he played football. I like looking at all the newspaper articles and pictures about him. I have pictures of him on my wall in my bedroom. I also have one of his trophies.

When I went back to school I remember the kids asked me how my dad died. I said I didn't know. They knew my dad because he had helped out in the class a few times. They asked me if he died from smoking, because they knew he smoked, but I really didn't know.

I went to a support group for kids who had somebody they loved who had died, but I don't remember too much about it. I guess I told the kids in that group that my dad died from depression. I don't know where I got that idea. Maybe I heard someone say it. No one said it was suicide for a long time because the police had to do a lot of tests first. Now I am learning about the difference between the kind of depression my dad had and the kind other people have once in a while when they get upset or have a bad day.

My mom said my dad had clinical depression and suffered from it all his life. He took medicine for it, but the medicine didn't work. She says he never really experienced joy, and that is pretty sad. I have experienced joy lots of times like when we win at soccer or when I do really well in school. I don't think I really understood anything about depression when I was five. I don't know if it really mattered to me how my dad died. What mattered was that he wasn't with me anymore.

Now that I am older I understand more about what happened, but I still feel kind of confused. I like to talk about my dad, and my mom will tell me stories about him when I ask. That makes me happy. I am the point guard for my basketball team and I am pretty fast. My mom told me my dad was really fast, too.

We go to the cemetery once a year and I like that. Getting away and being alone with my family to talk about what has happened makes me feel more comfortable. I like to look at the other graves near my dad's grave, too.

I think about my dad a lot. Sometimes just before I play soccer I wonder if he might be watching. I always hope so and I always want to play my best, just in case he is.

*   *   *   *   *

Six to Nine

By the age of six, most children begin to conceptualize the permanence of death, although they don't think it will happen to them or anyone they know or love. They tend to personalize death, and may create bogeymen or monsters. Their interest can be almost obsessive at times, leading to relentless questions about details. Morbid curiosity is not uncommon, particularly around a suicide death, which may involve violent acts or weapons.

When I relate in my support groups that my mother shot herself with a gun when I was a little girl, the boys invariably ask me what kind of gun she used. They also want to know where on her body she shot herself and if there was blood. The girls generally ask fewer detail questions. They make more comments such as, "That's sad. That's scary. Why did she do that?"

Indeed, the concept of a person choosing to end her own life is confusing to all of us, but it is particularly so for children who may never have heard the word "suicide" before or imagined that people do in fact take their own lives. They often express bewilderment and fear when confronted with the reality of suicide, worrying that maybe someone else they love might also leave them this way.

In my work with a shy, introspective nine-year-old named Sarah, I heard how, with increasing alarm, she had watched her mother's sadness and anguish grow following the suicide of Sarah's father. Sarah talked worriedly about hearing her mother weep at night. She would often hover anxiously outside her mother's bedroom door, unable to go to sleep. Night after night she would crawl into her mother's bed for comfort—and to comfort her mother in turn. She was reluctant to sleep in her own room for fear that "Mommy might hurt herself, too." Sarah thought if she could be with her mother, she might be able to assure her safety. Her mother had to reassure her many times that even though she was very sad, she would not take her own life like Daddy had done. She would take care of herself and Sarah. Suicide would not be an option.

Because children this age are beginning to form their ideas about death—how and why it happens—they often "try on" explanations that make sense to them. As they try to develop a perspective on what suicide is all about, they easily misinterpret facts and information.

I learned this first-hand one Monday morning when I spent time with a group of third graders whose teacher had hung herself the previous Friday evening. The children had learned of her death over the weekend and had many theories about what had happened. Several were convinced that their behavior on the school field trip to a museum that afternoon had caused her to take her life because she had said to a particularly rowdy group of boys, "You kids will be the death of me yet!" Other children were convinced that she had an accident because "no one would do that on purpose."

As we spent time exploring each perception, I talked with them about the reality of mental illness. I explained that their teacher had been suffering for a long time with a brain disorder. I let them know that because this illness made her feel extremely sad and confused, she didn't believe she could get better. We talked about how she wasn't able to think clearly and didn't really understand how upset her students would be when they learned she had died. Their teacher had been someone they had always felt comfortable talking with about their worries and fears. They were sad that she didn't know she could find someone to help her.

During this discussion I stressed the importance of finding an adult to talk with about troubled feelings, and I acknowledged that none of them were responsible for their teacher's illness or death. The idea of someone taking her life "on purpose" was hard for them to fathom, but our discussion led to other deaths the children had experienced. We talked about pets and grandparents who had died, and one student announced that her uncle had died of AIDS the week before. They shared their ideas about what they believed happened after death, and several children expressed concerns about loved ones who were ill. The "why?" of suicide continued to be a mystery, as it often is. I wished I had some magic words, but I didn't. I just tried to explain simply what had happened, and I made room for their thoughts and feelings. This was a hard chapter in their learning about life and death.

Body Concerns

Since children this age and younger are also very interested in their own bodies, their comments often express their concerns and ideas about how bodies function biologically. They may wonder if death hurts, particularly with suicide, which is often violent. They may be curious about what happens to a body when a person dies, and may ask questions like, "How do you eat or sleep when you are dead?" Although these questions may surprise adults, not all children make the connection between death and the complete shutting down of the body. They may need to be educated on how a body stops working when a person dies. This explanation is best done by using very specific words. "When someone dies, his heart stops pumping and all his organs (heart, lungs, kidneys, etc.) stop working. He can't eat or see or hear. He can't talk or go to the bathroom or breathe. When someone is dead, his body can't be fixed."

Many children in this age group experience somatic problems. Tummy aches or headaches are common. Concerns about leaving a surviving parent and going off to school or other activities are often experienced at a body level as children try to cope with their feelings of distress and uncertainty. Let your child know that his body is his friend, and that sometimes aches or upsets can help him recognize that he has troubled feelings. Help your child understand that all of his feelings are O.K., and provide him with information on appropriate ways to express his emotions. Many children need physical outlets as well as opportunities to express themselves through art, music and play.

Rituals

Many children at this developmental level like rituals. They are often eager to do drawings or choose items or pictures to go into a casket. They may like saying "Daddy prayers" or wearing an article of clothing that belonged to their deceased parent to bed each night. Baking a birthday cake or choosing a special Christmas tree ornament for the parent who has died may provide some comfort. The children whose teacher died decided to have a rummage sale to raise money for a school garden in the teacher's honor, since she had been an avid gardener. Encourage your child to come up with his own rituals.

Matthew, an outspoken nine-year-old with a mischievous smile and an affinity for baseball caps, shares this about rituals and remembering: "My dad died three years ago when I was six and a half. He hadn't been living with us for about a year before he committed suicide, but I still remember him. He was funny, and he liked to go bike riding with us. After he died he was cremated, and we have some of his ashes under a tree at our house. We built a little bench next to the tree, and sometimes we just sit there and talk about our memories. On Father's Day my mom gets helium balloons and we write messages on them, tie them together, and let them go. I did that last year, but this year I just watched while my mom and sister did it."

Holidays and anniversaries are often opportunities for creating additional rituals. (See Chapter Eleven – *Holidays, Anniversaries and Special Events,* for more on this topic.)

* * * * *

Caroline is a beautiful, articulate, almost sixteen-year-old Hispanic young woman with a lovely smile and soft brown eyes. She now has an excellent command of English, but at nine, when her father died, it was difficult talking about the overwhelming trauma of his death in a language not native to her. Caroline is bright, motivated and exceptionally polite. As she charts her way through adolescence, she exhibits maturity beyond her years.

CAROLINE'S STORY

"It was like we lost our mother and our father so suddenly."

My dad committed suicide six years ago when I was in the third grade. I will never forget that day, hearing my mother cry out when she discovered him. My brother and I looked past her and saw him hanging in the garage. We were screaming and crying and feeling so terrified. We didn't know what to do. We called 911 five times and the police finally came. I thought maybe my dad was still alive, and I kept praying for God to please bring him back. But he was dead.

My brother, sister and I had to go to our aunt's house for three days and we barely saw our mother. We missed her so much. It was like we lost both our father and mother so suddenly. We were frightened and confused and in shock, but we had to stay with relatives because my mom couldn't stop crying. She felt someone else should take care of us for a few days, but it was very hard for me not to see her.

At first I was really afraid that he had killed himself because of something I did. I was having problems the night before with my homework. I didn't want to do it and I was taking a long time. We kind of argued about that, so I was worried that maybe that's why he hung himself. I know that probably isn't the reason, but when I feel depressed and miss him, I sometimes think it is. And sometimes I think that he killed himself because that's what God really wanted. I just don't know.

The days following his death were so hard. We couldn't believe this had happened. When I went to the funeral home, I wasn't prepared to see him in that casket. He was all dressed up and looked like he was sleeping. I felt like screaming at him to wake up. We put some things in his coffin, a toy truck and some musical instruments, and I kissed him. I thought his cheek would feel warm, but it didn't. Seeing him there in that coffin made me feel as if the world fell on me.

I miss my dad every day, but I miss him more during holidays or special events. Last year I graduated from middle school and seeing everyone there with both parents made me sad, since I just had my mom. My mom gave me a ring, earrings and a necklace that she said my dad had wanted me to have on my graduation, so that made me happy. I felt he had given me a piece of himself.

Going back to school after his death was really hard. My teachers knew what had happened, and I felt they looked at me as a different person. I felt weird. They all knew my dad, since he had come to school events. They told me he would always be with me, but I still felt strange, different from everyone else.

When I returned to class and opened my desk there were cards that all the kids had made saying, "We love you and missed you." That was the sweetest thing anyone had ever done for me, and I felt loved. The kids in my class sat around me and I felt better. I was kind of glad to go back to school because then I was busy and didn't think about what had happened every minute. I was having nightmares every night, but being at school was kind of a relief.

I remember a couple of months later some kids I didn't really know that well asked me about my dad and where he was. I didn't want to tell them what had happened so I said he was in Mexico. You have to choose who you tell things to because you can't trust everyone. A boy whose parents were getting divorced teased my younger sister. There were several kids talking about parents at recess and he turned to my sister and said, "Well, at least my dad didn't commit suicide." I was mad when I heard about that boy. I wanted to yell at him to leave my sister alone, but we decided not to make a big deal about it unless he brought it up again. My sister cried when he said that to her, so maybe he realized that was a mean thing to do.

My mom took us to a support group at hospice about four months after my dad died. I really liked that group. At first I was shy and didn't want to talk, but after a while I felt like the group leaders were part of my family. It was good for me to talk about what I felt, and to hear all the other kids tell their stories. I realized I wasn't the only person who had someone they loved die. It was still hard to say suicide, but I got used to it. I learned in that group that there are some people you can trust and learn to love. I am grateful to all of those people who helped me through very hard times, and I love them all. We talked often about how a suicide isn't a child's fault, and that made me feel better.

I always try and look for the positive in people and situations. I believe everything happens for a reason. I am a strong person. I learned that about myself. I don't let bad things get me down or change me. I don't want people to feel sorry for me or think my family is crazy. I have worried that I might be an outcast if more people knew, but so far, the friends I have told don't treat me differently.

We had a father-daughter dance at my school this year and my friend invited me to go with her and her father. That was thoughtful of her and I appreciated her invitation, but I didn't think I would feel comfortable. I guess I will have to deal with that dance every year and I will feel sad, but I don't really want to go with anyone who's not my dad.

I go to a good school, a private Catholic school, and I am proud of myself for working hard. It costs a lot of money to go to my school, but I am getting some scholarships to help. I am kind of unique because there aren't many Hispanic girls at my school, and no one really speaks Spanish. We speak Spanish at home, but we all speak English everywhere else. Some of the girls are a little cliquish at my school or think they're more or better because they have more material things, but I mostly ignore that. I think I have become pretty confident about who I am.

I think my mom has helped me a lot. She has taught us to look for the positive, and she is very strict. I don't always like how strict she is. This last summer we fought a lot. I am growing up and I need responsibilities and more freedom. Sometimes she doesn't seem to understand that. I don't know where all this fighting behavior came from, but after a while I was sick of fighting. We love each other, and I know she wants me to do well in school and get a good education. I was being lazy, but now I am working harder again.

I want to go to a good university and be an international lawyer. I want to be an important person and help other people. Sometimes I worry that I won't make it. I think I have courage and I have goals, but sometimes I feel scared. My dad used to always tell me I could do whatever I put my mind to. I try and remember that.

We moved out of our house a few years ago, and I felt sad leaving that place with so many memories. I remembered all those piggyback rides my dad gave us in that house, but there were too many sad memories there, and we never liked going into the garage. In our new house we have pictures of my dad, and we talk about him once in a while. We go to church on his birthday and on the day he died. Sometimes we watch home videos that always make us laugh. We don't want to forget him. I think our family has gotten closer since he died. My brother who is one year younger than I am is my good friend. He makes me laugh. I love my younger sister, too. We all miss our dad. I don't remember ever seeing my dad mad or being mean. I still wonder why he died. Wasn't he scared? Didn't he love us? I won't ever know why he killed himself for sure, so I try not to think about that part too much.

My mom has a boyfriend now. At first it was kind of weird, but it makes her happy, so I am glad about that. She has done so much for us, and I want her to be happy. When I turned fifteen, she organized my *Quinceañera*, a celebration for becoming a young woman. She worked so hard to have everything just right, and I had a wonderful time. I felt very special. I loved having my family and friends there on my special day. I wished my dad could have been there, too, but I think he was watching me from heaven. I hope he is proud of me.

*   *   *   *   *

Ten to Twelve

Ten-to-twelve-year-olds are in the "in-between" years, and can have a difficult time knowing where they fit. Although not yet teenagers, many have nevertheless developed physically, with bodies well on the way to maturity. Others cling to behaviors and have physical attributes of their younger peers. Socially, children in this age group can vary tremendously in their perceptions and maturity, depending on their geographical location, parental and community values, and exposure to media. Because some children in this in-between time, particularly girls, may look older than their years, we may have unrealistic expectations about their ability to understand and integrate their experiences.

While some pre-adolescents have an almost "adult" understanding of death, others express ideas and opinions that reflect their immaturity. Grief responses will differ accordingly, with some able to confront it directly and others managing their grief primarily through play. You may want to read the previous section if your child is on the younger side or review adolescent issues if your child is more mature.

Some pre-teens demonstrate very little emotion at all, resuming everyday activities immediately and acting as if nothing has happened. Others will be clingy, tearful, and withdrawn, or express increased irritability. Some develop somatic difficulties: headaches, stomachaches, or flu-like symptoms. They worry about the health of their parents and other loved ones. They need reassurance that sometimes their bodies reflect their worries and stress through various aches and pains. Let them know that talking about their worries—or finding a way to express their tension through physical exercise or artistic outlets—will often make them feel better.

Many boys in this age group have not begun to develop physically, and their social development may also lag. They are less likely than girls to talk about emotional issues, preferring to engage with peers through sports or other physical activities, video games, or hobbies. If you are trying to support a boy following the suicide death of his parent, it may be helpful to let him know that his friends may not know what to say or how to deal with him in an appropriate manner. While some boys demonstrate a morbid curiosity about death and may ask many questions about the suicide, they are often uncomfortable talking about their feelings and may even joke or make sarcastic comments.

On the other hand, girls are more likely to try saying something comforting to a grieving friend, but may just as easily make a hurtful comment or behave in a way that alienates a classmate. Pre-teen girls are often struggling with self-esteem issues and can be particularly cruel or insensitive as they navigate friendship concerns.

Thirteen-year-old Alyssa, who was almost eleven when her mother died, relates how hard it was to know what to say about her mom's suicide. "I wanted to tell my friends about my mom, but I didn't want everyone to know, so I just told my two best friends. I didn't want rumors to spread all over school, so I told them not to tell anyone else, but they did. I guess it was just too hard to keep it a secret, but then everyone just looked away when I walked by. Then some girls I didn't even know came up and said they were so sorry about my mom, but one of them sort of giggled. I felt they were making fun of me. Some of my friends even got mad because I didn't tell them first. They were like fighting over who was my best friend. I didn't know what to say. All I could think about was that my mom was dead and my friends were mad at me."

Like many children, pre-adolescents may equate their actions as somehow being connected to the death. Fifteen-year-old Jonathan, who was twelve when his mother died from an overdose of prescription medicine, says that he still feels that if he hadn't been such a "troublemaker," his mother would have stayed alive. "I was starting to skip some classes I didn't like. The school called my mom a bunch of times. I had detention and was going to get suspended, and she was really upset with me. My dad wasn't around very much since the divorce, and I think she just got too frustrated with me. My grandma said my mom struggled with depression and it wasn't my fault, but I think I should have tried harder in school. I think maybe things might have been different if I had."

Jonathan has continued to struggle in school and act out in the community. His dad has remarried and Jonathan now lives with him. He has a new baby brother, a welcome addition to his family who has helped Jonathan begin to turn his life around. Jonathan wants to make sure his little brother doesn't get into trouble like he did, trouble which landed him in juvenile detention following a series of petty thefts. Now on probation, Jonathan sees a therapist, a woman who is helping him talk more about his mom and her suicide. "It's hard to talk about my mom," he says. "Sometimes I just don't know what to say, but we talk about how things used to be and what kind of a person my mom was. I really miss her. I have a lot of regrets. Sometimes I feel angry and really sad, but I am trying to become a person she would have been proud of if she had stayed around."

Like all children, Jonathan will need to revisit his feelings and memories about his mother's death as he matures and at certain milestones in his life. What he can begin to explore and verbalize at fifteen is different than what he was able to process and feel at twelve. Grieving his mom's suicide will be a lifelong process.

Not Quite a Teen

The in-between years can be confusing, but pre-teens, like all children, need information, love, support—and boundaries. We need to recognize that although they may be developing teen attitudes, perceptions and physical maturity, they are still children. We need to have realistic expectations of what they can manage and understand.

Diana, age ten, offers, "When your parent dies you need even more love than you did before that person died. You also need times where you get distracted so you don't think about it so much. Help your children by listening to what they worry about. Leave on a light and don't close your bedroom door at night."

Alyssa, whose story follows, told me, "We need space to get through this, but sometimes we might need to be pushed. But not too much, especially in the beginning, or we might freak out and back off too much. We need people who care about us to be there, but not pester us. We want to feel their concern, but please, don't dance around the issue or smother us. Be direct, but not critical. In the end it all comes down to how your kid is and what their personality is."

*   *   *   *   *

Alyssa is a spunky teen with an infectious smile who favors bright colors and big hoop earrings. Although she says she likes to talk, she found it very difficult after her mother died to talk with anyone about the death. It wasn't until she attempted suicide herself at twelve that she was able to begin to explore the impact her mother's life and death have had on her. Bright and curious, Alyssa, now in therapy, is becoming increasingly introspective. At thirteen, she is worldly and wise beyond her years in some ways—and also very much at risk. Fortunately, her father and extended family are working together to provide Alyssa with a stable environment and professional help.

ALYSSA'S STORY

"I don't want to rely too much on other people or get too close to someone, because I worry that somehow they might get ripped away."

I was almost eleven and in the fifth grade when my mom killed herself by overdosing on medication. That was about two and a half years ago and I am still grieving, although most people wouldn't know it because I'm doing O.K. at school and I have a lot of friends. I am an outgoing, fun-loving person. People think I am tough and strong, and I guess I am, but I am still trying to learn to let my feelings out. I am pretty independent. I don't want to rely too much on other people or get too close to someone, because I worry that somehow they might get ripped away. It's just hard to feel too trusting.

My mom was so optimistic, so sweet and pretty, and she would never say anything mean. I hope I will be pretty, too. I know I will be taller. My mom was really creative and loved to paint and draw. She was also an awesome cook who made great bagels and cookies and always made us special meals on our birthdays. She had a serious side and she was smart. She could stand up for herself and wouldn't back down if she believed in something.

I'm not sweet or calm like she was. I lose my temper more, and even though I love to read, I am not a good student with perfect grades. I am more of a troublemaker, and I tend to argue with my teachers. I love to talk, which sometimes gets me in trouble in class. I have an artistic side like she did. I like to design clothes and paint, but unlike my mom, I'm not much of a cook. I usually burn stuff. She loved to travel and I do, too. Our family lived in England and Sweden for a time and we have traveled in other countries.

My mom had problems with depression and sometimes I do, too.

I think her medication messed her up. She had too many prescription drugs from different doctors and she self-medicated with alcohol as well.

I remember one suicide attempt that happened when I was nine. My mom had been drinking and she and my dad got in a fight. My sister and I were worried about the fight. My dad was downstairs with us, trying to explain what the fight was about, when we heard her yell. We ran upstairs and found her standing naked in the bathroom, holding a razor. There was blood everywhere, and her eyes were unfocused and glazed over. She asked us if this was what we wanted. We were shocked and scared. My dad told us to go back downstairs and he would talk with us after he had handled my mom. I waited, but I fell asleep before I talked with him. I don't remember what happened after that.

The last conversation I had with my mom was upsetting. We were driving back from a conference with my teacher at school where I had gotten in trouble. At the time I was taking care of my younger brother a lot when my mom was wasted. I felt like I just didn't have time to focus on schoolwork, and I didn't do all my assignments. I got mad at her and said, "Maybe if you had been awake and doing the stuff moms are supposed to do instead of sleeping, maybe then I'd do my homework." I felt bad as soon as I said that, so I apologized, but my mom said she had to go, had to leave. I thought she meant she wanted to go away for a long time and I said, "You can't just leave. I love you." She said she was a terrible mother and ran into the house and out again really fast. I tried to tell her I loved her, but I don't know if she heard me. She just drove off and I never saw her alive again.

That afternoon in my room, I did my homework and I kept thinking about everything and going over and over what had happened. I worried that she would disappear and never come back, but I didn't expect she'd kill herself. But then again, I wasn't sure. I even tried to imagine what I would say at her funeral and then told myself not to be so stupid. I knocked over a clay mask and it shattered. That felt like a sign. It was really pretty and it broke.

I was worried that night when she didn't come home. We drove around with my dad looking for her, but I finally went to sleep. My brother woke me up in the morning to tell me she was dead. I didn't believe him and called him a liar, but then my dad told me it was true. I felt like I was in a dream. I didn't want to know the details or anything about her death. Everything seemed like it was going in one ear and out another. I just sat there on my bed in my room as people started arriving. I could hear bits and pieces of their conversations, but I didn't want to talk to anyone. I kept thinking that she might walk back in the door.

I felt like it was my fault she killed herself. My sister blamed me, too, but I guess all us kids blamed ourselves because we did fight a lot. Now I think that maybe it was all the medication that messed her up, but I don't know. I think she had a hard life growing up. She was born in El Salvador, and her parents got divorced when she was only three. She told me her stepfather was very strict when she was growing up. She didn't get to have much of a relationship with her real father, who didn't even come for the funeral. I never got to meet him. She always loved him and he said he'd visit, but he didn't.

I don't remember that much about the funeral except that they had her make-up all wrong. She didn't look like herself. I cried, but I didn't want to talk. My uncle was there and he's a really cool guy, big and muscular. It was so weird to see him cry. I remember feeling starved, and afterwards we went out for hamburgers. My mom was dead and we were eating hamburgers.

After she died it seemed like I saw a trillion shrinks, but I was really superficial and wouldn't let them in on anything about me or how I really felt. I don't even know if I knew how I felt. Of course I was sad and people kept telling me it was O.K. to cry. But I am the middle child and have always been the tough one who didn't cry. Since everyone saw me that way, I just continued to play along. I was in fifth grade and I just wanted to be with my friends and have things be normal instead of being around people who were crying all the time. I went back to school and got into my life while my older sister was the one who seemed to be falling apart.

But everything caught up with me, and eventually, I got depressed, too. Almost two years after my mom died I started feeling so sad and alone. I was home one night, talking on the phone with a guy friend after having had a bad day at school. He was going through some hard stuff, too, and we started joking about leaving or running away. I felt so discouraged about my life. I wanted to just get away from everything, but I knew I couldn't really go anywhere, so I took twenty-five Advil and twenty-five Tylenol and fell asleep.

At 3:45 a.m. I woke up and my stomach was hurting really bad. I went into my sister's room and told her what I had done. She woke up my dad and he drove me to the emergency room. They made me take charcoal and I threw up. I fell asleep, but I had to have a sitter, someone to make sure I was O.K. while I was recovering. I felt like I really did want to die, but I don't think I really thought about what that would mean. I ended up spending eleven days in a psychiatric hospital in a program with other kids who had emotional problems. And I finally started talking about what was going on inside me.

I went to stay for a few months with my aunt, my dad's sister, who lives in another state. She's a middle child, too, and I have always felt comfortable talking with her. I started seeing a therapist twice a week, and she taught me that I really needed to talk. I couldn't stay quiet about my feelings anymore. She was straightforward and patient, and I really liked her. The second anniversary of my mom's death passed. I felt really sad, but I could feel myself starting to feel a little happy again, too.

I came home a couple of months later and things were going pretty well until I took my dad's van one night to go out for a ride. A girlfriend was over and we smoked some pot. After she left, I felt bored. Even though I was twelve, I knew how to drive because once I got to try driving when I was with my dad in the desert on a road where there weren't any people, so I felt pretty comfortable driving the van. I was just planning to go out for a little while and come back before my dad got home. I drove around the neighborhood, but when I got to my driveway I saw the garage door going down and realized that my dad was home early. So I took off.

To make a long story short, I ended up going into my best friend's house, but no one was home. I knew where the house key was so I went inside. I was kind of freaking out about what I had done. I called my guy friend and he told me I needed to call my dad, but I was too scared and getting kind of panicked. Then my dad arrived and so did the police. They were worried I was going to try to kill myself so they broke into the house and found me hiding upstairs in the closet. I got in a lot of trouble and almost had to go to juvenile hall.

I ended up going to an intensive outpatient support group after that. I recently finished that group and I think I'm doing O.K. I know I am impulsive, but I really haven't done anything bad or criminal. I don't stay out all night or do bad things. Normally I am pretty good even though I probably talk too much in class.

I am not sure how my behavior is related to my mom. I am learning I have to keep talking about what is going on in my life and how I am feeling. I am taking a low dose of medication now, Zoloft, which some people think contributes to suicide. My dad and my doctor are watching my behavior very closely, and I try to be aware of how it makes me feel as well. My sister took it for a while, too, but she doesn't anymore.

Sometimes I get headaches or stomachaches and have to come home from school because I feel achy all over. I don't sleep well either. I am kind of a dramatic person, but sometimes I feel like I have no energy. I have ways of trying to make myself feel better. I am a Pisces and love the water, so I take hot baths to relax myself. I write in my journal, paint or go for a walk. I like to talk to my friends. I do yoga and stretch before bed.

Sometimes I worry about what I would do if someone else close to me died. I guess that is a normal worry, just like when I worry about how I am going to get through seventh grade. My dad is dating someone now and I don't really like her, but I try to be polite. I am excited about the future. I want to travel more and get my driver's license. I look forward to going to college and moving out, but I'm not sure if I want to be too far from home.

Most of the time I don't feel guilty anymore about my mom's suicide. If a person wants to kill herself, she will, yet I still wonder sometimes if I could have prevented her death. There is always that "what if?" in my mind. She promised me she wouldn't, but she did. That hurts a lot, and I know it's going to hurt for a long time, but I am learning not to let those feelings of grief and guilt consume me. I just can't let myself keep those feelings inside anymore.

CHAPTER FIVE

Teen Grief

"Sometimes I feel like I have a split personality. I get angry and don't understand how someone so talented, so beautiful and smart—she was a nurse and seemed to have the perfect life—how could she just end it all? But then my more mature side remembers she didn't choose to have this illness. Don't judge her for what she did. That wasn't her. That wasn't my mom. The person who killed herself was a stranger."

—PAIGE, AGE 17

Given the normal but profound changes of adolescence, a teenager's grief can be complex. Recent research has only added to the challenge of understanding the dynamics of teen development. It suggests that while teens may "look" physically mature and adult-like, the pre-frontal cortex of their brains is still developing. The pre-frontal cortex is responsible for setting priorities, organizing thoughts, suppressing impulses, and weighing the consequences of their actions.[1] This may explain why some teens are more prone to emotional outbursts, scattered thinking, reckless behavior, and the apparent inability to exercise good judgment—even without adding the staggering emotional weight of a parent who dies by suicide.

Parental disagreements and conflicts are common as teens attempt to establish autonomy. If a suicide occurs following an argument, or if a teen feels he was unresponsive to his parent's feelings prior to the death, he is likely to feel terribly guilty. A parent's suicide leaves him with no way to say good-bye or attempt to resolve comments made in anger. This is a particularly devastating experience for a teen. He is likely to experience reactions similar to those of adults, but will have fewer ways to cope.

Although some magical thinking may still occur, most teens are able to view death as final and irreversible. However, there is no getting around the fact that a parent appears to have willfully taken his or her own life. When death has been "chosen," which is how many young people define suicide, a prolonged and acute sense of unreality often characterizes a teen's response. Feelings of numbness, followed by anxiety and, on occasion, panic, will often occur.

The physical and emotional shock may leave a teen feeling jittery or light-headed, weak in the knees, or out of breath. She may experience heart palpitations, clammy skin, or an upset stomach. Her mind may simply "go blank" trying to comprehend what has happened. She may discover her short-term memory is impaired and that moments, days, even certain events cannot be recalled. Other teens report feeling a flood of emotions and are compelled to cry, scream, shout, and rage.

"At first I couldn't believe it," relates fifteen-year-old Amber. "I remember just standing there and everything around me seemed frozen, as if I was watching myself in the middle of a movie or something. I started yelling and screaming and saying that it wasn't true, that she couldn't be dead! And then I started crying. It seemed like I cried for a long, long time, for hours and hours."

Teens must be allowed to set their own timetable as they begin to integrate the death. They can be encouraged to ask questions when they are ready to learn the answers. They need to know they can decide how many details they want to hear and from whom. Honesty is best from the surviving parent and other important adults. An "I don't know" or "I don't understand, either" is better than deflecting or ignoring questions or making up answers.

Teens will grieve and try to take care of themselves consistent with their personalities. Initially, they may need to participate in activities to distract themselves from the pain. They may want to be with friends, go to a movie or out to eat rather than stay at home with family. Playing video games or surfing the Internet, shopping, reading, or watching TV may be a way of taking care of themselves. These reactions should not be viewed as a callous response to the trauma.

Don't be surprised if your teen makes comments like, "My dad had to go and screw up my life. I'll never be able to go to college now," or "What's everybody at school going to think of me?" Such responses may seem self-absorbed or insensitive, but they are honest reflections of a teenager's worries about the future as well as an expression of his hurt and anger.

It is important not to judge the response, but to know that shocking information can generate reactions that seem inappropriate as a teen's brain quickly moves into survival mode. Such automatic responses, made without thinking clearly or feeling the full anguish of the moment, allow them to counteract life-shattering news.

"Right after I heard that my dad had committed suicide, all I could think about was going to my soccer game," relates seventeen-year-old Dustin, who was thirteen when his dad died. "The first thing I said was, 'Who's going to take me to my game?' Everyone looked at me like I was crazy. My uncle blew up and said something about me only thinking about myself, as usual. I feel bad now that I said that. I don't know why I did. I just wanted to get away, I guess. I just wanted to be somewhere else."

Tears and Fears

Crying is a natural letting go of emotions that need to be released. It is a way to keep the body in balance. However, crying may not be a teen's first response. Numbness and disbelief may prevail, making it difficult for a teen to express all the emotions she is feeling inside. Not being able to cry is confusing and creates guilt, especially if she feels she should be crying and that others expect her to be emotional.

"I couldn't cry at first," states fifteen-year-old Ellen. "I felt horrible, so unbelievably crushed, like the wind was knocked out of me. I couldn't even stand up, but the tears just wouldn't come. It seemed like everyone was looking at me and I knew they were wondering why I wasn't crying. I didn't know why either. I felt so guilty, like how could I not be crying? My mother was dead. I was afraid there was something wrong with me. Later, when I did start to cry, I wondered if I could ever stop."

Some teens hold back their tears because they feel they need to take care of everyone else, and they worry that their crying would be hard on others. Others are angry or bewildered and prefer to keep busy with friends or activities as a way to ward off their tears. Many teens prefer to grieve privately, crying in the shower or late at night in bed. If your child does share her tears with you, it is important to be still and listen, rather than cajole her. Do not try to cheer her up or "fix" her pain.

Telling Friends

Teens are more likely than younger children to want to talk with their friends about the death. However, because peer relationships are so important at this age and many teens already feel concern about not fitting in, the suicide of a parent can magnify feelings of alienation. This makes it difficult to know whom to talk to about this traumatic experience.

Sometimes, well-meaning adults encourage teens to keep this information a secret, or even to lie about the death. This is not advisable. It puts a greater burden on a teen, and may place her friendships in jeopardy as friends may misinterpret the reason for her distance or discomfort.

Teens need to be encouraged to decide if, when, and with whom they want to share the information. They need reassurance that sharing what has happened with friends they trust can be a way to receive support from those who care about them. It is, however, important to acknowledge that telling one friend may lead to others also learning about the suicide. Like people of all ages, teens are often unable to keep such a big secret.

Some friends, even those with whom they feel a close bond, may not know what to say or how to support them. Friends can feel helpless and may respond with indifference, or attempt to change the subject as a way to cope with their own discomfort. Others, more often those who have gone through a loss themselves and understand the sense of isolation and confusion that may follow, are able to provide comfort and reassurance.

Grieving teens often do not know what they need from others following a traumatic death. Often it is simply a listening ear. Supportive friends can make all the difference to a bereaved teen who wonders if her life will ever be "normal" again. This is not a time to demand that a teen focus solely on family and thus be isolated from her friends, but to encourage her to spend time with them if she wishes. Many teens appreciate having close friends participate in memorial rituals and sit with them at the funeral. Letting her make those choices will help her feel more in control at a time when she may feel that her life is very much out of control.

Going Back to School

For some teens, going back to school is a welcome relief from the pressures and emotions on the home front following the death. Other teens avoid a return to school for as long as possible. Facing peers can be daunting, as teens wonder what information has reached the school community.

Often, information about the suicide precedes a student's return to school, and teens worry how peers will respond. They fear they will be talked about or possibly ignored by other students or teachers who may feel uncomfortable or judgmental. They worry about how to talk to others about a trauma they don't understand themselves. They wonder how they will be able to concentrate in class or manage homework. Many become keenly aware of identity changes, realizing they may no longer be seen in certain cherished roles. No longer identified as the goalie on the soccer team or the quirky drama student, they are now the one with the dead parent—the parent who killed himself.

Not wanting to be marked as an outsider, teens may suppress feelings or downplay the trauma, not knowing or not accepting how they feel. They will need choices about how they wish to be supported at school. Having a re-entry plan often helps, although some teens will reject emotional or logistical support from adults.

Before he returns to school, encourage your teen to have a private conference with his school counselor or a favorite teacher who can act on his behalf. He is likely to feel hesitant about making this contact, as many teens just want to go on as if nothing has happened. Others worry they will be singled out in some way. Offer to make the call yourself if he feels unable to do it on his own. Explain to him that without information about how his life has drastically changed, his teachers will be unaware of his needs and concerns. They may feel that any changed behavior or subsequent slipping grades are the result of indifference towards school or a change in priorities. Let your child know you are willing to accompany him to any meetings, or suggest he might want to take a friend with him. You need to let him know that there are ways to make school attendance and assignments easier to manage.

Arriving back at school with a friend is often helpful for a grieving teen, particularly if that friend shares some of her classes. Having a place to go on campus in the event a teen is momentarily unable to stay in class is also a good idea. Sometimes it is hard to focus on assignments or participate in class discussions.

Although your teen will grieve in a manner consistent with her personality, she may surprise you with her ability to face this trauma. I remember watching Paige, a seventeen-year-old who was respected by her peers for her athletic abilities and known for her pragmatic, caring personality, address her humanities class of forty peers two days after discovering her mother's body. Her two teachers, who shared teaching responsibilities, had gathered the class in a circle on a field outside the classroom. All the students held hands as Paige, accompanied by her boyfriend and best girlfriend, told them, "My mom was bipolar. We lost her a year ago when my parents separated. I don't know why this happened, but I have been told there was nothing I could do. Her illness is what took her from us."

Paige's teachers had done their homework. They had been in touch with Paige and her dad to determine what information she wished to share. They had invited me to help facilitate a class discussion. During the first hour of class, prior to Paige's arrival, her teachers had encouraged their students to make cards and write in their journals. We sat on the floor in a circle and passed around a "talking stick." Each student held the stick and had the choice about whether to share his or her feelings or thoughts about what had happened, or to pass the stick on. Their teachers went first, expressing their own feelings in a heartfelt way. Many students followed, choosing to talk about their own experiences with divorce and death. By the time Paige arrived her classmates were prepared to support her.

Unfortunately, many teachers do not know how to respond to a student grieving the loss of someone special, and they are even more tentative when the death has been by suicide. (See Chapter Nine – *Back to School: What Your Child's Teachers Need to Know*, for more information on how teachers can support grieving students.)

Changing Family Roles

When a death occurs, roles change in the family. A surviving parent may have to get a job or increase her workload to help support the family. This necessitates a shift in a teen's responsibilities, social life, and daily routine. Often an older child is expected to take on additional chores or to care for younger siblings.

This shift can be difficult for all family members, particularly if the changes aren't acknowledged or discussed as a family. A teen may be thrust into a parental role and resent being a disciplinarian for younger siblings who may not cooperate fully. While it is often necessary for a teen to pick up extra chores, too many responsibilities without the opportunity to be involved in the decision-making creates additional stress.

One way to contend with role and responsibility changes is to have family meetings. Although it may be difficult, try to sit down with your children and have a frank discussion about the inevitable changes that lie ahead. You may cry or find yourself feeling angry as you engage in this conversation. But as you and your children discuss and discover ways to cope with everyday tasks, you will find yourself moving forward. The path is likely to be bumpy, but you may also find yourself getting closer to one another.

You may want to suggest something like: "We are all going to be doing chores we haven't done before, and we have to support one another as we are learning. That means taking turns preparing food, doing the laundry, and taking care of the house without criticizing each other. We are going to talk about what needs to be done and plan a schedule together. I want each of you to let me know what you think you can manage and what you would be willing to do. We are going to figure this out and try hard to work together. When I am not here, your sister is in charge. This means she is going to do her best to be kind and make good decisions. If you are unhappy with those decisions, please cooperate anyway. We will sit down and talk about your feelings as soon as I am home. If you want, you can write down your concerns and put them in this suggestion box I have made. This is not going to be about who is right and who is wrong, but about us trying to work together."

A parent can also recruit other trusted and loved adults—the mother of their teen's best friend or a favorite aunt or uncle—to help a teen learn new skills. Your child might appreciate his grandparents' help in learning to cook or mow the lawn. Younger siblings need to be enlisted to help with family chores as well. Learning to do laundry, caring for pets or helping prepare meals may be challenging, but can also build self-esteem and a sense of mastery. It is important to work together so the burden of responsibility is shared.

Emotional Health Issues

Many teens report sleeping difficulties following the suicide death of a parent. Insomnia or oversleeping can occur, as can generalized fatigue and lethargy. Headaches, nausea, and stomach pain are also common. Grief can also trigger a suppression of the immune system, and flu-like symptoms can occur in a bereaved person of any age.

Teens also report concerns about feeling "crazy," describing instances when their thoughts or perceptions alarm them. A teen may think he saw his deceased mother at the mall or convince himself that he heard her voice or her familiar footsteps in the hall outside his bedroom. He may get lost walking to school or forget where he is going. He may try to call his deceased parent on the phone or talk out loud to his loved one. While these actions or perceptions may seem crazy, in most situations they are a normal part of the grieving process.

"Every time I saw a black Explorer I thought my dad might be driving it," relates Andrew, age seventeen. "I couldn't seem to get it through my mind that it wasn't him. A few times I even followed guys in black Explorers to make sure. Now that seems crazy, but I guess I just couldn't believe he was dead."

Teens need to be reassured that this "crazy" behavior doesn't mean they are having a "nervous breakdown," but are experiencing symptoms of grief. They need to be reassured these symptoms are temporary, and encouraged to forgive themselves for not being reliable, responsible, or clear-headed.

Talking About the Death—Or Not

Suicide can silence even the most talkative teen. A young person, who might normally always want the last word or is prone to offer her unsolicited opinion, may be unable to articulate what or how she is feeling. Adolescent boys, in particular, often have a difficult time talking about death. It is important not to push for conversation, but to let your teenager know that you are available to listen or simply spend time together.

Your teen may show you his grief more through his actions than with words. He may protest the death by acting out and/or withdrawing. He may have little to say, answering your questions reluctantly or speaking in a monotone, preferring to spend his time in his room. He may lose himself in video games or watching TV. Allow him time on his own, but insist that he join you for dinner whenever possible. Let him know you value his company and that you believe it is important for him to maintain some contact with you and other family members.

Risky Behavior

Your teen may feel he needs to test his own mortality by defying death through risky behavior. This, coupled with the natural inclination of many teens to believe that nothing bad will ever happen to them, is frightening for a parent. If you are concerned about such behaviors, you will need to have a serious discussion with your teenager. Explain to him that he is more at risk during this time of grief. Let him know that you want him to have time with his friends and opportunities to have fun, but you will curtail his activities or prohibit him from driving if you feel he is endangering himself or others. Tell him how important he is to you and how much you love him. Reassure him that you will get through this together.

Because he may want to try and feel better fast or escape from feelings of anger, sadness, and depression, he may engage in self-destructive behavior in the form of drug or alcohol abuse. He will need to be educated about how such substances may make him feel better for a short time, but this "high" is only temporary. It will be followed by a greater "low" as he comes face to face with the reality of the death. You may want to include your teen's friends in this discussion. Let them all know that while you understand about the natural inclination of teenagers to want to experiment, doing so at this time can be particularly dangerous for your child. In this way, you appeal to your child's peers as additional sources of support during this deeply troubling time.

Sexual Activity

It is not unusual for a teen to become sexually active during the grief process. She may need to feel close to someone, and often other family members are emotionally unavailable as they tend to their own grief. Becoming sexually intimate may serve as a distraction from her pain. It may also be seen or experienced as an antidote to feeling disconnected and out of touch. Sexual contact may initially feel comforting, but can leave a teen feeling embarrassed, ashamed, and even more depressed. A frank conversation with your teen about your concerns may help her make wise decisions, but not necessarily. If you are unable to address these issues, enlist the aid of another adult your teen trusts and respects.

The Challenge of Adolescence

Raising a teenager even in normal circumstances is enough of a challenge for most people. While not every teenager runs the gamut of rebellious or unpredictable behavior, many test the patience and resolve of those who love them. Your teen is likely to challenge you to look at your own belief systems and ways of being. Despite your love, you may not always like your teenager. Sometimes you will feel worn down by his or her energy and adventurous behavior. You will worry and wonder if you are doing the right thing.

If you are raising a teen and trying to cope with your own grief, you have a formidable task ahead of you. But it is not an impossible one. You will need the help of others—friends, family members and possibly professionals. Do not hesitate to ask for help. Remember that although you will try your best, your grief and a teen's natural reluctance to share information may make it more difficult than ever to communicate effectively. Do your best to keep the lines of communication open without trying to control your child's every move. Recognize her need to be with friends, but make time to be with her as well. Remember: You are still her parent, and as she matures, you will need to continue to maintain balance on that often shifting line between setting limits and letting go, of guiding her as well as trusting her own decision-making. When she falters or doesn't live up to your expectations, know that your responses will not always be perfect. You may say or do some things you regret, but the bottom line is that you love her. Never hesitate to reassure her of that fact, and that you will get through this together.

*   *   *   *   *

Blonde-haired and blue-eyed, Alicia is twenty and living with her boyfriend. She attends junior college and works two jobs. Her father killed himself six years ago. Alicia struggles with depression, but she is determined to get her college degree and become a teacher.

ALICIA'S STORY

"For a long time I felt like he was sleeping in another room or he was on vacation because it felt like physically he was still with us, that he hadn't really left."

I was fourteen when my dad killed himself by taking an overdose of Vicodin, mixed with alcohol. He had threatened suicide several times before, and we had taken him to a crisis clinic. They told us he would be fine, that he just wanted attention, so we didn't take him seriously. He promised me that even though he was depressed, he wouldn't do anything stupid. All I could think about when I heard he killed himself was that he had broken his promise.

I had been at a slumber party. When I got home the police were there waiting for the coroner. They allowed me to see my dad's body and say good-bye. He was in his recliner. I was in shock. I told him I loved him and to watch over me at my graduation, but I was in a fog. My camera was on a table near his body. The police took it to see if he had taken any pictures of himself beforehand. It was a long time before I got that camera back.

One of my relatives took me down the street, so I didn't see them take his body away. I felt numb and kept asking myself, "O.K., what should I be doing?" My mom was hysterical so I had to call family and friends to tell them about my dad. That seems a little weird to me now—that a fourteen-year-old was in this position—but I guess my survival techniques took over. My friends were shocked. I think they were expecting me to be crying more, but I was numb. I couldn't believe he was dead.

I was so worried about the future. I didn't know if we would be able to stay in our house because my dad had been the breadwinner and my mom didn't have a job. I had never seen her balance a checkbook or pump gas. I didn't know how we would cope. My sister, who is seven years older than me, finally arrived. She was helpful, but I felt embarrassed by my mom's behavior. She was crying on my friend's father's shoulder and I kept thinking, "God, they're going to think she's a freak or something." I don't know why that bothered me. I just felt sensitive about everything and couldn't make sense of things. For a long time I felt like he was sleeping in another room or he was on vacation because it felt like physically he was still with us, that he hadn't really left.

My parents argued a lot. They had separated before, but my dad was living back at home. I think they had a fight that night. I don't know all the details because my mom still won't talk about it. Sometimes I think if I had been there I could have stopped the fight, or maybe he wouldn't have gotten so upset. In some ways I guess I hold my mom a little responsible. You can't really say that anybody is responsible for someone killing himself, but I guess sometimes I wonder why they didn't just separate or get a divorce. They had so many problems. My dad had some serious physical injuries and was on disability. My mom suffered from severe depression and anxiety. There was a lot of medication in the house. Sometimes I think she made my dad feel like nobody loved him, even his two kids. Maybe he felt that if his wife didn't love him and his kids didn't love him, well then, why go on?

I think my mom has withheld information from me about my dad's death. I know he left a note, but she wouldn't show it to me. I found the note a couple of years later when I was snooping through her stuff. It said to "take care of the girls," but the handwriting was really sloppy. He never finished what he was going to write because apparently, the Vicodin had kicked in. I wish I knew more about what he was thinking in his last moments.

I've always had problems with my mom, but it's been harder since my dad died. She got overprotective because I guess she was scared that I was going to die or something. She also took out her anger about my dad's death on me. That was really difficult. She was upset all the time, and I had to be the parent. His death was hard for her. She didn't have many people to talk to because a lot of their friends held her responsible for his death. It seemed like her married friends didn't associate with her anymore because they felt too weird. There was such a stigma attached to his death. Even though I was mad at her, I felt angry with her friends for laying into her.

Our problems continued, particularly because she got together with another man who moved into our house less than a year after my dad's death. That was hard for me—it was so soon. On the one hand it took the pressure off me and I thought, "Terrific, I can actually go out with my friends again." But at the same time I couldn't help but think, "Yeah, you loved Dad so much, but you're already seeing someone else."

Two years after my dad's suicide my mom remarried. My sister and I were really mad and decided we didn't like him because we thought he was trying to take my dad's place. He wasn't really, but at the time we thought he was. It's much better now. We realize he never tried to step in as a father, and I appreciate that he never got involved in the arguments my mom and I had. He would share his ideas, but he never told me what to do or what was wrong or right. If we needed him, he was always there for us. If my car needed to be fixed, he would handle it. He was willing to take care of all those little things, and that meant a lot. I see that now.

Even though she didn't live with us, I am glad I had my sister to talk to, since I couldn't talk with my mom. We would reminisce and we could cry together. She's the only one now who tells me that my dad would be proud of me. When I get really discouraged with school or when I'm irritated and want to drop a class or hate a teacher, she's like, "Just keep going. You can do it." We have memories together.

No one else talks about my dad unless they want to figure out what the problem is with me. If I am in a bad mood, my mother or grandmother will say, "Well, that's because of her father." That is so annoying. My mom took down my dad's pictures and gave away or sold most of his stuff. She tried to get rid of every little memory of him, but I have the belt buckle he used to wear. It has an eagle on it, and is totally country-western because that's what he was, a cowboy. I like to wear it when I go country line dancing. It's kind of cool that I can wear something that he wore.

My dad was a hard-working guy. If he was sick or tired, he always went to work. He worked a lot of overtime. He was also very truthful. I knew I could count on him to give me an honest answer when I asked him a question. He was a quiet man who didn't show his emotions, which was part of his problem. I never saw him cry until my parents got separated. He fought with my mom, but he never yelled at me.

I'm a hard worker like he was, but I don't hold my emotions in. When people make me mad or upset me, I let them know.

I remember going back to school after my dad killed himself. My friends were supportive, maybe overly so, even kind of nosey. They hadn't had anyone close die. I don't think they really cared that much, but were more curious and trying to figure it out. My teachers were great. My mom called the school and let my counselor know, and my counselor prepared all my teachers. They were understanding and gave me extra time. Many of them didn't seem to know what to say, but I could feel their support.

I had one teacher who was really helpful. He pulled me out of class and said, "I understand your dad died. My mom died a few years ago, not in the same way, but if you ever need to talk, or you ever need to leave class early, go ahead. No questions asked. I'll understand." I relied on him throughout high school. I had him as a teacher in several classes and he got to know a lot about my situation and my problems with my mom. Sometimes he would come up to me and say, "Do you need to talk?" and most of the time, I did. There really wasn't anyone else I felt comfortable talking to, besides my sister, so I appreciated his support. He's still there at my old school, and I check back with him every once in a while. I was glad I had school after my dad's death. Being there and doing my work was my way of forgetting about my problems.

I slept a lot when I wasn't at school. I was always so tired. My mom seemed to sleep a lot as well. I didn't realize it then, but sleeping was probably one of my ways of coping. My mind was just too tired to do anything else. I often felt depressed and moody. When I got mad at my mom, I would throw things, not at her, but at the wall, trying to get the feelings out. I still get depressed easily. Sometimes I just feel drained and empty, like I want to curl up into a ball and cry. A lot of times I do.

I had been in counseling before my dad died because my parents were getting separated, but our insurance only paid for one more session after his death. I wished I could have continued. I tried a support group for teenagers. It was O.K., but I think it made me more depressed when I heard others talk about their parents or other family members dying. I wasn't always thinking about my dad when I would go there, and all these emotions would come up. I didn't always want to deal with those feelings, but overall it was nice hanging out with kids my own age.

I helped plan my dad's memorial service. He was cremated, and I helped pick out his urn. I gave a small speech at his service. I don't have a religious community and I kind of wish I did. I have had friends say that people who commit suicide go to hell. That really bothers me. Maybe if I had specific religious beliefs, I could better understand those questions about heaven and hell. I believe that God takes everybody in a certain way, but I don't think God comes and says you have to kill yourself. I wish people wouldn't say that about suicide to me. Unless they have had someone they love kill themself, they don't really understand.

My dad's ashes were in our house for a year or two, but now they are in a military cemetery that is kind of far away from us. My sister and I went there this year for the first time. We are the only ones in our family who have been to see him. I feel guilty about that because he's just sitting up there all by himself. I wish he were closer, because I would like to visit him more often. I miss him the most around big events like when I got my driver's license and when I graduated. I always wonder what he would have said. Would he have showed his emotions or told me he was proud of me?

I guess I will always wonder about that, but I am doing O.K. It's been six years since his death and I have grown up a lot. I get stressed, but I try to figure out what is bothering me and fix it instead of sleeping. I try to work through problems instead of letting them overcome me. I have a boyfriend who listens and accepts every part of me instead of being critical. We have been together three years and have worked through a lot of issues. I think we'll get married some day, but first I have to focus on school. School makes me happy. I feel good when I see my hard work pay off. I work as a waitress to help pay for school and living expenses. Sometimes when I wait on doctors, I feel intimidated, but, hey, I am going to get my college degree. Whenever I talk to people who are well-educated, I'm very intrigued by them. I thirst for knowledge and I want to succeed.

As I've gotten older, I understand my feelings a lot better. I know when I'm numb to things, and I'm learning how to deal with change.

Life can change so suddenly. I am learning how to pick up the pieces, put things back together, and move on.

Sometimes I get really depressed and, if I'm going to be completely honest, I have to say I have thought of suicide myself. It's not like I want to be with my dad, and I don't think I would ever do it, but sometimes I just don't want to deal with the emotional pain I feel. I worry that if I talk about my suicide feelings to someone else, they might be scared. Maybe they will think it runs in the blood and because my dad killed himself, I might, too. But that makes me ten times more against suicide. I know about the grief and pain that follows suicide and all those unanswered questions and how people look at you in certain ways. So I don't tell people about my suicide thoughts. I just say I'm depressed and I do talk about that. I talk with my boyfriend and cry. Sometimes that's what I really need, the chance to talk, cry, and be held. Dealing with my depression is one of the challenges I see ahead of me, that and getting through college.

My biggest worry about my future is that I don't have an emotional or financial safety net. My mom still doesn't work, and because there is tension in our relationship, I can't really trust her to be there for me. That really scares me. I hope to be a high school teacher some day, and I want to have a house and a family. I just can't think about that too much right now. I have to get the basics taken care of first.

I have learned that the intense pain of a parent's suicide doesn't last forever. At first it's so hard, and you feel numb. When that numbness goes away, it hurts even more, but then, after a while, you hurt less. You begin to understand your feelings and deal with them, and life does get better. You have to learn to trust your own feelings. Some people may tell you it was your fault, or that you should have done something to make it not happen, or that the person who committed suicide went to hell. You can't listen to any of that. I try to remember that my dad loved me. He didn't kill himself to make me mad or get revenge.

If I had any advice for parents it would be to remember to be a parent. I know that parents have difficulty dealing with their spouse's death, but your child still needs you. You can say, "I get scared, too, sometimes," or "I can't always be perfect," but you need to pick yourself up. We need to be reassured that you will always be there.

* * * * *

Dustin, nearly eighteen, is a bright, thoughtful young man who prides himself on his independence. Although his mother tried to get him into counseling following his father's suicide five years ago, he refused. Like many teens, he engages in some risky behaviors. He agrees that sometimes he needs to exercise more caution, but maintains he is not as "crazy" as he used to be.

DUSTIN'S STORY

"He was dead. I felt like I was the last man standing."

I was thirteen when my dad died. I remember being shocked, but somehow not surprised. He never talked about it, but I always sensed his depression. I could look into his eyes and see something was on his mind, something wasn't right. I would often think, as I was saying good-bye to him, that this might be the last time I'd see him. But I didn't really expect he would kill himself.

I remember our last conversation. He had taken me to Target to get some candy. When he dropped me off at home he said all the usual stuff, "Don't do stupid things. Don't be hard on your mom about the divorce," things like that. The last thing he said was, "What are we going to do tomorrow?"

I didn't think it would be the last time I saw him alive, but it was.

The next day I was at a friend's house when my mom's best friend came to pick me up. That was kind of strange, but when I saw my uncle's car in our driveway, I knew something had happened to my dad. When I walked into my house and saw everyone crying, I was stunned. My grandmother told me my dad had killed himself. I knew it was true, but I couldn't really believe he had died. I knew he was struggling, but the worst thing had finally happened. He was dead. I felt like I was the last man standing.

My dad had been battling manic depression all his life. I guess he felt he just couldn't go on. My parents were getting divorced, and he was financially insecure. He struggled with alcohol and substance abuse. I guess he was too overwhelmed and felt suicide was the only way to get rid of all that pain and suffering.

I remember that before he died I was feeling really connected to my dad. I had always been a "momma's boy" until I was ten or eleven, but by twelve I was beginning to break away. My mom and I weren't getting along that well, but things were O.K. with my dad. Life seemed pretty cool. I felt like I had everything.

Then my parents separated. That was such a shock. It seemed everything was fine before that, but then they started having all these deep discussions and my dad "went away on a business trip" for two weeks. I knew something bad was happening, that my life was going to change. When he came back they told us they were separating, that the love wasn't there anymore. They never told me why. We all cried. I remember that was the last time I thought that everything was perfect. I never really felt a part of our family after that.

After he died, I didn't want to talk to anyone about how I was feeling. I took out my feelings in sports, played soccer the next day. I remember it seemed like everyone was bugging me to talk to a counselor. That made me mad, like they didn't feel I was capable of handling myself. All that nagging about seeing a grief counselor or going to a support group just made me shut down. My counselor at school would call me into his office, but I never talked about it with him either. I didn't feel like I needed to share my feelings with anyone. My counselor was a good guy, but it wasn't his responsibility to make me feel better.

My mom and our family doctor were concerned about me, thinking that since my dad was manic-depressive, I might be at risk for serious depression. They insisted, so I did take an anti-depressant for about six months. I think it probably helped me, but after a while it seemed like I didn't need it anymore.

After my dad died I wanted to see his body, but no one would let me. He had taken an overdose of medication, mixed with alcohol and food that his doctor had told him was dangerous mixed with the medication. But I didn't think his body would look messed up. My mom and my uncle said he didn't look the same, but I still wanted to see him. He was my dad. I felt I should be allowed to see him. When they said no, I felt like they were hiding something, and that made me mad, too. I guess I am still mad about that time in my life.

I thought the memorial service was kind of lame. Everyone was looking at me, expecting me to behave a certain way, I guess. I didn't show much emotion. I wasn't going to be the way they wanted me to be. I think I am like my dad in that way, somewhat of a rebel.

Going back to school wasn't too bad. In some ways it helped, provided me with something to do, a distraction from what was happening at home, a way to get my mind off the death. All the kids knew. I remember walking down the hall and hearing whispers, rumors. I just kind of let it roll off my shoulders. It didn't really bother me, and sometimes I was able to get out of stuff I didn't feel like doing, so that was O.K. Maybe I used my dad's death as a way to get out of school, but that is what you do when you are thirteen. I think everyone thought I was different in some way, that I had changed because of his death. They expected me to cry or act nuts, but I just went to school and acted like nothing much had happened.

My friends were kind of weird around me. We were that age when we were kind of shy, didn't talk much about anything. They didn't know what to say. I guess what would have helped the most would have been comments like, "Dude, I'm sorry. That's a hard thing that happened. I'm here if you want to come to me for anything, but I'm not going to push it." I think saying it once, getting it out in the open is best, but after that, let it go and try to get on with things.

My teachers would take me out of class and offer support. I would thank them for trying to help me, but I felt like I didn't need any help. I think teachers should treat kids pretty much the same after a death happens. It's important to acknowledge what has happened, but don't dwell on it or make a big deal out of it. I didn't want them to loosen up on me or treat me differently. Maybe some kids need extra help, but not me. I was never into school anyway, never felt all that connected or motivated. My stepfather says I haven't been challenged yet. I hope that is true, since I quit school this year and am going to take the GED. I have a job and I am a good worker, but I plan to go to college in the fall. I got an 1140 on the SAT and I didn't even study, so I can probably do better. I want to study psychology and work with kids.

Now that I am almost eighteen I realize I wasn't old enough to know my dad as a person. I missed out on that. I knew him as a father, a protector, and a provider. We played sports together, but who was he really? My grandparents won't talk about him. It's too hard for them, I guess, but that makes me kind of mad. They moved away after he died and I haven't really seen them that much. They have all the pictures of him when he was young and all the stories. I wish I knew more about him.

I think we are a lot alike. He was athletic, and so am I. He was smart and funny, and I am witty like he was. I am stronger, however. I have more self-control, and I don't dwell on the bad things. My philosophy is that life happens, so deal with it. I don't see the point of getting stressed out. I believe things will eventually work out. I'm not afraid of the future or failure. I like to take chances, and I get excited about all the possibilities ahead.

Before my dad killed himself I used to think he might, and I would say to myself, "Well, if he does, I will, too." And then he died and I knew it wasn't my way. I always knew I wouldn't kill myself. I thought of it, like most teenagers, but those thoughts have only been thoughts, nothing solid. I'm pretty O.K. with my life, I guess. I like being in nature, music, hanging out with my friends. I like the feeling of accomplishing things, like doing a good job at work or when I built a tree house as a kid. I like being acknowledged for my hard work. I like girls, particularly the chase, but once that's over, I change girlfriends. I like playing with my two-year-old brother. I don't think my dad's death changed me that much. What changed me was growing older.

What I really miss about not having my dad here is talking with him. My step-dad is a nice guy, but he's not like me. He was never rebellious. If my dad was here, I would like to ask him about what he was like when he was growing up, if he felt like I do about things. I wish I could talk to him about what to do in certain situations with school, jobs, girls, etc. I have a lot of girlfriends, and I like to party. I think he did, too. Sometimes I take risks like getting stoned and driving around with my friends. I would like to see if he did stuff like that, too, and what he thinks about what I am doing. Once in a while I have dreams about him where I see he's back. I smile and say, "Oh, you're back. That's cool." Sometimes I have talks with him in my head.

Every year, near the anniversary of his death, we go to the cemetery. Everyone goes—my sister, brothers, my mom and stepfather. It's O.K. I don't mind going, but I feel it's a little weird for my stepfather, and I feel awkward for him. We see my dad's grave and put flowers on it. I don't remember the exact date of his death, but I know it is at the end of January. He is always on my mind around that time.

I think if he were here he would be proud of me and how hard I worked to earn the money for my first car. It was a cherry red '65 Mustang. I worked three jobs to get the money for that car. Now I have a Nissan 300 ZX. He would have really liked that car, too. I wish he could have seen my hard work and dedication to get those cars, but he probably knows.

CHAPTER SIX

Grieving Responses:
How Nature Heals

*"There is no normal life that is free of pain.
It is the very wrestling with our problems
that can be the impetus for our growth."*
—FRED ROGERS
YOU ARE SPECIAL: NEIGHBORLY WISDOM FROM MR. ROGERS

The death of a parent is an extreme event for any child, and suicide only compounds the emotional weight. But we should never assume we know exactly how a child feels or how he or she will react. Each child is unique and will respond according to his or her personality, life experience, and temperament.

A number of feelings may occur all at once and seem overwhelming, or they may surface weeks, months, even years after the suicide. An incident or memory may trigger a rush of feeling that upsets a child, who will likely confront periodic emotional upheavals as he enters new periods of development.

It is critical to let children know that whatever they feel is O.K. We must encourage them to express those feelings in appropriate ways that do not allow for hurting themselves or others. They also need to know that if they want to keep those feelings to themselves for a time, that's O.K., too.

We have learned that children grieve in doses, and they are more capable than adults of putting their grief aside. We know that some children may not show many outward signs of grieving, but feel the loss acutely. Expressing feelings in some way—verbally, or through art, movement, or other creative outlets—helps children cope. Some young people need to be coaxed to express what is inside of them. No one will have magical powers to take their pain away, but children can learn to face their pain, say the word "suicide," and confront the reality of how their parent died.

Following are some of the reactions your child may have to the suicide death of a parent.

Denial

"I tell myself that he is in Mexico, visiting our cousins. He isn't really dead—just gone on another visit." —PAUL, AGE 10

Denial can encompass a variety of emotions: shock, disbelief, numbness, even indifference. When a suicide occurs, denial provides an emotional and sometimes physical numbness that initially helps screen out and manage intense pain, allowing it to surface in shorter spurts as reality sets in.

I often hear from parents who worry that their child is "in denial" following the death of someone special. They are surprised and sometimes angry that their children seem undaunted by the death, preferring to be with friends, watch TV or play video games, rather than talk about what has happened. You needn't feel alarmed by these responses. Denial isn't such a bad thing. It is a natural defense mechanism that allows us to cope. Engaging in customary activities can help a child survive the initial emotional trauma while he begins to integrate what has occurred.

At the same time, do not mistake indifferent behavior as your child "taking the death so well." Although you may feel relieved that he seems to have his feelings in hand, it is important not to minimize a child's grief. Do not reinforce the notion, adhered to by our grief-avoidant society, that stoicism and suppression are appropriate ways to handle feelings. While denial may be part of how a child takes care of himself, at some point, when he feels safe and ready, it will be necessary for you to discover what he understands has happened and how he is experiencing this loss.

Some children will insist "Daddy is coming later," or that "Mommy isn't dead, she's sleeping." Such comments are painful to hear, as we recognize they reflect a child's anguish and her inability to comprehend what has happened. While acknowledging the reality of a parent's death is a necessary task of grieving, children must be allowed to take the time they need to accept and begin to integrate their loss. For some children this takes weeks, even months.

Emily, who was six when her mother died in the hospital following an overdose of prescription medicine, had been told the truth about her mother. Her father had explained, "Mommy died because she was sick in her mind. Some people die of serious diseases like cancer, where parts of their bodies don't work right anymore and can't be fixed, so they die. Mommy had a disease in her brain that made her all mixed up. She thought she couldn't get better, so she took too many of her pills and died. The hospital tried to help her, but it was too late."

Emily attended her mother's memorial service where she sat quietly with her thumb in her mouth. Weeks later she told me, "The hospital is hiding Mommy." She wasn't ready to accept her mother's death. We talked about how hard it was to believe that her mommy had died, because Emily remembered saying good-bye to her in the morning and going off to school. By the afternoon her mother was dead. Emily wanted to believe that since she never saw her mother after their morning conversation, maybe she was still in the hospital somewhere. We continued to talk about Emily's wishes and how much she missed her mommy. ("It is so hard to understand how you could hug Mommy good-bye and never see her again. You just can't believe she really died. You miss her so much and wish she was still in the hospital. I am so sorry she died.") Emily nodded, changed the subject and started talking about the tooth fairy coming, since she had just lost another tooth. Eventually, with time and gentle reminders, Emily began to accept the reality of her mother's death, although the concept of suicide remained difficult for her to understand.

Regression

"I couldn't sleep in my own bed for a long time. I didn't want to be alone in the dark, and it didn't help to have the closet light on. I was too sad and too scared." —RACHEL, AGE 13

When faced with a traumatic experience, children often demonstrate behaviors they have outgrown. Regressive behavior allows them a return to times when they may have felt safe and protected. It signals a need for additional love and attention, and is most apparent during the first year or two following a death. These behaviors are usually temporary and may include having a difficult time separating from the surviving parent or caregiver, talking "baby talk," soiling or wetting pants, bed-wetting, or thumb-sucking. A young child may also need help doing simple tasks which he had previously mastered, such as feeding himself, dressing, tying his shoes, or making the bed. Many children want to be held, rocked, or nursed.

Your child might also express a fear of the dark. Even teenagers may want a nightlight, or they may become anxious about going to bed, wanting to sleep with a parent rather than alone. Going to school can also become an issue. Children and teens may have trouble sleeping and then feel too tired to get up in the morning, or be fearful about being away from the surviving parent. Others develop stomachaches or headaches that make attending school problematic.

It is important not to punish or humiliate children who regress. Without support, they may bury feelings, making it difficult to move through grief. While you will need to offer additional affection and security, it's also important not to over-protect or over-indulge your children. Sometimes it is hard to distinguish between offering support and over-indulgence. One simple guideline: If your child's regressive behavior seems to escalate over time, he may have needs that are not being met.

Seven-year-old Timmy, a first grader in one of my support groups, became increasingly withdrawn after his mother died. He didn't want to go to school and often complained of a stomachache. He had several friends he played with regularly, but after his mother's death he was reluctant to be away from his dad and uninterested in having friends over. He spent his time playing video games by himself, but needed to check on his dad's whereabouts frequently, often following him from room to room. His dad had taken time off from work and tried his best to reassure him, but Timmy's stomachaches worsened. He was spending more and more time at the nurse's office at school. He started wetting the bed again, a behavior he had managed to conquer midway through kindergarten. He had difficulty settling in at bedtime and would often crawl into his dad's bed in the early hours of the morning. His dad felt inadequate and frustrated in his inability to help his son, particularly as he, too, was not sleeping well. Timmy's older brother, Daniel, age eleven, seemed less impacted. He returned to school right away and continued to play on a basketball team where he was a star player. Daniel did have trouble concentrating in school, however, and he was often irritable.

With a counselor's help, Timmy's dad instituted a bedtime routine where he would read with the boys and talk about their mom. They would look at pictures of her from happier times and recall special moments together. Their dad talked to them about their mother's depression. He reassured them that even though he was very sad, he did not have the same illness and would always be there for them. He also took Timmy to their family doctor for a visit. The doctor thoroughly examined Timmy and talked to him about how stomachaches sometimes happen when kids are worried or feeling sad and unable to talk about their feelings. He reassured Timmy about his and his dad's health, and suggested that Timmy might enjoy listening to relaxing music at bedtime.

Timmy's dad got him a small tape recorder with headphones that Timmy could put on at night or even during the day. Timmy chose music that sounded like the ocean. He liked the idea of playing it whenever he wanted to hear something soothing. Timmy and his dad also met with Timmy's teacher. They made a schedule for school attendance whereby Timmy would go mornings and return home after lunch. The plan included eventually increasing the time spent at school, and a break each morning when Timmy could call his dad at home. After about five months Timmy was able to make it through the school day without a stomachache. The bedwetting stopped, but he still needed to occasionally crawl into bed with his dad.

Regressive behaviors are usually temporary. If we can be patient and provide a supportive presence, most children will move through them. Sometimes, however, because of a parent's own grief, finding the strength to face these behaviors is difficult, and reinforcements are necessary. Don't be afraid to enlist the help of other supportive adults, including a mental health professional.

Backlash

"I am mad at everyone: my mom for leaving, my dad for fighting with her, my brother for going off to college and leaving me here alone. My counselor keeps bugging me to talk and I have nothing to say. Don't they see my life is totally messed up now?" —JASON, AGE 14

Backlash refers to angry outbursts that include expressions of hate, blame, and resentment. These feelings often mask underlying (and unexpressed) emotions of pain, helplessness, frustration, and fear. They can be directed at anyone—the parent who carried out suicide (particularly if there are unresolved issues with that parent), the surviving parent (for not being able to prevent the suicide), God (who isn't supposed to let bad things happen), the doctor (who couldn't seem to help), even the world at large (which may no longer seem like a safe place).

Anger may be part of a child's grief work, but it is not a requirement. Some children may have minor angry outbursts or none at all. Others will seem edgy and irritable, defiant, and quick to pick a fight. Teens frequently experience the suicide as an event that separates them from their peers and "messes up their chance for a normal life." However, contrary to what many believe, adolescents do not *always* act out.

Children and teens may also be angry—and deeply hurt—by what they perceive as a parent's deliberate abandonment. Underneath the anger and protest often lies the child's feeling that if a parent "chooses" death over life with him, perhaps he is unlovable. He may ask himself,

"If Mommy loved, me, why did she leave me?" He may act out to prove he is indeed "bad" in some way. Acting-out behavior may take the form of temper outbursts, defying authority, bullying, or starting fights at school. Teens may demonstrate increased risk-taking behavior, engage in stealing, or ignore curfews. They may act as if they don't care about themselves or anyone else.

These behaviors are troubling to adults and caregivers, who may feel helpless, threatened, or uncertain how to respond. It is important to recognize that such expressions of anger assist children in coping with their anguish. Protesting allows them to function and survive. Having a place to outwardly direct their pain, rather than hold it internally, may also help prevent a host of other problems—disabling guilt, chronic depression, low self-esteem, and physical ailments. However, it is important to be alert for anger turned inward, which may be characterized by withdrawal, self-deprecating comments, and/or self-mutilating behavior.

Supporting a child's need to express her angry feelings without arguing or retaliating can be a challenge for adults who are also grieving. Care must be exercised not to shame or induce guilt. While destructive behaviors need to be curtailed, angry feelings should not be judged as good or bad, right or wrong, but acknowledged as a natural part of a child's grief experience.

Children who are acting out need to know that despite their actions, they are lovable. They need adults to help provide external controls and limits as they are learning to develop their own inner controls. This may mean a safe place to express anger and anguish, as well as alternative ways to redirect explosive feelings. It is important for the surviving parent to be neither punitive nor overly permissive. Children must know that hurting themselves or others is not O.K., and that an adult will intervene if they are unable to control their impulses.

Claire was nearly thirteen when her mother was found in a motel room, dead from an overdose of prescription medication. Following the suicide, Claire's nineteen-year-old sister slid into depression and made a suicide attempt herself. Her sixteen-year-old brother was uncommunicative, spending most of his time with his friends. Claire felt alienated from her sister as well, but she was unwilling to talk with anyone about her family isolation. She was a good student, had friends, and felt she could handle her life without any adults intervening. However, she and her older sister fought fiercely, often coming to blows, and she found herself frequently slapping her younger brother, who was six at the time. When her brother's bruises came to the attention of a counselor, Claire's father, who felt overwhelmed with managing four children and his own feelings around his wife's death, insisted on the family entering counseling. This was not a negotiable arrangement. Claire and her siblings needed alternatives to physically acting out.

Guilt and Regret

"My mother felt guilty because the last time we saw my dad, he wasn't feeling very well. I think maybe he was drunk. She told me to give him a hug, but she didn't hug him, so I didn't want to either. That was the last time I saw him. He killed himself the next day. I wished I had hugged him. Maybe he wouldn't have died." —CHRISTIAN, AGE 10

Most of us will experience guilt at some point after the suicide of a loved one. We can't help going through the "if onlys" when we think of those days, weeks, and moments prior to our loved one's death. Children, like adults, replay incidents that may have occurred before the suicide, feeling guilty and regretful about things said or not said, wishing for the opportunity to go back and do things differently.

Seven-year-old Maggie, whose parents were divorced, told me that her dad was often late picking her up at daycare. The day before he hung himself, she was the last child left at her daycare center. She felt embarrassed and was mad at her dad. "I sat in the car and looked out the window when he told me he was sorry. I didn't want to talk to him. When he asked me if I wanted to listen to the radio, I said I didn't care. I said I wanted a different daddy—but not really. He dropped me off at Mommy's and I never saw him again. I shouldn't have been so mean to him. He would still be here if I wasn't so mean."

Young children are particularly prone to magical thinking, believing that just by thinking about something, they can make it happen. When a suicide occurs they feel remorse and guilt if they have had any negative thoughts about their parent or have made comments that might be construed as harmful.

Maggie had fierce temper outbursts before her dad's death and also had trouble focusing in school. However, since her father's suicide, her emotional outbursts have increased dramatically. She has become more aggressive, striking out at others, and picking fights on the playground. Her teacher reports that Maggie has had trouble sitting still in class and is often irritable. She has threatened to run away because she no longer likes school.

Maggie has begun therapy, and her psychotherapist is helping her understand that her father had a mental illness that contributed to his unreliable and erratic behavior. Her counselor has encouraged her to see that she is not a "bad" girl who deserves to be punished. Rather, she is a sad girl who misses her dad and who sometimes feels angry with him for ending his life and leaving her. Because Maggie's father had bipolar illness, Maggie's mother is aware that her daughter may also have a genetic predisposition to the disorder. If Maggie's disruptive behavior continues or she begins to demonstrate other troubling symptoms, her mother plans to have her evaluated by a pediatric psychiatrist specializing in mood disorders.

Some children feel guilty when they experience relief following the death. Fifteen-year-old Andrea remembers her first thought following the suicide of her father was that she would no longer have to worry about whether he would be dead, alive, or drunk when she got home from school. He had been depressed for years following an injury that prevented him from working or fully participating in family life. He drank heavily and he had made several suicide attempts. She always knew "something bad would happen," and felt uneasy about bringing friends home, not knowing what to expect. "But when he was feeling better, he was fun," she said. "We'd watch *Jeopardy* together and he was smart and funny. How could I be glad he died?"

Andrea needed time to sort through her anger, sadness and guilt. She worried that her feelings of relief meant she didn't love her father enough. When she began having fun again—getting a boyfriend, going to the prom, having friends over—she continued to struggle with guilt, feeling that being happy again was being disloyal to her father's memory.

Her mother and aunt kept telling her it wasn't her fault and that she should go on with her life. But it seemed to Andrea that they were impatient with her and unwilling to talk about the death. "I know they just want to cheer me up, but they don't listen. They are always trying to talk me out of what I am feeling, as if I am silly or being too dramatic. I just want them to listen."

While it is important to clarify for children and teens what may have contributed to a parent taking his life, we often do not know for sure. Trying to talk a child out of her guilt, rather than encouraging her to explore her feelings and perceptions, may give the message that her feelings aren't valid, causing her to withdraw or feel disconnected from others.

Eventually Andrea began to come to terms with her guilt. She participated in a teen support group where she did a lot of writing. She also talked with her best friend's mother, who as a child had experienced the suicide of her father. And at the suggestion of her friend's mother, Andrea and her mom saw a therapist who helped them listen to one another.

Hyper-maturity

"I felt like I was the parent instead of my mom. At first it was O.K. because I wanted to do something to help, but then I got frustrated because my younger brothers wouldn't listen to me and there was always so much work to do. I wanted to be with my friends. I needed my mom to be a mom again." —JAMIE, AGE 13

Sometimes well-meaning adults, who believe they are helping a family get back on their feet, encourage children to take on too much responsibility. Statements such as, "Now that Dad is gone, you are the 'man of the house,'" or "In your mom's absence, it's up to you to take care of the house for your dad," are confusing to children, who may miss out on childhood by internalizing these messages. The oldest child of the same sex as the parent who died is often the one cast into this role.

Other times, children may unconsciously adopt these behaviors on their own as a way of continuing to identify with the parent who has died. This may keep the parent "alive" and thus soften the impact of how the family's lives have changed. Adopting a grown-up role in the family can also be a way for a child to ward off his own sense of helplessness. It can provide a structure to follow and a set of behaviors that he may also view as a way to help his surviving parent cope. But sometimes there is a price tag.

Thirteen-year-old Danny, the oldest of three children, felt that it was up to him to manage his younger siblings and keep the household running smoothly after the death of his father. He quit his baseball team and stopped hanging out with friends after school, so he could take care of his two little sisters while his mom looked for work. He was very strict with them and spanked them when they did not put away their toys. His father had been the disciplinarian in the family, often insisting the kids eat everything on their plates and sending them to their room at the first sign of disagreeable behavior. Danny developed into a stern taskmaster, more authoritarian than his father had been, making the girls sit at the table long past mealtime. If they didn't finish their food, he would send them to bed early. Danny's mom was so sad and exhausted from her grief, as well as discouraged about the family's finances, that she had a hard time supporting him or providing parental limits. Danny, who had been a good student, began to miss assignments and do poorly at school. Fortunately, his uncle stepped in. He worked out a plan with Danny's baseball coach for Danny to rejoin the team, and he enlisted the aid of a neighbor who began caring for the girls after school.

Helping a parent can provide child survivors with heightened self-esteem and a way to respond to the trauma of suicide. However, a surviving parent needs to help her children find ways of feeling better without sacrificing their childhood. Providing extra hugs and reading stories to younger siblings might make a child feel involved and more connected to her family, but staying up late and discussing family finances with her dad puts more responsibility on her shoulders than is appropriate.

Karen, now fifty-six, recalls that prior to her mother's suicide when Karen was twelve, she had already taken on the role of managing the household because of her mother's alcoholism and mental illness. "I had three younger sisters, and my dad was in the military. He loved my mom very much and tried desperately to keep things together, but she was always in bed sick. She was often violent, screaming and hitting. She was in and out of mental hospitals because of her severe alcoholism. When she died, I was angry and confused, but also relieved. And I just went on taking care of things. My father and I were very close. I was sort of a surrogate wife to him. He had color photos of my mother in her casket that were taken at the funeral. He would look at those pictures every night, especially several years after her death when we moved back to the states from being overseas. The reality of her death had truly set in and he missed her, but he began to break down. He wouldn't shave regularly and he went into a deep depression. I got upset and burned the photographs. I was sixteen. I felt that he wasn't functional. I told him he had to lift his head up and move on because he had kids. He heard me and began to perk up, started shaving again and focused more on his career and family. Looking back, I feel that this role I took helped me by giving me great strength and compassion for others. It's like a wound—when it heals the scar tissue is actually stronger than regular skin, like a shield. You eventually heal, yet you are never the same. The price tag, however, was incredibly high, as I had no childhood, no female role model. I was emotionally damaged with issues of abandonment, trust, anger, guilt and never truly knowing what was 'normal.'"

A grieving spouse may unconsciously reinforce a child's adult behavior, as it is difficult to be both father and mother while also contending with grief. Surviving spouses need the support of other adults as they take on the role of being a single parent. Even if a parent has been divorced or separated from the person who takes his or her life, family dynamics are likely to change dramatically. While extra responsibilities and chores may need to be assigned, it's important to ensure that children are not inadvertently or unconsciously placed in a parental or replacement spouse role. Such roles can negatively impact self-esteem, resulting in confused self-identity, missed childhood opportunities and experiences, as well as possible long-term depression.

Anxiety and Fear

"Who's going to make my lunch and tuck me in bed?" —ARTURO, AGE 6

The shock of suicide can send family members into a tailspin that can descend into near panic. Some children become increasingly anxious and overwhelmed with fear. They may be full of questions concerning their own survival and that of others they love. You may hear expressions such as "What will happen to me? Who will take care of our family? Can we stay in our house? If this happened to my dad, could it happen to my mom or someone else I love? Could this happen to me?"

These feelings of anxiety may suddenly come and go for some time after a traumatic death. Sometimes survivors find themselves crying uncontrollably over something seemingly unrelated to the death. Others report feeling frozen or unable to participate in activities that previously brought them pleasure. Some children develop hyper-vigilance, concerned that something bad will happen if they are away from their remaining parent.

Eight-year-old Tiffany began attending a support group with her younger brother several weeks after her father died. Initially, Tiffany liked the group and was eager to participate in the art projects. She quickly became a group spokesperson, telling each new member the "rules" and expectations, although she was quick to "pass" when it came to talking about her father. As big sisters sometimes do, she was prone to interrupting and correcting her little brother. The group leaders gave her lots of support, encouraged both children to talk or not, and provided creative outlets for their feelings. Tiffany reported that she "loved the group and loved the projects and loved the snacks."

After attending the group enthusiastically for a month, she surprised her mother and the group leaders when she suddenly decided she didn't want to go anymore. She adamantly refused, preferring to stay with her mother. She became increasingly anxious, stopped wanting to be with friends after school or go to Brownies—activities that she had previously enjoyed. She didn't want to go to Sunday school unless her mother came with her. She attended school reluctantly, and often had a tummyache or expressed worries about her heart beating too fast. She was fearful at night and could not go to sleep without her mother lying on the bed next to her. She awoke frequently during the night with nightmares that she couldn't remember.

Tiffany's anxiety upset her mother, who felt overwhelmed by her own grief and ineffectual as a mother. "I don't know what else to do," her mother reported. "I have tried everything I can think of—reassurance, long talks, soft music at bedtime, reading stories, special time with me away from her brother, seeing our family physician—nothing is working, and I am exhausted. When she doesn't sleep, I don't sleep."

Even though her mom had told her many times that she wasn't going anywhere, Tiffany continued to worry that her mother would get too sad and go away or die. Eventually, with a counselor's help, they talked in more detail about her father's illness (bipolar disorder) and his alcoholism. Her mom reassured Tiffany, "Yes, I am very, very sad about Daddy's suicide, but I am not going to kill myself. I don't have the brain illness that Daddy had, and you know I don't drink at all." When Tiffany tearfully asked who would take care of her if her mother died anyway, her mom responded, "If I were to die while you were a little girl, which is very unlikely, Aunt Keri would take care of you and you would live with her and Uncle Jim and your cousins. But, even though I am sad and tired and cry a lot, I am healthy and planning to be around for a long time." Even with these reassuring words, it took months until Tiffany felt safe again.

Rational feelings can go out the window following a suicide death, and fears can accelerate. Survivors may develop behaviors that plague them for some time, and even though they know their fears are unrealistic, they are unable to alter their behavior. Christine, who was eighteen when her father jumped off the Golden Gate Bridge, recounts, "It was many years before I could cross the bridge without breaking into a sweat. For a long time I couldn't drive over it, but had to have someone else drive—and I would just close my eyes. Even now, twenty-five years later, I still feel a knot in my stomach when I cross that bridge."

When a child's parent dies, especially by suicide—a mysterious and confusing death—anxiety is sure to be present. As time passes and children mature, most anxiety will diminish, but occasionally a child is unable to cope because of unrelenting fear. Some children are naturally more sensitive and fearful. Sometimes night terrors make it difficult for a child to sleep. This is particularly true for children who discovered their parent's dead body or witnessed the suicide. It is hard to see children suffer in this way, and difficult to feel like a good parent if you can't seem to alleviate their suffering. But some children will need more than you can give them, especially if you are steeped in your own grieving. If your child's anxiety is getting in the way of her ability to feel pleasure or participate fully in life, it is time for help from a mental health professional. Ask your family physician for a referral. Your child may be suffering from Post Traumatic Stress Disorder (PTSD).

The last time I saw Tiffany, she told me her counselor had given her a stethoscope so she could listen to her heart and to her mom's heart, too. She had tried to listen to her cat's heart, but that didn't work very well. She was back at Brownies and working on getting her "Friend to Animal" badge. She didn't want to talk about her dad, but she did want to let me know that she had decided to become a doctor or a nurse or someone who took care of animals.

Sadness

"When I heard she died, I cried and cried and cried." —CARRIE, AGE 10

A child's inconsolable sadness is perhaps the hardest experience to bear as a parent. As reality sets in and a child begins to accept that Mom or Dad isn't coming back, the sadness can be overwhelming. Eleven-year-old Kristi described it well: "There's a black hole in my heart."

Sometimes this emptiness comes much later in the grieving process, surprising some children and the adults who care for them. Adolescents in particular are prone to bouts of sadness months after the death of a parent. A meaningful song or sad movie can overwhelm a teen, making him feel very much alone or wonder if he is "going crazy."

Many children worry that if they express sadness, they will make their parents sad, too. This is very scary. You will need to reassure your child by letting her know that tears are O.K., saying, "I am crying because I am so sad. Daddy has died and we will never see him again. Sometimes I can hardly believe this has happened, but I know it has, and that makes me very sad. When we feel sad, we cry. I will probably be crying for some time, but I will still be able to take care of you. I might need extra help, but I am going to be O.K."

While a child might be uneasy about seeing her surviving parent's anguish, she may be equally disturbed by *not* seeing her parent's tears. Fourteen-year-old Elise related, "When I saw my mom being so stiff, so cold about my dad, I felt mad, like she didn't really care about him. Then I heard her in her room at night crying, and even though I felt sad about that, I also felt relieved."

While some children wail and sob, others cry quietly or don't cry at all. This doesn't mean they aren't anguished by the death of their parent. Sadness often increases as the reality of the death sets in and a parent's loss is felt day to day. While many children are more able than adults to put sadness aside and engage in life's activities, they often have specific times when their sadness is more accessible. Bedtime is frequently a time when children will express sad feelings and need a little extra time to be hugged and comforted.

Sadness can also occur when a special event is at hand. "I remember when I went to the prom," relates twenty-three-year-old Beth. "I was sixteen and my mother had died two years before. I wanted her to be there to see me in my dress and help me with my hair and do my nails. We always loved doing those things together. When I was getting dressed, I felt so sad because she wasn't there to share my excitement. I cried even though I was looking forward to the dance."

Some events or memories bring intense sadness, while others elicit a wistful longing. Sadness comes and goes. Child survivors learn to grieve over time, longing for what has been lost and what might have been. Often, this aspect of mourning will need to be addressed later in life, when maturity brings a new awareness of what was missed in childhood. Sad feelings, like all feelings that come with the loss of someone special, have to be acknowledged and expressed, becoming part of the fabric of who we are and will become.

Shame

"I told my friends at school that he died of a heart attack. I didn't want them to know what really happened." —DEREK, AGE 15

Because suicide is a stigmatized death, family members often feel shame. Children and teens wonder how their friends will react to the news. They fear others will think their parent was crazy or a bad person. They relate experiences where people glance away or change the subject in their presence. They talk about peers whispering behind their backs, making them feel like outcasts.

Because suicide and mental illness remain stigmatized, shame and embarrassment continue to flourish. Shame is a divisive emotion that may occur if we feel so guilty about the death or the events that led up to the suicide that we condemn ourselves and feel that others condemn us as well. Such feelings lead to a sense of isolation at a time when what is most needed is support and a safe place to sort out feelings.

The reality is that even sensitive and aware people can feel mystified about how to respond to suicide. They simply have no idea how to react, and may thus withdraw or avoid survivors at a time when friendship is needed more than ever. While there are always people who are inappropriately curious or judgmental, many others are afraid about saying the wrong thing. They are uncertain about what, if anything, to do. And some people pull back out of concern that they may make the survivor feel worse by intruding too much, or they assume that the family prefers to be alone.

Such discomfort and assumptions come from the instinctive fears and shock that most people have when it comes to suicide. Understanding how someone could take his or her own life is difficult, if not incomprehensible, for the majority of us, given that our most basic instinct is self-preservation. But for those children, teens and adults who are reeling from the suicide, withdrawal or a change in the comfort level of friends is a severe blow.

Seven-year-old Elizabeth discovered her mother's body, and the following months were especially traumatic. She reported that a neighborhood girl who had been her friend kept talking to other kids about how Elizabeth's mom had died. "She just won't stop talking about it, and that makes me mad." Although she didn't call her feelings "shame," she knew she felt terribly hurt and uncomfortable. That's the trademark of shame: having a gut experience that something feels bad and isn't right, but not necessarily being able to put your finger on it. Elizabeth loved her mom and worried about what other people would think of her. She wanted to tell them about all the special things she did with her mom, how they made cookies together and cuddled. She loved having her mom work in her classroom and remembered the funny jokes her mom used to tell. Elizabeth didn't want people saying or thinking bad things about her mom. She felt compelled to defend her, all the while wondering: "Didn't she love me? Was she crazy? Why is everyone looking at me funny?"

Since we are social beings who need the approval of others, we often do not want to openly discuss family problems. But suicide does not occur without severe problems being present. Survivors have to cope not only with the personal anguish that follows, but also the inevitable social implications of profound family "secrets" made public.

Alcoholism or substance abuse is often involved when a person attempts to end his life. While there is more understanding today that alcoholism and other addictions are diseases rather than choices or moral failings, these illnesses continue to be stigmatized. If drug or alcohol use was a problem for the deceased, it can be doubly stigmatizing for survivors if the details become common knowledge.

Reducing the stigma associated with suicide begins with being open about what has happened. Children are perceptive and often know intuitively when things are amiss. Disguising the suicide as "an accident" or avoiding simple, straight-on discussions of what behaviors precipitated the death implies that something shameful or frightening has occurred that must be kept a secret. If children are given inaccurate information or are told *not* to speak about the death with people they trust, they are denied an avenue for healing.

Knowledge counteracts shame and embarrassment. Children need to know it is O.K. to ask questions and to talk about the death with those they trust. They also need to know it is O.K. *not* to talk to people if they do not feel comfortable.

Courtney, who was nine when her father took his life, shared with me that a few months after her father's death she had gone to the dentist. The hygienist who cleaned her teeth had heard that Courtney's dad had died and wanted to know what had happened. Courtney didn't want to talk about it, but because she had been raised to be polite to adults, she felt uncomfortable declining. With downcast eyes she told me that she wished she hadn't said anything. "The lady looked at me with this shocked face and it got real quiet in there. Then she started talking about something else—I can't remember what because I was too upset. I was trying not to cry, and I got a stomachache. I felt there was something wrong with me." Courtney still felt unsettled about this incident weeks later. She felt she had betrayed her dad. We talked about how it can sometimes feel scary not knowing what to say to grownups or anyone who asks questions that are too hard to answer. I reassured her that if this ever happened again, it would be perfectly fine to say, "I don't really feel comfortable talking right now," or refer the inquisitive adult to her mother or someone else. Saying no is O.K. She didn't owe an explanation to anyone.

Relief

"After Daddy died the house was more peaceful and quiet." —MOLLY, AGE 7

Relief may occur if a parent's suicide followed a long history of self-destructive behavior or previous suicide attempts. No matter how much children love their parents, living with someone who is abusing alcohol or drugs or experiencing continued mental torment is frightening. Even though a child may miss a suicidal parent immensely following the death, she might also experience a renewed sense of safety if her household begins to feel calmer and more predictable.

"Daddy and Mommy fought a lot and yelled at each other," states seven-year-old Molly, whose stepfather died after overdosing on alcohol and prescription medication when Molly was nearly six. "Sometimes Daddy would get in the car and drive off and Mommy would cry and cry. I could hear them fighting in the night. I felt so scared. I tried to keep out the noise by putting my head under my pillow. But I could still hear them. After Daddy died, the house was more peaceful and quiet. Mommy still cried, but it was different. It was kind of better. I still miss Daddy, but I am forgetting what he looked like. He used to throw me up in the air and catch me. I miss him, but I don't miss the yelling."

Guilt often accompanies relief. We need to accept that relief can be a normal response when a parent's behavior has been frightening. Our task becomes learning to put those feelings into perspective and encouraging children not to let relief grow into inappropriate guilt.

Ailments

"My daughter had so many stomachaches. I felt so helpless when she would curl up, hold her tummy and cry. I couldn't seem to comfort her."
—ROBYN

Children may experience all kinds of physical responses to the death of a parent that are real and must be acknowledged. Some children feel tightness in their chests or have difficulty breathing. Stomachaches, headaches, and flu-like symptoms may occur. Grief can suppress the immune system, making a bereaved person more susceptible to colds and the flu.

Some children will lose their appetite while others may want to snack often. Infants may need to nurse more frequently or have a bottle readily available. Sleep is often disrupted and nightmares may plague a child who once slept comfortably through the night. Conversely, some children, particularly teens, may want to sleep more than usual. While some children feel fatigue or a lag in energy, others experience increased restlessness, giddiness and hyper-activity. Tummyaches or "owies" are messages from children that all is not well. Often, such physical symptoms are related to fears of separation from a surviving parent. Such ailments are real, not simply imagined. They reflect the anguish children experience as they face the reality of the death.

Sometimes a child will unconsciously take on a "sick" role if he feels a need for extra emotional support, or if that support has been denied. Children who assume this role do not do so on purpose, but feel out of control of their bodies and unable to find another way to express feelings. A visit to a friendly family doctor is often an excellent idea when a child is sick or displaying physical symptoms. A good general physical examination will alert you to any need for a medical intervention. In addition, a medical consultation may allay a child's fears by creating an opportunity to talk more about the death.

All parents want to try to relieve their children's suffering. Sometimes it's impossible to do much more than give extra hugs and try to be patient, trusting that physical "hurts" will diminish over time if children are given support and reassurance. The loss of a parent is extremely stressful. Most children will demonstrate some physical responses as they try to adjust to the loss. However, if physical ailments become so pronounced that a child is unable over time to separate from her caregiver, go to school or resume normal play activities, professional help is advised.

*   *   *   *   *

Grieving is hard work. There are no shortcuts through the pain. Watching your child grieve while coping with your own feelings will likely be the hardest thing you ever do. No one can tell you or your child the "proper" way to grieve. Each person touched by the suicide will grieve in her own way, in her own time.

There is comfort in the words of Rabbi Earl Grollman, who states in his book, *Suicide—Prevention, Intervention, Postvention*: "The only cure for grief is to grieve. There is no getting around the pain that a loved one willfully took his or her life. Grief is an emotion, not a disease. It's as natural as crying when you are hurt, eating when you are hungry and sleeping when you are weary. Grief is nature's way of healing a broken heart."

CHAPTER SEVEN

Funeral Rituals

"He looked like he was sleeping.
I wanted to tell him to just wake up, but I knew I couldn't
because he was never, never going to wake up again."
—BLAKE, AGE 11

Funeral rituals offer us the chance to say good-bye and honor the person who has died. So often the focus following a suicide is on the suicide itself, the last act, rather than the fact that the deceased was also an individual with hopes, strengths, and challenges. A funeral or memorial service gives us the opportunity to remember how our loved one enriched our lives. Encouraging children to help plan and attend these rituals allows them to acknowledge the reality of the death. It also provides them with comfort and support as they mourn.

However, as you may be discovering, grief can be incapacitating. The idea of putting together a funeral or memorial ritual may feel overwhelming. If so, *ask for help*. Family members, friends, clergy, and funeral directors are all potential resources. Try to have some way to commemorate the death, but do not feel guilty if you are simply unable to manage this on your own. The service does not need to be long or elaborate; it is more important that it accords to family wishes, cultural traditions, and spiritual beliefs.

Children should not be forced to attend memorial rituals. Although young children may not completely understand the ceremonies surrounding death, if given loving encouragement and information about what will happen, very few will refuse to attend. Teens, on occasion, may resist and need additional support. Suggest that friends accompany them. Having close friends share this experience is comforting, and it strengthens the bonds of friendship.

Preparing for the Service

A visit to the church or mortuary prior to a service is a good way to prepare your child. She can see where she will sit and learn about the ceremonies of death. Educating her about the viewing, the funeral, and other traditions allow her to more readily accept the reality of the death.

This is also a time to tell her who will be coming and how long the service will last. Talking to her about how people will be expressing many different feelings helps prepare her for the inevitable tears she will encounter. Let her know that crying is a natural part of grieving, and that memorial services allow for laughter as well. If she hears stories that make her laugh, that's O.K. Encourage her to talk with the minister or person in charge of the service beforehand, suggesting she might want to share stories or memories that he can include in his remarks. This will help her feel more involved, and it often adds a special dimension to the service.

Viewing the Body—or Not

If the body is in good shape, a private viewing before the service can be helpful for a child *if he chooses to, if he is adequately prepared, and if he is accompanied by you or another adult he trusts.* Seeing the dead body of his parent in a casket confirms the reality of the death. This can be helpful because children easily imagine that their parent is just away temporarily and will return at some future time. The important point, however, is to ensure that the body is presentable and that the child is prepared, in detail, for what he will see. If the body is badly disfigured, allowing a child to see his parent is not advisable, but the truth about why you have made that decision is important.

Young children are often curious about touching and seeing a dead body, while many teens are reluctant. No child should be forced to see or touch her parent's body, but unless your instincts tell you otherwise, or the body is not presentable, it is important to give her the choice. If she does elect to view the body, let her know what to expect. This means describing in detail the condition and color of her parent's skin, how make-up has been applied, how her parent's hair looks, what clothes she is wearing, any facial expressions, etc., as well as information about any items that have been placed in the casket. Do not be surprised if even your best description does not adequately prepare your child. Children, particularly teens, often comment that their parent "just didn't look like Dad (or Mom)—the make-up was weird and the hairstyle was all wrong." Some young people say they wish they had never looked, despite their initial insistence. Some, while tearful or even stoic, convey resigned recognition that a parent is indeed dead. Viewing a body or deciding not to takes courage. It is important to support your child with whatever decision she makes.

Addressing Common Concerns

Some questions you may face, followed by possible responses:

Why doesn't Daddy wake up?
Even though it looks like Daddy is sleeping, he is not because he is dead. Remember, "dead" means Daddy is no longer alive. He is no longer able to breathe, open his eyes, talk, hear or feel.

Daddy's skin feels weird. Why is he so cold? Is it O.K. to touch him?
The blood circulating in our body is what keeps our bodies warm and our skin soft. The temperature is controlled by a place in the brain. But when someone dies, their heart and brain stops working, so the heart cannot pump the blood around the body anymore. That's why Daddy's skin feels cold and firm. It's O.K. to touch him. You can hold his hand or even kiss him good-bye if you want. That is up to you.

Why is just the top of Daddy here? What happened to the rest of his body? Did his legs get cut off?
No, this casket has two parts and only the top part is open. Would you like us to talk to the funeral director about opening the bottom part of the casket so you can see the rest of Daddy's body?

If the casket is closed:

What if he isn't really dead but trapped inside that box?
It's so hard to believe that Daddy is really dead, but he is. I saw him before he was put in the casket, and so did Grandpa and Uncle Ted. His heart had stopped and he was no longer breathing. The doctors tried everything they could, but they couldn't save him. His injuries were too damaging and he died.

What did he look like after he died?
What do you imagine he looked like? (After finding out what your child imagines, respond with a simple explanation—describing the injuries without going into great detail. Some children worry that not all body parts are inside, so if she brings this up as an issue you can tell her that his body is intact, but bruised and discolored. She could be told that his skin is pale and his eyes are closed. You can then move into more descriptions about what clothing he was wearing and how the picture she drew especially for him after he died was placed in the casket with him. This will be enough for some children while others will want more.)

Why can't I see Daddy's body? I want to—why won't you let me?
(If you believe the body is too badly damaged, you will have to insist that the casket remain closed, and then deal with your child's feelings of disappointment, anger or confusion. You can say something like:) Daddy injured his head when he shot himself, and he doesn't look like Daddy. I'm sorry to disappoint you, but Grandpa and I think you will feel better remembering the way he looked before he died.

Sometimes it is also helpful to encourage a child to have a silent conversation or even talk out loud in the presence of the body. You can explain to her that while her dad can't hear her because he is dead, it might feel good to say her last thoughts or relay a message she wished she had said to him before he died.

Involving Children in the Ritual

There are many ways a child can be included in funeral rituals. Begin your discussion by asking him if he has any ideas. He may want to choose a special item of clothing for his deceased parent to wear, or write a note to be included in the casket. Some children will want to participate in the service by telling a story or reading a poem, but most will prefer to let others do the talking. You can ask your child if he has something he would like to have read or said for him. Many children like to look through pictures and pick out favorite photographs to be included on a picture board, while others know exactly what special items they may want to place on or near a casket.

Twelve-year-old Kim, whose father, an out-of-work musician, shot himself, knew right away what she wanted to include in a display for her father. "I put his guitar and guitar picks on the table and his membership card to his gym. He loved music and used to play for me. He had big muscles from working out at his gym. He used to take me there and we would go swimming together. I also put a picture of me in my soccer uniform because he used to come to my games and cheer for me."

Teens often like to have input into the design of the program handed out at the door, or contribute ideas for what might be included in the service. Some like to choose special poems or readings to be shared by them or someone else. Many teens appreciate the opportunity to choose certain songs or burn a CD for the ceremony. Children of all ages seem to like placing flowers on or in the casket before or during the service. Others like to light candles or blow them out. Some like to choose colored helium balloons and write messages on them, releasing them outside the service or at the cemetery. I have also seen toddlers and young children blowing bubbles during a service, as well as young people greeting guests at the door or passing out memorial programs.

Not all children will want to participate in planning or be an active part of the service. They may simply be too shy or too stunned to be involved, but ask them to tell you what feels best, and try to incorporate their ideas if possible.

Behavioral Concerns

Be prepared that your child might not show outward signs of grief at the service. A lack of tears doesn't mean he isn't grieving. His grief may be internal at this point as he attempts to integrate the reality of the death. Sometimes children and teens worry about not crying. They need to be reassured that whatever they are feeling is O.K., and whether or not they cry is not a reflection of how much they loved their mom or dad.

Often, words are less important to young people than is physical contact with you and others they love. Hugs or hand-holding provide comfort, although facing large numbers of sympathetic adults offering hugs can be daunting. It is wise to let your children know that people are likely to come up to them and ask them how they are doing or say, "I'm sorry." Let your children know it is O.K. to just nod and simply say, "Thank you." You can also talk to your child about what she can do to help you, like holding your hand or snuggling next to you during the service.

Keep in mind that it is unrealistic to expect young children to attend a viewing or funeral for a prolonged time. Developmentally, they have limited attention spans. Having a familiar family member or older teen friend accompany a child can be helpful. You and other family members need the opportunity to grieve without having to chase down little ones or be responsible for monitoring their behavior. If a young child is having trouble, the "helper" can take her outside or to another room.

Some funeral homes have a children's room with toys and games where children can come and go. Reassure your child that it's O.K. to have fun in the playroom. Many children need to move around more following a death as a way to cope with trauma and stress. You may also want to educate older siblings about this. Sometimes, older siblings, already feeling upset and anxious about the ceremony, may become irritated by a younger sibling's behavior and feel they need to take on a parental role. Reassure them that someone else will be in charge.

Discussing the Suicide at the Service

Whether to directly address the issue of the suicide during the service is often a quandary for survivors. Some people feel that since the suicide is on everyone's mind anyway, making a straightforward but compassionate statement is comforting. Others prefer to barely allude to the suicide, or not mention it at all. Discuss your feelings and concerns with your clergyperson or whoever is conducting the service. It is important to know and trust that individual, as you don't want any surprises. This is not a time for judgmental attitudes from anyone. Be firm with what you feel will be most comforting for your family. If the suicide will be mentioned, let your children know. This is another opportunity to reassure them again that the suicide was not their fault. Let them know they are loved and that their family and friends will be there to support and comfort them.

Cemetery Burial

If a cemetery burial is going to follow the service, explain beforehand what happens there, and again give your child the option of attending or not. If the service is at a church or funeral home that does not have an adjoining cemetery, let him know that he will travel to the cemetery in a car with other family members. Tell him that a special vehicle called a hearse will transport the casket and lead the way. Let him know that other people who have attended the service will be following with their car lights on.

 If your child chooses to attend the graveside service, let him know that in most cases, the casket will be lowered into the ground with a special machine. This is a sad and somber moment, and it can be scary for children. Perhaps you or someone else he loves can remind him that the body is just a shell now, carefully protected from the elements by the casket. This is no longer a person who can breathe or feel, but a special person who will live on in his memories. Your child also needs the option to leave the graveside service early if he does not feel comfortable seeing the casket lowered.

Let your child know that after the funeral or memorial service most families hold a reception where food is served and people gather. Many children enjoy this time, particularly if young cousins or friends attend. It is important to encourage children to relax and have fun during these gatherings. Let them know it is all right to enjoy themselves and even laugh. Grief will come and go over time.

Cremation

Young people are often curious about the cremation process. Adults sometimes feel squeamish about explaining it, but a simple explanation is often better than what a child may conjure up in her imagination. You or someone she trusts can remind her again that a dead body does not feel pain. Explain that the deceased body, enclosed in a casket or container, is taken to a place called a "crematory." Here the body is heated in large, kiln-like ovens to a very high temperature. It changes into ashes that are then gathered up and placed in special containers (urns) or cardboard boxes. These containers, which hold the ashes or "cremains," are then given to the family. Some families like to order special urns that are custom-made and reflect the deceased's taste or personality.

Sometimes people place the container in a regular cemetery grave or put it in a columbarium, which is a building, room, wall, or alcove designated to hold urns. Others prefer keeping the ashes of their loved one in a special place at home, perhaps on the mantel alongside a picture of the deceased. Others are more comfortable putting the urns away on a shelf.

Many children want to look at the ashes. If you are comfortable dealing with this request, look at them yourself first so you can describe what they look like. Share this information with your child and let him decide whether he wants to proceed further. While in years past cremains often had small bone fragments and we would tell children they looked a bit like kitty litter, they are now processed into small particles resembling fine gray or white sand.

While this may sound macabre to some, children's curiosity is natural. As a children's bereavement counselor, I have learned to expect questions and surprises. I remember one support group where a nine-year-old boy brought his grandfather's ashes for "Show and Tell." We had a discussion about how cremation is a little like recycling, a concept that made perfect sense to the kids.

Children are often eager to share their opinions on what should be done with the ashes. "My dad's ashes are buried in our yard," said ten-year-old Sean, "and my mom saved some for me and my brother, too. I keep mine on my shelf in a box I decorated. I put pictures of race cars, baseball, and our family on the box, since those were things my dad loved. He died three years ago and I used to look at it a lot, but I don't much anymore. I know it's there, though."

Still others prefer to scatter the ashes someplace meaningful, which was the case for me. My paternal grandparents immigrated to the United States from Northern Ireland in the early 1900s. My father was born here, but always longed to see Ireland. When he died, I decided to honor him by taking a small amount of his ashes there. I found a lovely field of green rolling hills, dotted with sheep and newborn baby lambs, where I released some of his ashes. The rest I planted under a tree at my home.

Visiting the Grave

If your child's deceased parent is in a cemetery, encourage him to visit at least once, but don't force it. Some families choose to visit the cemetery on the anniversary of the death or on holidays, but make visiting the grave a choice. Let your child know he can stand at a safe distance, or stay in the car if it is near the grave. Reassure him that the visit doesn't have to be long. Some children feel frightened by graveyards, but once they visit, they usually find it's not so scary. Find a way to make the visit meaningful for them by bringing flowers or encouraging them to write a note or bring an object that might have special meaning. Most cemeteries will leave flowers or items on graves until they wilt or begin to look untidy. Theft is a risk, of course, which needs to be explained before children decide to leave anything special that they may eventually want to retrieve.

Nine-year-old Chris likes to visit his father's grave each year. "We have been going for four years now, every May near the anniversary of my dad's death. My brother and sisters don't like to go, and sometimes they don't, but I always do. I like to look at the other graves near my dad's grave, and I like to bring flowers. Once I left one of my 'hot wheels' there. I don't remember my dad too much, but I still like to talk to him and tell him stuff. When I was little, I brought a picture I drew. After we visit the grave, we go out for pancakes. I want to keep going every year."

CHAPTER EIGHT

Sharing Religious and Spiritual Perspectives: Questioning Our Beliefs About Life

Dear God:
Instead of letting people die
And having to make new ones
Why don't you just
Keep the ones you got now?
—JANE, AGE 6
CHILDREN'S LETTERS TO GOD

Before we can help a child or teen reflect on spiritual issues, we have to acknowledge that each of us has our own unique belief system that reflects our views on the existence or not of something greater than ourselves. Some people express their spirituality through adherence to a particular religion. Others prefer to define their beliefs by their relationships with others or how they operate in the world.

Our spiritual orientation evolves as we mature. What we once believed as children changes as we explore our inner landscape and encounter life along the way. When someone we love dies, we naturally question our beliefs about life—the meaning of life and where we fit in, why some people die young, and why others live a long time.

Children are constantly trying to understand their world. In his work, *The Spiritual Life of Children*, Robert Coles calls them "spiritual pioneers," eager to press on and explore issues of meaning, even though the territory is new and not fully understood. Your children have already begun their spiritual journey. They will continue to explore their beliefs as they grow. A parent's death will become part of that ongoing process.

The Loss That Shakes Their World

A suicide death poses complex spiritual questions. While losing a loved one to suicide becomes just one part of a survivor's spiritual journey, that loss can dramatically shake one's world.

Some survivors have a faith crisis, questioning how a loving God could allow such a traumatic death. Others embrace their religious beliefs and find that their faith sees them through this life-altering experience. Still others, who may not have a clearly defined spiritual path or who reject the notion of religion altogether, will have different reactions.

After a suicide, you will naturally look to what has helped you before in times of stress or trauma. Noting these examples can empower you, or you may find yourself rejecting notions that no longer provide comfort. You may seek answers and explanations from new sources, since spiritual beliefs are often challenged by sudden death. You are likely to encounter others who may, without your asking, want to "help" by sharing their own religious or spiritual viewpoints. While their efforts may come from kind intentions, you may have to let them know that you are on your own journey. Perhaps the solace and support you need will come from a spiritual community, or cherished friends, or a profound internal search in the depths of your own soul. Most likely some combination of these will enable you to discover those values and perspectives that will help you come to terms with your loss.

As you explore your spirituality you will find your children exploring theirs as well. Although their experiences and perceptions will differ from yours, you cannot help but influence them. Tempting as it is, try to avoid pat answers or clichés. Allow them instead to explore their own beliefs. Ask them to share with you what they believe. Feel free to tell them you don't know all the answers, and you have some of the same questions yourself. You can encourage them to talk with others you trust, and let them know you will help them find ways to feel more comfortable.

Why Is Heaven a Better Place Than Here With Me?

Children frequently parrot what the significant adults in their lives believe or say. "She's in a better place," is a phrase we often hear. While such statements are meant to be comforting, they can also be confusing, as children wonder, "Why is heaven a better place than here with me?"

Daphne was five when her dad hung himself from a tree in the backyard of their home. Her family was deeply religious, and the term "suicide" was initially avoided. Daphne's mother tried her best to talk with Daphne about her father's death, but was so distraught herself that she couldn't accept that her husband had ended his own life. In the days following his death Daphne's mother questioned whether someone else had killed her husband. When she faced the inevitable truth that he had died by his own hand, she had trouble talking with Daphne and her sister. Trying to find some way to soften the trauma, her mother told her, "Daddy is now with the angels because God wanted him." Daphne was confused by this explanation. She wondered what kind of a God would want her daddy so much that he would take him this way. She also worried that maybe "God would want me or my sister or my mom." While she continued to say that her dad was in a better place, she seemed bewildered about what that meant for her and other important people in her life.

Because every child is unique, each must be encouraged to explore his own feelings about life and death. There is no one "correct" spiritual response to a child's questions of "Why?" or "How could God let this happen?" that fits all situations. Helping children find their own answers means meeting them where they are and avoiding answers that may make adults feel better, but confuse children.

Pat, a grandmother who describes herself as someone with "strong convictions which are based on what the Bible teaches," was faced with telling her grandchildren, two and five, that her son, their twenty-four-year-old father, had ended his life. While she notes that, "Heaven is described in the Bible as a beautiful place which truly is a 'better place,'" she believes children need to be told the truth rather than "warm and fuzzy" things which confuse rather than explain. "When Josh died," she explains, "we told the girls that their daddy was sick and hurt himself so badly that he died. We wanted them to understand that we do not make the choice to leave for this 'better place' because we'd rather be there than here with our families. They seem satisfied with this answer and don't dwell on it. I think that sometimes adults, because they are so uncomfortable talking about death, say things that make them (the adults) feel better, rather than what makes sense to the kids."

Sometimes children express feelings about wanting to be reunited with their deceased parent. Such responses are normal, although hearing your child fantasize about her own death or her elaborate plans to "visit" her deceased parent in heaven can be disconcerting. ("If I swing high enough, I can land on a cloud and visit Daddy," or "I want to die, too, so I can be with Mommy.") While troubling to adults, such comments do not usually mean a child wants to end her life, but are more often an expression of her longing and a lack of understanding about death.

Occasionally such comments are generated by well-meaning adults who have gone overboard in their explanation of heaven. Most kids like the concept of heaven. It gives them a place to put their deceased parent. However, when adults describe in glorious detail a fairyland location high in the sky, a young child is likely to express his wish to visit this appealing and seemingly easily accessible place where his missing parent now resides. ("If Daddy flew to heaven and it's a better place, I want to go there, too.") If the concept of heaven is fundamental to your family's religious life, consider presenting it in general terms as a peaceful place without the pain that Daddy experienced here on earth. Emphasize, however, that it isn't a place we can visit. The goal is to comfort a child rather than create a glowing explanation that may confuse him.

The point to remember is that young children often take comments about God and heaven literally. If you tell your child that the angels came for Daddy, you might be surprised by a response like, "Why couldn't we have locked the door or kept him in a closet so the angels wouldn't get him?"

While perspectives from your own religious or cultural traditions can be immensely comforting to your children after the suicide death of a parent, it is also helpful to allow them to express their own thoughts about what happens after death. You may discover your child has his own creative explanation, like a pre-school child who had this to say: "The insides go up and the outside goes down."

Suicide Is Not a Punishment

Some children will ask about the morals of suicide, worrying that their parent will go to hell or that survivors will be punished in some way. While some continue to subscribe to this notion, many religious leaders have moved away from using fear as a deterrent to suicide, as they acknowledge the role of mental illness in suicide deaths.

I remember the relief I felt when I met with the staff at a Catholic school following the death of a teacher. As a representative of hospice I took no religious or spiritual position, but feared that I would be encountering a belief that death by suicide meant their beloved teacher would be remanded to hell. Knowing how frightening that could be to children, I was relieved to discover the staff had a more benevolent viewpoint. They expressed to me that they felt "God was merciful and forgiving." They told the children that suicide is not a punishment or sinful, but is something that happens when emotional or physical pain exceeds a person's resources for coping.

Twenty-three-year-old Colleen, who was eighteen when her mother died, doesn't feel her mother's suicide impacted her spiritual or religious beliefs, but maintains, "The only thing that makes me upset is that in some religions, people say that a person who commits suicide will not go to heaven. It frustrates me because I believe that if a person had such a hard time in life, they should be peaceful in death...no matter how they die."

Many Survivors, Many Beliefs

What is true is that each person responds differently to the trauma of suicide. Richard, who says he is "as atheist as they come," says, "I don't look at my wife's death as anything related to God, but I think that each of us must adapt to our surroundings, and one of our tasks is to help those around us. Of course, my kids are the most important people in my life, and that is where I put my energy. My wife was Catholic, and my kids will develop their own belief systems as they mature."

Robert, whose wife was diagnosed with bipolar illness, echoes Richard's sentiments: "My wife's suffering had nothing to do with God. It was a mental illness. I would have done anything I could to help her, but her suffering was out of my hands. Maybe people are just here for a short finite time that may be O.K. for them, but hard for us. We want to hold on to them, and their leaving causes us immeasurable pain."

Theresa, whose ex-husband shot himself when their daughter was nine, recalls meeting with her parish priest following the death. "He was at the house with my ex-husband's family when I arrived with Danielle. He thought maybe I expected him to tell her about her father's suicide. He looked at me and said, 'Not having children, I really don't know how to handle this. I haven't been in your shoes.' He suggested we pray for strength. I appreciated his honesty and his prayers. He helped me find the words to tell her myself what had happened with her dad."

Judy, whose son took his life, adds, "I don't know what to say to my grandchildren about their father and God. I left the God of my childhood in the dust and could no longer believe in that God. I don't even know if there is a God, as how could he be so cruel? And don't tell me that God will never give me more than I can handle. That just makes me mad."

Thirty-six-year-old Doreen, whose mother died by suicide when Doreen was seventeen, recalls a near-death experience she had when she was twenty-one: "As the speeding car hit me head-on I felt engulfed by my mother's love. I knew she was O.K. and in heaven with God. I asked her in our encounter if I could stay with her. She said no, that I had a lot of work to do. I knew then that I had to take her death and make it meaningful. I have always believed in the connection of all beings, that we are a part of a much larger plan. This near-death experience validated for me that I was on the right path."

Twenty-one-year-old Hannah, whose father took his life when

she was sixteen, feels that she began her spiritual journey after her father's death. "When I returned to public school after he died, I felt overwhelmed. My teachers didn't seem to understand, and some of the kids were cruel. I transferred to a private Christian school and everything changed. I found a sense of belonging and learned that God is always with me, here to comfort me and guide me. Believing in his love and wisdom sustains me. I have been involved in Christian organizations on my college campus, and we do God's work in poor neighborhoods. I don't know how my dad's suicide fits into all of this, but I do know that my faith has led me to helping others."

Staying Connected

Grief is not a time-bound process that ends in detachment, but can be a continuing connection. As Therese Rando says in her book, *How to Go on Living When Someone You Love Dies*, "Although death ends the life of the person you loved, it does not necessarily end your relationship with him. You can have an appropriate, sustained, loving, and symbolic relationship with the person who has died." This may begin with the funeral or memorial service, but can also include rituals that children create—sharing stories of a parent on his or her birthday, releasing balloons with messages, or creating a special place in the house or in their room where photographs or keepsakes are displayed. Visiting and caring for the gravesite or creating a shrine or altar may allow bereaved children to create an imaginary place where they can "visit" with their deceased parent.

Ask your children if they have any ideas about whether and how they may want to stay connected to their parent. Not all children will be comfortable with this idea. It is important to be sure you don't act out your own agenda. Let your child lead the way.

Some families like to have a memorial candle in a special place, to be lit if a family member is thinking of the person who has died. Children like to light candles and honor their parent in this way, but, needless to say, candle lighting requires supervision and a timeframe. An adult must be responsible for making sure the candle is extinguished.

Some children report being connected to their deceased parents through dreams or extraordinary experiences. I have heard children talk about "feeling Mommy all around me." Sarah, age seven, shares a dream she had several months after her mother's death: "Mommy was there in the doorway at my birthday party. She said she had forgotten her keys. I thought maybe she wasn't dead anymore, but I knew she was," she says, wistfully. "But I liked having her visit me. Maybe she is my guardian angel."

Children need to be allowed to share their experiences with what may not be easily explained. This is part of their ongoing spiritual journey.

More Questions Than Answers

Your child's spiritual beliefs will be challenged no less than yours after the suicide of her parent. She will have many questions about how her parent could die this way—and you will not have all the answers. No one has a complete understanding of why people suffer. For now, your child needs reassurance that it's all right to question and be angry and confused. As she matures, she will revisit these questions and begin to formulate her own answers. She may get to the place that some people do, which is to acknowledge that the answer is a mystery, and what is important is how we respond to and manifest our beliefs—how we live a meaningful life.

CHAPTER NINE

Back to School:
What Your Children's Teachers
Need to Know

"It was almost like she read my mind sometimes
when she would ask me if I needed to talk
or have a break from class.
I think she will always be someone
I can talk to about things that worry me."
—DANIELLE, AGE 12

Returning to the routine of school after a parent's suicide is an important part of healing. School provides children with a sense of normalcy, reassuring them that life goes on, even in the face of tragedy. The timing of a child's return varies with each child and family, but a week is a good frame of reference. Some children choose to return sooner, as they feel being with friends and the predictability of school is preferable to the confusion and sadness at home. Other children become increasingly anxious about being away from family members, and they resist returning to school. These children may need a few extra days at home or the flexibility of attending school half days for a short period of time. If your child seems exceptionally fearful about returning to school you may need to consult with a mental health professional.

You may have already heard from your child's teacher, principal or counselor. If not, contact them and discuss your concerns. News of a suicide often finds its way into the school community, so be prepared to tackle this issue. Decide what you wish to share. You are not obligated to give details, although a simple explanation of what your children understand or have been told will be helpful to the adults who will be working with your child. Discuss when your children will return to school, and plan a time when they can meet privately with their teachers or school counselor before class begins. Teens sometimes balk at this idea, so you will need to involve them in these discussions. (For more information on helping teens get back to school, see Chapter Five – *Teen Grief*.)

It is important to prepare your children for what they may encounter when they return to school. Because suicide is difficult to understand, their friends may be awkward around them and not know how to offer comfort. Let your children know that their friends care about them and want to be supportive, but may not understand what it is like to have a special person die. (Refer to Chapter Three – *Telling Your Child*, for more information on how to help your child respond to others.)

Many educators find it difficult to help child survivors. They may have had little or no experience themselves with suicide. The rest of this chapter offers information and suggestions for school personnel. You may wish to share some or all of it with your child's teacher or counselor.

Suggestions for Teachers

If you are a teacher committed to supporting a grieving student, it is important to look at your own experiences with grief and loss. Examining your attitudes about suicide is also imperative, as those feelings and beliefs will be transmitted to your students. Because of the stigma of suicide, children need their teachers to be compassionate and understanding. You may not have encountered an experience like this before, and you may find that talking about it isn't easy. That's O.K. Our culture as a whole doesn't talk much about death or dying. Trust yourself to rely on your skills and concern for children to see you through this challenging time. What your student will need most is someone to listen if he feels like talking. The "right" words aren't as important as an open heart and a willingness to create the space for him to let you know what he needs.

Bereaved children are aware of a teacher's body language. A stiff posture, poor eye contact or an overly cheerful façade when you are feeling ill at ease may send a message to a child that he is somehow not O.K. He is already likely to be feeling confused, guilty and uncertain about his place in the world. He will be looking to you for reassurance and acceptance. Of course, you are shocked and saddened by the suicide. You may be feeling angry. If you find you are feeling judgmental about his parent's death or about suicide in general, it is important to talk about those feelings with a trusted peer or someone who can support you. Your school counselor may be able to assist you.

Be sure you find someone who understands the dynamics of suicide or who has had personal experience surviving the suicide of a loved one.

You might also contact your local hospice agency and request a consultation with a bereavement counselor who is knowledgeable about the grief of children and teens. Your student needs you to welcome him back into the classroom with a caring, non-judgmental outlook, a willingness to work with him as he grieves, and the belief that he will be able to cope with this trauma.

What to Say to the Class

If you are the child's primary teacher, check with your school principal to determine who will contact your student and his family to express condolences. Young children appreciate hearing from their teachers. Find out what information the family would like shared with classmates. In the high school setting where there are multiple teachers, a school counselor, principal, or favorite teacher can be designated as the contact person.

When you have the information a family wishes to share, give your students a simple explanation about what has happened as the class day begins. Some families are comfortable mentioning the suicide, but many are not. You will need to respect a family's wishes without participating in a deceptive story. If you are asked specifically about a suicide, you can say, "I know there are many stories going around, but

I am not sure of all the details right now. What we need to focus on now is the fact that Tyler must be feeling very sad. How can we let him know we are here for him?"

This is an opportunity to talk about feelings, and to explore with your students ways to support someone who is grieving. Encourage them to write personal condolence notes, and provide them with the materials to do so. Let them know that honest expressions of friendship, support and concern can help a bereaved student feel less isolated and more connected to friends and the school community. ("I am sorry your mother died. I don't know how that feels, but I am here for you." "I miss you and care about you.") Grieving children also like to have memories of their loved one acknowledged. ("I remember when your mom was Room Mother. She made the best cupcakes." "I remember when we went to your dad's work and he let us play on his computer and took us out for ice cream.") Depending on a child's age, drawings or special "We miss you books" can be created and delivered to a bereaved child. Children and teens also appreciate a handwritten note from their teachers.

Sometimes a school community will have already heard that the death was a suicide and begin speculating or making comments that require intervention. Often people who have never been impacted by a suicide personally are quick to judge or place blame on the deceased or on other family members. You can support your student and teach compassion by attempting to diffuse those statements with comments like, "I know you are feeling shocked and confused about this death, but I don't feel it is helpful to place blame on anyone. We need to recognize that someone who takes his life is feeling overwhelmed, desperate and alone, regardless of how much his family loved him." You might also educate impressionable students by adding something like, "Sadly, he/she didn't know how to get help. It's important to remember that no problem is so great that we can't work towards a solution."

You may discover that even in tragic situations there are opportunities for learning. As you listen to your student's feelings and fears, your job will be to clarify the information, reassure your students, and help them respond with compassion.

Some years ago I was invited to assist a third grade teacher who planned to tell her students about the suicide death of a classmate's mother. As the class grappled with the impact of that information, one eight-year-old boy somberly related to the class that, "Maybe it happened because they were getting a divorce. People do that when they get divorced. They think they can't live without their husband because they love them too much and think they will miss them too much. That's why."

Several students looked shocked. Anticipating that other children who were in divorce situations would be frightened, I responded by saying, "I can understand that the idea of someone killing herself is very scary, but Susanna's mom didn't end her life because she and Susanna's dad were getting divorced. Lots of people get divorced and even though they are very sad about that, they don't kill themselves. We don't know why Susanna's mommy killed herself, but it wasn't because of divorce. Sometimes what happens is that a person's brain gets an illness. They get very confused and don't know they can get help. We need to remember that this is a very sad time for Susanna." Susanna's teacher added, "We want to be kind and support her in any way we can. Would you like to do some drawings for Susanna and her family to let her know we miss her and are thinking of her?"

Some of your students may express an interest in attending the funeral or memorial service if it is a public ceremony. Given the suicide and the fact that this may be a child's first experience with death of any sort, you will want to encourage parents to accompany their children. Older teens may not want their parents to attend, preferring to go to the service as a group or with another friend. In any event, you may also find yourself in a position to educate your students about what to expect, and about appropriate funeral behavior.

Most bereaved children appreciate having their teachers attend a funeral or memorial service. To them, having their teacher share this difficult time conveys a message of caring and acceptance. They feel validated in their grief and special at the same time.

When Your Student Returns

Many children will have trouble facing their friends after a suicide death. For others, going back to school provides stability in an uncertain world, and being with friends feels good. It's important not to make a judgment about the length of time a child needs away from school before he is ready to return. Some children need several days or a week or two to cope with their feelings, while others are more comfortable returning right away.

To help a young child integrate back into the classroom, set up a time to meet with him and his remaining parent or another concerned caregiver prior to his return to school. Let him know you will be sensitive to his feelings and are prepared to give him extra attention if he is feeling sad or needing extra help. ("I know you are sad and maybe a little confused about your dad's death. I will be here to help you in class and we can have a special talk time at recess if you would like some extra attention.")

Facilitating a teen's return to school is more complicated. Many teens resist parental involvement, preferring to handle things themselves. Because multiple teachers are involved, it is important to have a designated contact person, a favorite teacher or school counselor who is prepared to meet privately with a teen upon his return to school. That person can help a teen come up with a plan to negotiate homework, missed classes, and what to do if he needs classroom breaks from time to time.

It is important not to hover or make assumptions on how a child or teen will react following the suicide. Do not push them to talk about their experience. Often they simply do not know what to say or how they feel. Keep in mind that teens in particular may be ambivalent about how they want others to respond to them. They are often reluctant to be singled out, yet upset if no one says anything. Despite their need to maintain a "normal" façade, they need to have the death acknowledged. They need to know their teachers are willing to work with them as they deal with the impact of their parent's suicide.

When you talk with your student, speak directly, using simple, straightforward language. ("I am sorry your mom died." "I can't know how you feel exactly, but I want to be here for you in any way I can." "Let's talk about what might help you feel more comfortable in class." "I missed you and I am glad you're back.") Do not impose your religious beliefs, and be careful about empty phrases like "He's in a better place," or "I know just how you feel." You won't know how he feels unless you, too, experienced the suicide of your parent at his age. If you feel comfortable sharing a personal experience, sometimes that exchange can create a bond. However, it's important not to assume he will feel the same way or follow the same grieving path that you have. Let go of your own expectations and let your student teach you what he needs you to know. Listening is more important than talking, guiding or advising.

Children react to their grief in different ways. Some will appear withdrawn, while others may demonstrate aggressive behavior. Anxiety, fear, anger and sadness are all normal responses. Many students experience somatic difficulties—stomachaches, headaches, listlessness and fatigue. Your student's grief response is likely to reflect his personality. A child who is usually boisterous and physically active may need more time on the playground while a student who is more reserved may appreciate quiet time in the library. A child with behavioral issues may need to attend school half-days for a time, working towards full-day attendance as he becomes more able to manage his behavior.

A bereaved child often needs a private place to go when he feels overwhelmed with his feelings. Setting this up ahead of time is comforting. Students feel reassured if they know they can go to the library or their school counselor's office as a refuge. If they don't want to leave the classroom, other work can be assigned like writing in a journal or reading a book. Some children need the reassurance of a family member's voice and may need to be released from class to call someone at home or work.

Teachers can also help by monitoring the amount of work given students, acknowledging that bereaved children and teens may have a difficult time concentrating in the classroom. Following her father's death, Jenny, a bright, artistic teen who had previously excelled in school, remembers, "After he died, I couldn't concentrate at all, for what seemed like months. I felt I was failing him and failing my mother by not being able to keep up. It seemed all my creativity stopped and I couldn't remember anything. I was impatient with my friends, and schoolwork seemed so irrelevant. But, little by little, I went back to writing poetry and drawing. Most of my teachers were great and gave me opportunities to do alternative assignments. I decided I couldn't give up. I had to keep going, but I felt like I lost a year of myself after he died."

By offering peer tutoring or academic support after school, teachers can help grieving students keep up with their work. While it is essential not to place too many demands on bereaved students, helping them keep up with their peers allows them to continue friendships at a time when those relationships may sustain them. Confer with your student and his family to develop a compassionate, realistic plan for handling schoolwork. This may mean limiting or suspending homework for a time. Allowing a child to change seats to sit next to a friend can also be supportive.

Children coping with the suicide of a parent need room to express their feelings without disrupting the continuity of the classroom. If a student acts out or behaves in a troublesome manner, he will need support to channel those feelings in an appropriate way. Underlying his acting-out behavior are feelings of abandonment, low self-esteem and anxiety. He will need the sense of security that comes with clear boundaries and appropriate discipline. He also needs warmth, attention and affection. While it is important to acknowledge the death and provide comfort and stability in the classroom, it is also essential not to be overly attentive or solicitous. If you are patient and observant, your students will teach you what kind of support they need.

Grief is a potent and painful emotion, which must not be ignored or minimized in an attempt to help the child "get over it." Do not expect your student to feel better in a prescribed timeframe or to go through the grieving process in certain, predictable stages. Grief is not linear. Sometimes the pain and sadness can deepen in the second year.

Curriculum Concerns

Some teachers wonder if they need to alter their curriculums to exclude topics related to loss or death. While it is important to be sensitive to classroom discussions and assignments on these topics, avoiding them altogether prohibits students from learning valuable lessons and developing tools to cope with the inevitable losses they will experience as they mature. Death, after all, is part of life. Hopefully, you have already taken advantage of natural, everyday encounters with life and death to talk with your students about their concerns and feelings. When children are exposed to natural events happening around them—the death of a prominent world leader or celebrity, a new baby in the family, the death of a pet or a favorite grandparent, or a discussion on seasons and how we experience the life cycle in nature—they are more likely to grieve in healthy ways.

So, rather than eliminating these lessons, be aware of how these topics may impact your grieving student. Postpone an assignment that deals directly with suicide and come up with an alternative. Let your student know beforehand what the lesson or assignment will be and offer her other options. By meeting with her privately before you assign the work, you can check in with her and see how she is faring. ("Jessica, we are going to be reading a book, discussing it and writing a responsive essay about a young person's experience with death. I imagine you are feeling vulnerable right now, sad or confused or maybe you don't know how you feel. I would like to involve you in this project in whatever way works best for you. That may be by providing you with an alternative assignment. I care about you and I want to help you in any way I can. Would you like to talk about how things are going or how I can support you?")

Trust your instincts as you work with these topics. By being willing to examine your own attitudes and experiences with grief, loss, and suicide, and by listening to and observing grieving students, you will be better prepared to plan a curriculum designed to be sensitive to their needs.

When to Refer

If your student develops behavior problems that interfere with his learning—increased difficulties with friends, acting out, temper outbursts, frequent absences, excessive clinginess or withdrawal, stuttering or tearfulness over a long period of time, he may need to see a mental health professional. Depending on your school's protocol, consult with your school counselor or arrange a meeting with your student's surviving parent to discuss your concerns.

Educate yourself about the warning signs of depression. (See Chapter Seventeen – *When More Help Is Needed: Depression and Bipolar Illness in Children.*) Self-mutilation (cutting, pulling out hair or eyebrows, picking excessively on one's face or other parts of the body), alcohol or drug use, suicidal thinking or statements indicating possible self-harm, demand immediate attention. Notify your school counselor and administrator. Familiarize yourself with resources in your community. If you feel a young person is in danger, don't hesitate to ask him if he has thought about, intends to, or has made plans to end his life. You won't be giving him any ideas about suicide, and you may save a life by asking. If a child admits to feeling suicidal, stay with him and get professional help immediately. Always collaborate with another school official in these situations.

Understanding Vulnerabilities

Know that your student will continue to grieve over time, and that the expression of grief can be delayed until years after the loss.

Children are often particularly sad around holidays or when special events occur. If you are accustomed to doing projects around Mother's Day or Father's Day, be aware that these are vulnerable times for bereaved students. Talk with them about how they would like to be involved. Remember that even school events like Back to School Night or a classroom Open House can be difficult. Your student may experience sadness or regret as these events approach. It is helpful to make a note in your student's record, indicating the date of his parent's death. This way, subsequent teachers can be sensitive to a student's feelings when anniversaries, special events, or holidays approach.

Graduation is another bittersweet event, a time of marking a significant accomplishment and looking to the future. I often hear from teens, regardless of when their parent has died, that they long for that one person who is missing. Depending on your relationship with your student, you will know whether to comment or not. An apropos statement might be, "I know your dad would be very proud of you completing your senior year and would support your decision to go on to college," or "If your mom were here, she would be so happy for you and very proud of the person you have become." Such sentiments can be validating for a student mourning her deceased parent.

Being a Mentor and Friend

As you know or may be discovering, the suicide of a parent leaves a child, his family, and the community in shock. Life has been turned upside down. Your student will need time, support, and love as he copes with this trauma. Your job is very important. Since children spend a good part of their day at school, it can become almost a home away from home. As a teacher, you are in the unique position of imparting not only information, but modeling compassion, sensitivity, and character.

I often hear from children and teens about the importance of their teachers and the impact of those who disregard their feelings, as well as those who treat them with respect and compassion. Your willingness to go that extra mile can make a tremendous difference in the quality of your students' lives.

Danielle was nine when her father killed himself. Three years after the fact, she remembers feeling good about her experience with her third grade teacher. "When Daddy shot himself, my mom called my teacher and told her what happened. She came to my house after school and brought us cookies and letters from the kids in my class. She hugged me and I felt kind of embarrassed, but mostly I felt happy to see her. She told me that her mom had died a few years before. She said she still felt sad and cried sometimes. We talked about what she would say to the kids in my class when she told them about our visit. I was scared they would think my dad was a bad person if they knew he had shot himself, and he's not a bad person. My mom said he had a sickness in his brain that made him feel all mixed up and he didn't understand what he was doing. She said everyone in our neighborhood would hear about my dad anyway, so we decided it was O.K. for my teacher to tell my class that he killed himself. She said she could tell the kids in a way that would be O.K. because everybody loved me and would want to comfort me. So, I guess she did, because when I went back to school, everyone seemed really nice and no one said anything to hurt my feelings. At first everyone kind of surrounded me and hugged me. All the girls wanted to play with me and even the boys were nicer. Then it seemed like everyone pretty much forgot and life went on O.K. at school, even though I started having more trouble concentrating. I had bad dreams and worried a lot, but my teacher always seemed to understand. It was almost like she read my mind sometimes when she would ask me if I needed to talk or have a break from class. I think she will always be someone I can talk to about things that worry me."

CHAPTER TEN

Memory Building:
Stories That Speak to Life

"I didn't want people to stop talking about my dad.
We did so many fun things together; rode bikes, flew kites,
and wrestled. I don't ever want to forget him."
—MATTHEW, AGE 9

One of my biggest regrets about my mother's death is that I never got to know who she was as a person. Because she took her own life and no one knew how to talk to me about it, they essentially erased her. In an effort to help my brother and me "move on," someone quickly packed up her clothing, took down the pictures of her, and removed all traces of her presence. When we discovered that asking questions about her brought embarrassed silences and pitying looks, we stopped asking.

I am sad that I never learned all the stories about who she was as a girl, as a young woman, as a mother. She had a life and qualities that made her special, interests and adventures before her death, a personality that was unique. People loved and cherished her, but because of the trauma of her death, most of those stories died with her. Before long I got a "new" mother who was kind and cared for me, but all vestiges of my "real" mother were relegated to a cupboard to be saved for one day "when I was older." I had no pictures of her then, no treasures that belonged to her, and no permission or encouragement to speak of her.

People are often uncomfortable talking about someone who has died by suicide. They are concerned that such conversations will evoke too much emotion. But a child needs to hear those who loved her parent talk openly without idealizing or blaming the departed. Children of all ages like to be reminded or told about special times they shared with their parent. Most of all, they long to know how their parent felt about the son or daughter left behind. Trying to "move on" too quickly creates confusion for children. It denies them the opportunity to build memories.

Continuing to talk about the parent who has died, telling stories, looking at pictures, and giving children mementos to treasure, are essential to helping a child cope with loss. Without that connection she will feel adrift and isolated, cut off from a part of herself. Our memories ground us, providing familiarity and an acknowledgement of special bonds, of continuity over time. They afford us the opportunity to appreciate and understand the past.

Helping Children Remember

If children are old enough when a parent dies, they often remember certain smells associated with their parent and wistfully recall the feeling of a cozy lap or a loving hug. They are also able to picture a parent's face. Sooner or later, however, these pictures fade, no matter how hard a child tries to remember. The younger the child, the more difficult it becomes to conjure up an image or a memory. This can be very upsetting. Children need reassurance that even though their mental pictures may fade and the intensity of their feelings may change, their love remains.

They also need tangible ways to remember their deceased parent. Photographs are very important. Special keepsakes or personal items that belonged to the deceased parent also provide a link.

When eleven-year-old Melissa's mother died, Melissa appropriated an old afghan her mother had often used while watching TV. "It smelled like my mom for a while, but even though it doesn't anymore, I still like to wrap myself up in it," she says. Andrew, age seventeen, has a San Francisco Giants cap and a signed baseball that belonged to his dad. "My dad was a huge Giants fan. We went to some games together and he always took his mitt. He never caught a fly ball, but he was always prepared, just in case."

Family members or friends who want to help a child remember a parent can assist by creating a scrapbook with pictures and stories. Such a memento, particularly if it depicts all sides of a parent's personality—strengths as well as vulnerabilities—provides information a child survivor will treasure, especially as she grows older.

Even now, these fifty odd years later, I find myself drawn occasionally to a small-but-heavy, dented black doll trunk on the upper shelf of my closet. Its antiquated lavender lining is tattered, and the lock no longer works, but this trunk remains a repository of my memories. Inside are a few pictures, an announcement of my birth, the guestbook from my mother's funeral, and several letters she wrote to my grandmother. In an ancient Mother's Day card she writes, "You will always be the grandest mom a girl ever had, and if I can be as good to my daughter I will count myself a perfect mother." I feel her love and longing in those words. They connect me to my past and to her.

Storytelling

Perhaps the greatest gifts someone can give to a child whose parent has died are the stories that speak to the life of her parent. She may want to know what made her father laugh or what challenged him growing up. She may be curious about what his hobbies or talents were. As she matures, she is likely to wonder about her parent's belief systems and values. Recollections of a parent's anguish or illness can also be shared in more depth, without excluding joyful memories.

Chris, whose ex-wife, Pam, took her life after several unsuccessful surgeries and years of addiction to pain medication, recounts a trip he took with his daughter a year after Pam's suicide. "Pam and I were divorced for ten years before she ended her life. I was angry with her a good portion of those ten years because of what I saw as inappropriate parenting. I always had to be the bad guy who enforced the rules, while she treated the kids as little adults, setting very few limits and exposing them to people and experiences that were not good for young children. After Pam died, my nineteen-year-old daughter decided she wanted to attend college in Colorado where Pam's sister lived, and where Pam and I had grown up. So, I drove her there from California. I took her to all our favorite haunts and showed her where her mother had lived as a child. On the trip out, during our hours together in the car, I shared with my daughter as many stories as I could remember of her mother's childhood. I talked about why I fell in love with her mother in the first place. I feel good about that trip, and I hope it meant something special to my daughter, too."

Preserving Memories

As you consider ways to help your child remember his parent, keep in mind that he will let you know what is helpful. Some children are anxious to talk or participate in projects to memorialize their parent. Others, most notably teens, may express discomfort and even resentment if they feel a conversation about their parent is contrived. Be respectful of a child's temperament and developmental stage as you encourage memory building. Make sure your efforts are in your child's best interests and not primarily from your own needs. Be aware that a child's needs change over time. As he matures, he may want to change or discontinue rituals established during the first years.

Following are suggestions to help your child build memories of his or her deceased parent.

- Encourage him to collect favorite pictures for a memorial board to be exhibited at the funeral or memorial service.
- Make sure she has a picture of her parent to keep with her, or to have in her room if she chooses.
- Consider showing video recordings of his parent when he is ready.
- Ask friends and other family members to write stories, memories or observations about the deceased parent, and include them in a scrapbook with pictures.
- Encourage her to make a collage of pictures she finds in magazines that remind her of her parent. She might also like to use actual photographs of her parent.

- Suggest that your child help you go through pictures and pick out photos he likes to place in an album. Reminisce about the pictures as you go through them, and talk about what was happening at the time the pictures were taken.
- She can also make a memory box and decorate it with stickers, glitter, drawings, artificial flowers, shells, pictures, or other decorations. Encourage her to be as creative as she wants, and suggest she might want to fill it with photos, poems, or other keepsakes to memorialize her relationship with her parent. She can add to her memory box over time.
- Put together a keepsake box yourself for additional special items such as jewelry, letters her parent wrote, or other personal items. Boys often love to have their father's wallets. Include news clippings, funeral announcements, memorial programs, etc. You may make one box for now and one for when your child is older.
- Check out websites on the Internet for survivor memorials. Encourage your child to set up his own virtual memorial.
- Suggest he might want to write a letter to his parent recalling special times they had together.
- Pick some flowers from your garden or purchase a bouquet and invite her to come to the cemetery with you. Let her know the purpose of the visit is to remember happy times.
- Encourage your child to help you plant a tree as a living tribute to his parent.
- Consider finding a support group for your child. Most support groups for children and teens include activities and art projects designed to help with memory building and expression of feelings.
- Ask her if there are any clothes or personal items from her parent that she may want to have, either now or saved for the future. If she is unable to choose anything now, make some selections for her and put them away.
- Enlist your child's help in choosing a charity for you to make a donation to in honor of his deceased parent.

- Research opportunities for a visual memorial marker. Many communities welcome financial contributions or physical work on a special project. For example, a parent's life can be commemorated by a plaque on a park bench or a brick in a children's playground walkway.

Group Events

Many organizations sponsor group events or memorial projects as a way for survivors to honor their loved ones. The American Foundation for Suicide Prevention (AFSP) sponsors an annual National Survivors Suicide Day where survivors are invited to view a live broadcast at many sites throughout the United States. They also have community "Out of the Darkness Walks," where survivors join together to walk and raise money for suicide awareness, education, and prevention. The Lifekeeper Foundation has a quilt project. Their goal is to place a "Face on Suicide" by creating a visual image of suicide in America. Nearly all fifty states and a number of specialty groups are represented in their quilt display at the National Suicide Awareness Event held every September at the Lincoln Memorial in Washington, D.C. This event is sponsored by the Suicide Prevention Action Network (SPAN), whose chapter representatives also bring letters from people in their communities asking elected officials to support suicide prevention efforts. They hand-deliver those letters to congressional representatives and senators, a process many participants feel is very empowering.

As you search for resources to help you and your children through the aftermath of a suicide death, you will discover other organizations and events for survivors. Your family may find it comforting to be involved in such activities. Please refer to the resource section at the back of this book for more information.

CHAPTER ELEVEN

Holidays, Anniversaries and Special Events: Exploring What Fits for Your Family

*"My mom made a cake for Daddy's birthday and
we talked about our memories. The cake was good
and we looked at pictures of when we were little.
I liked the one of me and Daddy riding bikes."*
—EMILY, AGE 5

The first year following any death can be especially difficult as families chart their way through holidays, birthdays and annual events that evoke memories both painful and joyous. Often the approaching day creates increasing anxiety, as family members struggle with how to acknowledge a day that was special in the past, but may now be a reminder of what has been lost.

With a suicide death, surviving parents often feel conflicted. They want to provide their children with a semblance of happiness, normalcy and fun, but find it difficult imagining how to celebrate in a time of darkness. Sometimes just finding the strength to get through the days, weeks and months following the suicide precludes having the energy to prepare for a special holiday.

That being said, it is important to find a way to acknowledge and observe holidays and other special occasions. Ignoring an approaching holiday creates more anxiety and disappointment than does facing it squarely. Since many holidays have become large-scale media and commercial events ("Just Nine Shopping Days Till Christmas!!"), they can't be escaped anyway.

Children rely on holiday traditions. They want to know that even though their parent has died, the family will still find a way to celebrate Christmas or Hanukkah, or plan a birthday party. While acknowledging the special day will be different, family members can be encouraged to blend familiar traditions with newly created rituals that commemorate the day and also promote healing.

Meeting as a family is the best way to plan holiday events. Talking together and brainstorming—encouraging each family member to participate in the discussion—helps families acknowledge the reality of the death. It is also an opportunity to connect with one another at a difficult time. Some families decide they want to celebrate the day somewhere else, feeling a change of scenery might be beneficial. Other families prefer to find a way to include past rituals, feeling that consistency and the familiar are more soothing. Not everyone is likely to agree, but a family discussion will give each family member the opportunity to express his or her needs and wishes.

"Last year after Daddy died Grandma took us to Hawaii for Christmas," reports eleven-year-old Michaela. "We all talked about it and it seemed like a good idea, because everyone was so sad. Hawaii was pretty fun, but we didn't have our tree or our stockings. It was fun to play on the beach, but it was too sunny. I missed the snow and I missed waking up before everyone else and going downstairs to see all the presents. We still got presents and that was good, but I missed being home. I missed Christmas Day with our cousins, but most of all, I missed Daddy. This year we decided we are going to stay home. It won't be the same without Daddy, but I think it will be O.K."

Michaela's mother adds, "I couldn't be home for the holidays last year. I felt guilty about not giving the kids a traditional Christmas, but I just couldn't imagine dragging out all the decorations or shopping for everyone. Even thinking about getting a tree and decorating it threw me into a panic. My husband always did that. He was a chef and he always cooked a big dinner for all the relatives. Having Christmas the old way seemed beyond anything I could manage. I think this year we can ease back into it and figure out some new traditions. I hope so, anyway."

Often, other family members or friends will offer to host holidays or help you create new rituals. You may feel confused about how to proceed. Trust your instincts. You can always try something different next year. Don't be surprised if your children are inundated with gifts from family and friends looking for a way to express their own feelings of sadness and helplessness. While gifts don't make up for the absence of a beloved parent, the gesture is sincere, and your kids will enjoy the presents nevertheless.

Children's Suggestions for Hanukkah and Christmas

Try to find a way to bring memories of your spouse into the holiday or event, since he or she is on everyone's mind anyway. Children I have talked with have come up with the following ideas:

Christmas/Hanukkah:
- Hang up the missing parent's stocking (if he or she had one) and fill it with greenery or candy canes. Some children like to make a stocking if one isn't available, choosing to decorate a commercially made felt stocking or create one from construction paper or felt.
- Pick out a favorite photo or possibly a holiday picture from a prior Christmas or Hanukkah and place a candle next to it. Allow anyone to light the candle at times during the holiday season when they are thinking of their special person. Young children will need assistance with lighting the candle. Safety rules about not leaving candles burning during family absences or at bedtime need to be acknowledged.
- Decorate a box with seasonal wrapping paper and cut a slit in the top. Ask people to write down memories of the person who has died, then place them in the box. Set aside a time to read all the stories.
- Pick out a special ornament each year to commemorate the deceased parent.
- Make an ornament out of construction paper with a picture of the parent who has died on it, then have it laminated.
- Suggest that each family member do something special to honor the missing parent. Write it down and put it in an envelope to be placed on the tree or near the menorah.

Examples might be donating a gift to an organization that serves the needy, singing in a holiday choir, making a financial contribution to a charitable organization, working in a soup kitchen or food bank, or cooking something special that the parent who has died used to cook or enjoy.

- Since the Hanukkah tradition is about finding light in the darkness, some Jewish families create a ritual around the lighting of the menorah. They share memories with each candle lighting, and talk about ways to bring light to the current dark time.

Every year the hospice organization where I work has a non-denominational memorial service where we invite everyone in the community to let us know the names of their loved ones who have died, whatever the cause. We read those names aloud at the service. As a special feature, we invite children who have been in our support groups to be in a youth choir that performs two songs at the ceremony. Some children and teens come year after year, choosing this performance as a way to remember their loved ones, and there are always new participants each year. In addition to our older children, we have had children as young as three participate, sometimes holding teddy bears or wearing Santa hats. They may not know all the words, but no one expects a professional performance. They always touch the audience's hearts with their sweet voices.

In my support group for adult survivors, one man has decided that his way to get through the holidays and honor his wife is to volunteer to be Santa at the annual Firefighters' Toy Drive. He and his wife hadn't been married very long before she took her life. They hadn't had children yet, but he feels comforted and useful as a Santa stand-in. "I couldn't do this the first year after my wife died, but I tried it the second year and found that even though it was really tiring and pretty demanding, I felt good about myself. I didn't get to be a father, but I can get into the Santa role and try to relate to the children. I think maybe I do a good job listening to all those kids and being kind to them. My wife had a mental illness and she took her life, but she was always kind, and she cared about people."

Birthdays

Chances are that young children will not know or remember the actual date of their deceased parent's birthday, though teens often do. Nevertheless, with guidance from the surviving parent, some families like to acknowledge the deceased parent's birthday in some way. Ellen, the mother of two young children who was estranged from her husband when he took his life, decided to make a birthday cake that first year, and she used the opportunity to encourage her children to share memories of their dad.

Children of all ages like their own birthdays, and they are likely to miss their deceased parent on their special day. Some children worry that they may not be able to celebrate their birthdays, and many express feeling out of sorts. Grief bursts (temper tantrums, crying episodes, depressed moods) can happen when a child realizes that his parent will be absent on his special day.

If possible, try to arrange some sort of birthday celebration for your child, or ask another family member or friend to take on the task. If the death occurred recently and is close to a child's birthday, having a big party may be too difficult. While it may be necessary to postpone a celebration or do something low-key on his special day this year, it is still important to acknowledge a child's birthday.

When Kristen's mother ended her life twelve days before Kristen's thirteenth birthday, Kristen knew she would always equate the death with her own birthday. "The first year we didn't celebrate in the same way, but we tried. My dad made my favorite foods and all the relatives came over. They kept watching me, and everyone tried to be happy that I was now a teenager, but, of course, we were all really sad. But I appreciated getting together and it was still good to get presents."

Anniversaries

While we generally think of anniversaries as a yearly occurrence, some people experience them on a monthly or even weekly basis. If a loved one died on a day of the week or a certain time of year with special significance, that day each week or season may stimulate painful awareness of the absence. "My husband died just before Thanksgiving three years ago," relays Monica, the mother of seventeen-year-old Hillary. "We live in an area where the seasons are spectacular, and Thanksgiving is when we always get together with our extended family. Seems like now when I see the leaves starting to change, I know it's the time of his death, and I just feel a kind of gloom. I want to do all the traditional Thanksgiving things, but I have had a hard time." Her daughter has instituted lighting a candle on the Thanksgiving table for her dad. "We talked about putting an empty chair at the table, but that was just too sad, too much of a down thing, so we light a candle instead," says Hillary. "We don't think so much about the actual day he died. We just remember him at Thanksgiving."

Young children are less likely to remember the actual date of the death, although teenagers often do. Most prefer to let the date come and go without making a big deal about it. You may want to comment that the date is coming and ask your children if they want to do anything to mark it. Sarah, whose long-term partner jumped to his death from the Golden Gate Bridge, invited her sixteen-year-old son to help her come up with a ritual. "Although my partner was not my son's father, he helped raise my children. At the one-year anniversary of Ron's death, my son and I honored his memory by writing him notes and placing them in a bowl along with a candle. We sent the bowl into San Francisco Bay toward the Golden Gate Bridge and watched it until it sank."

Sometimes families like to go to the cemetery or acknowledge their loved one by having a meal together and sharing memories. Other families find comfort by having a mass said or engaging in a ritual that has personal meaning such as listening to special music or visiting a site that feels comforting. "I like to take the kids to the beach near my husband's anniversary," states Dana, the mother of two daughters. "We don't talk much about their dad, but we throw rose petals into the water and have a picnic. I don't know how long we will do this, but for now, we like to be together in this way."

Some families choose not to do anything on an anniversary, but simply acknowledge the day and feel relief when it is over.

Sometimes anticipating the anniversary of the death is more difficult than the anniversary itself, especially when well-intentioned people ask how the family may plan to commemorate the death. "I don't know if it is worse having people ask or if they say nothing at all. I don't really think of the death on a particular date. I just remember the weeks leading up to her taking her life and all the struggles we went through that winter," comments Jim, who was left with three young children following his wife's suicide. "I don't want to do anything on that day. It isn't a day for celebration, but a sad day."

What is important is deciding for yourself what fits for you and your family. That can change as the years go by. Sometimes acknowledging an anniversary will have more significance for the partner left behind than for the children. If that is the case, you will want to find a way to recognize the day on your own or with a trusted friend, rather than insist your children participate in a ritual that may have no meaning for them.

* * * * *

You may find it hard to believe you will ever be able to truly "celebrate" holidays again, but you will. Combining the support of family and friends with the healing balm of time, you will find new ways to mark these days and open yourself again to the simple joys of celebration.

CHAPTER TWELVE

Support Groups: Solace and Safety

*"At first I didn't want to go, but we made fun art
and did drawings. It was hard at first to say how she died,
but the counselor helped me. The other kids were nice.
I got used to saying my story, and it was O.K."*
—BRIANNA, AGE 10

People of all ages can benefit from attending support groups, often offered through counseling centers, hospices, schools or hospitals. These confidential groups are generally offered at little or no cost and may be either time-limited or open-ended. Many meet weekly or bi-monthly. Support groups are not for everyone, particularly those with a history of serious emotional or behavioral problems who may benefit more from individual therapy. However, many people feel that support groups offer a needed refuge after the suicide death of a loved one. Being with others who are struggling with similar issues, in a non-judgmental atmosphere, can feel like having an extended family that understands the pain and isolation you are feeling.

Children's Bereavement Groups

Mourning is a necessary task for those who have lost someone special. Unfortunately, our society often fails to support or understand the unique nature of a child's grief. If his grief is unacknowledged, a child will feel isolated and confused, particularly when the death has been by suicide. Depression—or acting out his pain through destructive behaviors—may follow.

Support groups allow children to talk about the death in a safe environment with facilitators who are trained to work with each child's individual grief experience. Most groups offer a variety of play and art activities to help children express their feelings, share personal experiences and build memories. Being with other children who have lost a special person normalizes the grief process. It helps young people realize they are not the only ones who have suffered a loss.

Some grief educators believe children and teens are not ready for a support group until three to six months following a death. While it is true that the reality of the death often doesn't sink in immediately, I believe children can benefit from a support group sooner. I prefer to look at each family's needs individually. A bereavement counselor or children's group facilitator can help you decide on the timing of a group for your child.

It is not critical that children attend a support group designed solely for those who have experienced the suicide of someone special. Although suicide-specific groups may provide additional support and a unique sense of camaraderie, children coping with the suicide of a parent can be successfully integrated into groups dealing with other types of death.

Young children may discover that the concept of suicide is new and mystifying to their peers. Since children are naturally curious, other participants are likely to ask surviving children more questions, particularly if the death has involved guns or weapons of any sort. With this in mind, parents and caregivers need to prepare a young person for the inevitable questions he may encounter.

"At first I was worried that my children would feel ostracized or somehow different from the other kids, since their dad had killed himself rather than dying by some other means," states May, whose two daughters, Madison, age eleven, and Bethany, seven, attended a children's group following the death of their father. "But no other group was available, and I wanted them to get some help. The girls were shy at first. They said some of the other kids didn't know what suicide was. They were asked why their dad had killed himself. We had talked about how to answer that question before they started the group. The group leader also helped them explain how some people have an illness in their brain and don't understand they can get help. Madison had more trouble talking about her dad, but that is her personality. She is a little more reserved. Her younger sister didn't seem to have much trouble at all, and she surprised me with how matter-of-fact she was. I guess what reassured me was they both wanted to keep on going to the group. We were able to continue talking about their dad with every art project they brought home."

Most children are shy about attending a group. Meeting new people and having to talk about such a private and painful matter feels scary. Teens are particularly reluctant to attend support groups, because they often feel vulnerable and don't want to be different than their peers. They worry about losing control, crying or not knowing what to say.

I suggest that parents tell their children that they want them to try a support group, emphasizing it as an opportunity to be with others who will understand their loss. Tell your children that you want to be the best parent possible, and that it's your responsibility to provide them with people and situations to help all of you as you grieve. Rather than ask a young child if he wants to attend a group, let him know you want him to try it a couple of times. If he seems reluctant, assure him that if he is really uncomfortable, you will explore alternatives. If you are also attending a support group yourself, you can model your belief that talking with others who understand can be helpful.

Art, games, discussions, and, of course, snacks have natural appeal for children. The difficult part of a group is talking about the suicide. I encourage parents to "coach" their children prior to beginning a support group, practicing with them what they might consider saying. A counselor or the group's facilitator can help with this. Surviving parents, who are trying to cope with the trauma as well, often feel hesitant about what to say to their children, and may not trust their own abilities. A little preparation is a good idea, though children must also have the option not to talk.

"At first I didn't want to say how my dad died," reports eight-year-old Curtis. "The counselor said I didn't have to if I didn't want to. But then I did say what happened, and the other kids asked me a lot of questions. They wanted to know what kind of gun he used and where he shot himself. I felt weird talking about it at first. Then I got used to it and it was O.K. The kids weren't mean and they didn't tease me. I kind of felt better because I didn't want to keep it a secret anymore."

Teens may refuse to attend a support group, and if they are adamant about this, I don't think it's a good idea to insist. Offer them an alternative, which might include talking individually with the group facilitator or attending a meeting with a friend. I often meet with teenagers who don't like the idea of attending a group. I like to get to know the teen and hear his perspective on what has happened. I ask him if he would like to share his view of himself and other family members. We talk a little about the grieving process, and I share my own experiences. I also tell him about the group, specifically how it works, what we do, as well as general information about who is attending. I stress that this is a confidential situation, and that our groups are comprised of kids from many walks of life, who might not all be friends even if they attended the same school. We come together because grief and losing a loved one is an equalizing experience. A support group is one place where others do understand.

Teens are curious about their peers. They may consent to attending a group if they have information about how the group works, and have the option to stop if they are not benefiting. Teenage boys, however, rarely think a talk group is for them. Encourage your teenager to give a teen group a try, but don't be surprised if he balks. You can insist he attend once. With luck, he will be intrigued by the other participants or actually enjoy himself. Providing adolescent groups with some structure to help participants focus on their experience and ease their awkwardness usually makes it worthwhile for them.

Some bereavement programs provide outdoor-based support groups or grief camps. These experiences may provide teens, especially boys, with an alternative to traditional grief support groups.

Adult Support Groups

One of the best ways to help your child is to find a suicide survivor's support group for yourself. Although you may believe that what you are feeling could not possibly be experienced by anyone else, or that no one will truly understand the depth of your pain, support groups help you discover you are not alone. No matter how horrific or unbelievable your experience has been, you will find others who understand and are willing to listen. Others who have experienced the suicide of a loved one know about the sense of isolation and abandonment that accompanies this trauma.

Unlike the situation for children, I believe it is important for adults to find a support group focused specifically on suicide, rather than a general bereavement group. I have talked with survivors who have tried other groups and have felt uncomfortable or misunderstood. Despite the best intentions, other grievers may subtly or openly discriminate, feeling that a death by suicide indicates a "choice," or that somehow the survivor is responsible or inadequate in some way. Attending a group where all participants are survivors allows participants to share painful experiences and discover that each person in the room can relate to the guilt, confusion and anguish that follows suicide.

In addition, participants learn that suicide survivors come from every socio-economic group, from all ethnicities and every religion or spiritual tradition. As group members, we don't stand out in any particular way, but are simply a mix of caring friends and family members who are hurting from our loss. No one will insist that your loved one is "better off now" or that you need to grieve in a certain way. We know you have to grieve at your own pace, and may need to go over and over what led up to the suicide. In a support group you can be yourself. You do not have to take care of anyone else or put on a "together" face. You will discover that there is room for you and what you are experiencing.

Generally, the format for a survivor group begins with a check-in. Participants introduce themselves and then may choose to speak about their loved one or not. Confidentiality within the group is assured, and while participants are invited to share, some choose to remain quiet as they get their bearings. Some groups are time-limited, with participants starting together and attending for a specified number of sessions. Others are ongoing where group members can come and go. Sometimes people attend for a few weeks or months, and then decide to take a break. Others come consistently for longer periods and develop friendships that grow beyond the group.

Most of our time together is spent sharing stories of our loved ones or how we are coping day to day. We bond over how people don't really know how to relate to us, walking around tiptoe or acting as if nothing ever happened. We acknowledge the friends who have left us and the new friends who may surprise us with their compassion and understanding. We gain strength from sharing our experiences. Sometimes we are able to offer hope or an insight to someone else, and that feels good.

I have found that support groups for survivors welcome new participants wherever they are in their grieving process. For some, attending a group soon after the suicide can help combat the early isolation. Others may need more time before they feel they can talk about what has happened. They are simply too raw and need to talk to someone individually first. And in some cases, participants who were unable to talk about their trauma at the time may come to a support group years after the suicide, finally ready to explore their experience.

New members learn from the veterans that initial feelings of hopelessness and anguish change and eventually lessen in their intensity. Older members are reminded of those early days of despair, and are able to see that they have moved forward. We share stories of those moments where grief comes unbidden and unexpected, even as our lives seem to be getting better. Tears flow, anger and frustration is expressed, and sometimes we even laugh, which surprises us all.

Starting Your Own Support Group

If you feel like a support group would be helpful for you and there isn't one in your area, you might consider starting your own. You may be able to contact your local mental health clinic, hospital or church to see if they could help you, or if they might have a room where you could meet. You might advertise in the newspaper or ask the leader of your faith community to make an announcement in the bulletin. You might be surprised at how many people respond. More lives have been touched by suicide than most of us imagine.

Some survivor groups operate without leaders, or they rotate leadership. While many of these groups work very well, I feel it is better to have at least one trained facilitator, someone who is also a survivor, but has worked on his or her own grief and understands the dynamics of grief, suicide, and group process. As you will discover, this is a tumultuous time, and survivors experience significant upheaval and distress. A facilitator who has had bereavement training or is a mental health professional can often help with the group dynamics, drawing out shy participants and helping the group keep its focus. Sometimes participants may need more than group support, and having a facilitator who is able to assess and refer makes the group feel more secure.

*   *   *   *   *

Although support groups are not for everyone, everyone needs support following a suicide death. Your task is to find that support for yourself and your children.

"I don't know what I would have done without my support group," comments Suzanne, the mother of two young children. "It took me almost a year to get there because I was so overwhelmed at first. From the first day I felt at 'home.' The other participants knew my struggle. It was like I could finally be myself. I had been so busy taking care of my kids, my parents, and my husband's family—always trying to make everyone else feel better. I finally found a place where I could talk about my guilt and my anger. I wish I had gone sooner. I'll never be the person I was before he killed himself, but at least I don't feel so crazy anymore."

CHAPTER THIRTEEN

When Your Spouse Carries Out Suicide

"I thought we loved each other
and would find a way to work things out,
but he deserted me and the kids.
Weren't we worth living for?"
—JULIA

A spouse's death by suicide leaves a surviving partner reeling, feeling abandoned, alone and betrayed. This death was not inevitable. Its apparent deliberateness can contribute to profound feelings of inadequacy, anger and guilt.

As you struggle with the aftermath, you will be flooded with questions. Who was this person I married? What could have been so wrong, so intolerable, so upsetting to make him choose to end his life? How could he abandon the children and me? How can I help them when I can barely cope with my own rage and sorrow? What could I have done to prevent this terrible act?

You may believe that by working together you and your partner could have found a solution. Perhaps you tried to convince her that nothing is bad enough to end it all. But the reality is that a suicidal person is almost always unable to think clearly or see beyond her desperation. Maybe for a time she was capable of waging a battle against her thoughts, tried to believe that hope existed. But she finally reached the point where she was no longer capable of fighting. This is one of the costs of mental illness—it can take lives. Most of the time, properly prescribed medication or other treatments work, but sometimes they don't.

Research and clinical experience have convinced most suicide experts that in the moment when someone takes his life, his emotional, physical or spiritual anguish is so overwhelming that he sees no other options. It's as if he is in a dark tunnel with no hope of finding any light. He is unable to see that you and your children love him and will suffer from his death. He may believe he is a burden, and that ending his life will release you from the pain he feels he has caused you. But ultimately, his death is not about you. It is about ending the intolerable pain he is feeling.

Most of us who experience deep anguish are able to find a way through. We know there are solutions to problems if only we hold on. You may wonder yourself if you are going to get through the grief you are feeling over your partner's suicide. Such concerns are normal, but *if you have thoughts of ending your own life, you need to seek professional help at once.*

Common Responses to Grief

As you are discovering, grief can feel overwhelming. As the surviving spouse, you are particularly victimized by this death. Your loved one has ended his suffering, but you are left to pick up the pieces—to cope with your pain, go on with your life *and* take care of your children. You may be surprised by the incredible amount of energy it takes to grieve. Perhaps you are wondering if certain feelings or behaviors are normal. Following are common physical and emotional responses of survivors:[1]

- Feeling of tightness in the throat or heaviness in the chest.
- An empty feeling in the stomach, loss of appetite (or wanting to snack often).
- Emotional numbness and lack of motivation to do necessary daily tasks.
- Alternating anger and guilt.
- Restlessness in looking for activity, but finding it difficult to focus.
- Feeling as though the loss isn't real, and expecting to see the one who has died.

- Sensing your loved one's presence and talking to him or her.
- Wandering aimlessly, unable to finish what you've started.
- Difficulty sleeping, exhausted all the time.
- Intense preoccupation with the life of the deceased.
- Dreaming of your loved one frequently, or wanting to.
- Assuming his or her mannerisms or traits.
- Becoming easily frustrated, more irritable than usual.
- Wearing clothes, jewelry or other personal items of your loved one.
- Feeling you need to "take care" of other people who seem uncomfortable around you by not talking about your feelings of loss.
- Confusion about religious/spiritual beliefs.
- A need to tell and retell stories of the relationship and the loss.
- Mood changes over the slightest things.
- Crying often and sometimes unexpectedly.
- Low self-esteem.
- Difficulty thinking (forgetfulness, memory lapses) and making decisions.
- Anger that the world goes on and that you seem so alone in your grief.

Is There a "Proper" Way to Grieve?

Each person grieves differently. Grief is not just an emotional experience, but physical, cognitive, behavioral and spiritual as well. You will find yourself grieving not only for your partner, but also for the hopes, dreams and expectations you held prior to the death. How you grieve will be influenced by who you are in the world—by your temperament, gender, culture and spiritual beliefs. Even such personal variables as lifestyle, health, and how you manage stress will factor into your grieving process.

"Grieving Styles" and Gender

In general, men and women respond differently to grief. Like all generalities, there are many exceptions, but most therapists and grief researchers recognize basic gender differences in what may be called "grieving styles." Women are more likely to respond to grief by expressing their emotions, sharing their feelings with others, and asking for help. They often have more difficulty than men in accepting and expressing their anger around the loss of their loved one. Men tend to grieve privately. They are more likely to cry alone while driving their car, whereas women cry with their friends over coffee. Men try to think through their grief with rational analysis. Anger and guilt may arise, but thoughts rather than feelings tend to dominate their response to grief.

The roots of these gender differences are complex, giving rise to questions of "nature-versus-nurture" that are likely to continue challenging psychologists and brain researchers long into the future. The important point for those suffering the loss of a loved one is that there is no "right" way to grieve. Some men grieve in the more expressive way common to women, while some women gravitate to the more private, analytical style of men.

New Hampshire legislator Roger Wells, who lost both his wife and teenage daughter to suicide, exemplifies the more male-oriented response to grief. "Men grieve differently," he says. "We want to talk, we want to spill our guts, but we clam up, especially in front of women. I couldn't talk about what had happened, and I had to get back to work. I had to make a living. I couldn't take the time to grieve. That's the way most men function. I was a racetrack veterinarian, and I remember I would often cry while driving to the track. But once I hit the security gate, I would imagine my emotions being like a coat. I would take off my coat and hang it on an imaginary nail at the security gate. I would work all day and when someone would say, 'Hi, Doc, how are you?' I'd say I was fine. But obviously I wasn't fine. You put on this false pretense and you do what you have to do. When I finished the day and I drove through that gate, my imaginary coat would come off the nail and I'd drive home, often in tears. I never felt like I had a choice about my grieving. I had to function."

Openly expressing their feelings with others may come more naturally to most women, but this doesn't mean grieving is easier for them—just different. "I had to find others who understood my pain," reports Jennifer, "but it took me a while to actually go to a grief group. I didn't even want to leave the house. My friends came through for me by bringing us food, helping with housework, picking up the kids, just being there when I needed to talk or cry. But when I got to the group I felt so reassured. They really knew what I was going through. We were going through it together."

Experiencing the pain of loss is a necessary part of grief work. There is no way around the pain, but it's important to acknowledge and respect individual needs and differences. Men, more often than women, choose active means of coping with their grief, such as engaging in competitive sports or hobbies, creating a memorial, or working harder at their jobs. They may thus *appear* to be less impacted, but their grief is no less deeply felt. Gender tends to influence the *expression* of grief, but not its existence.

An example comes from an address at a grief conference I attended several years ago. The speaker shared a story of a father whose daughter died after crashing into a neighbor's fence. The father went out the morning of the funeral with lumber and tools and began to repair the fence. Observing this, the neighbor came out of his house and said, "Hey, you don't have to do that."

To which the father simply replied, "Yes I do."

Another man, Michael, recalls: "When my wife took her life, I was completely blown away. I didn't know how to respond, but I knew it was up to me to take care of things. I had to continue supporting my kids, so I went back to work after a few days. I could talk to my sister some, but I didn't want to talk to anyone else. I went to one support group meeting, but I just couldn't relate, and I was the only guy there. I spent hours in the garage tinkering. Seems I had to be busy. But it took me forever to clean out her closet. Sometimes I just wanted to touch and smell her clothes. I didn't tell anyone about that for a long time. I was too embarrassed."

Recognizing that men and women may grieve differently allows us to identify and accept a variety of grief responses that promote healing. In the end, the most important task is to find the way that will most help get you through this tumultuous time.

Blaming Yourself

When your spouse takes his or her own life, you are likely to feel you were somehow at fault. Maybe you didn't realize the depth or severity of your partner's depression. Maybe you said something that you feel upset your spouse. Maybe you knew there were weapons in the house and you didn't remove them. Maybe you feel you should have monitored his medication more closely or insisted on a medical intervention. Maybe you had feared she would consider suicide, but you did not believe she would follow through. The list of what you think you "should have done" may be extensive. These "if onlys" may trouble you for a long time.

Laura, whose husband of eighteen years shot himself while she was at the store, struggles as she recalls her last interaction with Larry. "He had been very ill with pulmonary disease, and was upset with how dependent on me he had become. I liked taking care of him, but that last morning I was feeling frustrated because he didn't want to take his medication. I snapped at him a little and asked him how he expected to get better if he didn't take his medicine. We needed some things at the store. I could have waited until later, but I thought maybe a little break would do us good. I just keep thinking if only I had been more patient, if only I hadn't gone to the store, well, maybe he wouldn't have killed himself. I can't get that idea out of my mind."

In the survivor group I lead, much discussion centers on the motivation of the person who dies by suicide. The "Why?" question is closely followed by thoughts of what survivors could have done to prevent the death. After the fact, we can always see what we might have done differently. Of course, there is no way of knowing what might have happened if we had. Maybe the suicide would have been deterred in that moment, but carried out at another time. Maybe the person would have gotten the necessary help she needed, perhaps with a new medication to change her outlook and body chemistry. Maybe the suicide could have been averted—but maybe not. The hard truth is that there is no way of knowing.

In most situations, others will reassure you that your spouse's suicide wasn't your fault. In some part of your mind, you may know this to be true, but in another darker place, you may doubt yourself. You may feel you are not worth staying alive for, that you were in some way so unacceptable that your partner chose to leave you. You may feel you don't deserve to continue living or to experience pleasure. These feelings are a form of "survivor's guilt." They reflect the sense of helplessness and confusion we feel after a suicide death.

You will never be able to fully comprehend what motivated your partner to end his or her life, but the critical point is this: *The suicide was not your fault*. You would have prevented it if you could. At some point, you must come to know this, and thus surrender to the reality that there was nothing you could have done to guarantee the long-term safety of your partner.

If Others Blame You

As incomprehensible as suicide may seem, it is human nature to seek an explanation for such a tragic act. Unfortunately, one easy way to do that is to assign blame. And who better to blame than the partner of the person who carries out suicide?

You may sense that others hold you responsible. Perhaps you notice them looking at you differently, or avoiding eye contact, uttering insincere, uneasy pleasantries, or changing the subject. You may even be subjected to accusatory remarks or distressing questions.

Complicating this situation is the fact that surviving spouses often face a barrage of questions by the police, who must rule out foul play. This is a traumatic experience that can anger and unnerve grieving partners and their families. Joan, whose husband ended his life, recalls, "My husband's death was so blatantly a suicide. He had to actually tie a string around the shotgun because his arms didn't reach. It was obvious that he had made the gun fire with his foot. But the police still asked me whether he had any enemies. I understood this was standard police procedure following any sudden death, but it was still extremely upsetting."

If you find yourself in a situation where your children or other family members hold you responsible, try to remember that they are suffering, too. In moments of deep grief and despair, people can make cruel and hurtful remarks, comments that wound deeply. This is also a way, unconsciously, to attempt to absolve themselves of any feelings that they are somehow responsible for the death.

Perhaps you feel that your spouse's parents or siblings are culpable in some way. Your anger with them may make it difficult to be with one another. Rather than coming together for love and support, you may find yourself drifting apart as blame and anger overtly or even covertly drive a wedge into your relationship.

Hopefully, you will be able to weather this storm. It is important for your children to remain connected to their grandparents, who are a link to the parent who has died. Each of you must give up holding the other responsible if you are to maintain a relationship. However, sometimes keeping the connection is too upsetting or destructive. Some families do drift apart. But, if possible, put blame aside and try to talk with one another about your feelings. You might also consider seeing a bereavement counselor together as an avenue for healing.

Financial Concerns

In addition to the overwhelming grief you may be feeling, you also face a myriad of practical concerns. Despite your feelings of loss, loneliness and confusion, life must go on, and the world continues to make demands on you. Even though it may feel like time has stopped, you know you have to think about the future and how you are going to manage financially.

The American Foundation for Suicide Prevention, in conjunction with the National Endowment for Financial Education, offers a comprehensive guide to financial matters for survivors entitled, *Surviving a Suicide Loss: A Financial Guide*. In a clear, organized way, interspersed with survivor vignettes, this booklet covers the immediate aftermath of handling funeral, medical and insurance matters, and longer term issues such as planning for your children's education, managing your money and settling an estate. Particularly valuable is information about Social Security survivor benefits that may be available to you and your children. (See *Resources* section for more information.)

Having to worry about money is stressful, but unavoidable for most surviving spouses. Money issues arise fairly soon after a suicide, as survivors have to contend with funeral expenses, medical costs and everyday bills. Most experts and many survivors recommend not making any major financial decisions right after losing your loved one, but waiting several months or longer, if possible.

Who Am I Now?

You may wonder if you can live through this, or if you will ever stop crying. The term "widow" or "widower" may frighten you, make you angry or seem way off the mark. You may feel too young for such a label. You may wonder if there is a right or wrong way to grieve, and if you are up for the task. A friend of mine told me, "I remember feeling so inadequate and fearful that I would not grieve 'the right way.' People's comments were sometimes confusing. Many times their words were not helpful or comforting; sometimes I felt even worse. The turmoil of emotions within my heart did not correspond with their desire for me to 'be myself again.' Believe me, I certainly wanted to turn back the clock and be myself again, but that was not to be."

One thing is certain: You are still a parent with a big job ahead. Your child's grieving journey will be shaped by your response. You may feel lost in your own reactions, and you may question your ability to comfort or be sensitive to your children. Be assured—they need you now more than ever. Children often wonder following the death of a parent: "Are we still a family?" Because they no longer have both a mom *and* a dad, they may need help in redefining what "family" now means. They will need encouragement that you will make it through this trauma together. This is a time when you must call on whatever strength you have inside to reassure your children that you will be there for them. Summon other friends and family members such as aunts, uncles, and grandparents who can support you and your children. Avail yourself of whatever community resources you or your supporters can muster. You have a long journey ahead, but you will discover there are pathways through your anguish.

It's true that you aren't the "old you" anymore, and your life will never be as it was. But as you continue on this grieving journey, you will discover a new you. This will happen, inexorably, with the healing passage of time.

* * * * *

Olivia is a pretty, petite, thirty-seven-year-old Mexican-American woman and the mother of three children, ages fifteen, fourteen and twelve. Olivia's husband, Enrique, killed himself six years ago. Today Olivia's children are good students, polite and loving, active in school and sports. Olivia works as a classroom aide at a neighborhood elementary school. She is determined to provide her three children with a good education and the loving support she feels she didn't have as the oldest child of seven, growing up in Mexico City.

OLIVIA'S STORY

"I had to find a reason to go on without Enrique, and my children became the reason."

I fell in love with Enrique when I was seventeen. I was very shy and quiet. Enrique was twenty-one, a handsome man who was too much of a "lady's man," according to my parents. They didn't approve of him. We got married in a small ceremony. My father was upset that we didn't have a big church wedding. When I asked him who would pay for this big wedding, he told me it would be my responsibility. Enrique and I decided to buy a house in Mexico instead. A year later we moved to California to strike out on our own.

At first we lived with cousins and worked in the fields until we could pay for our own place. When I was twenty-one, my daughter was born. By the time I was twenty-four I had three children. Enrique found work first as a dishwasher in an Italian restaurant. I worked there, too, making salads. Then he worked construction and finally got a good job restoring antique furniture. I worked as a waitress in a Mexican restaurant and took classes to learn English.

Those early days were so full and lively. Enrique was a good father. He would always play on the floor with the children. He wrestled with them and made up games. He played the flute for us. We felt close as a family. I knew he had many difficult times when he was a boy. His father and older brother had beaten him, but he seemed to have found happiness with me and our family.

The night Enrique killed himself he picked me up from my job around 10 p.m. I was tired. I wanted to go to sleep. Enrique was watching a dance show on Spanish TV. He didn't want me to sleep. He said, "Let's watch this meringue lesson and go dancing." I laughed and said, "You learn the steps and teach me tomorrow." An hour later he woke me up to suggest we go out dancing. I told him I was too tired.

In the morning the light next to Enrique's side of the bed was still on, and the house was quiet. Usually Enrique would have been up and getting the children ready for school. His boots were still on the floor next to the bed. I called to the children to get them going. Then I walked through the house, looking for him. His truck was parked outside, but I did not see him. Then I noticed a crack in the door to the garage and saw the light on. I thought he was there working on a project. I opened the door and saw him hanging with a rope around his neck.

I screamed and cried. The children came running. They were frightened and shocked. My two oldest looked inside the garage, but my little girl hid because she felt so scared. My son—he was only eight years old—tried to help me cut his dad down, but we couldn't do it. I called 911 several times, crying and crying. The police and fire department came in about ten minutes, but it seemed like forever. One of the policemen was a friend of ours and he told me that Enrique was "gone." The police wouldn't allow us to go back in the garage. The children were taken to relatives, and we began to think about how we would be able to go on after this terrible, terrible death.

I couldn't believe Enrique had killed himself. The night before he had been so happy about his job. He had many plans for the future. I couldn't believe he would hang himself. How could he? He loved the children. How could he do this to them? I blamed myself. Maybe I didn't listen to him enough when he wanted to talk about his feelings. I thought if I hadn't been so tired that night, maybe I would have heard noises in the garage—something that would tell me Enrique was committing suicide. The worst thing that happened was when my sister came to my house right after. Instead of giving me a hug, she said, "Now you are alone, and it's too late. You didn't appreciate the wonderful husband you had." I felt so terrible because that made me think his death was all my fault.

I don't really remember the first few days after we found Enrique. I was crying all the time and I had to have someone else take care of the children. I knew they missed me and wanted to be with me, but I had trouble taking care of myself. I felt so alone, sad, upset, and very tired. I felt like I had no reason to go on living.

All I could think about was that I would have to work harder to support us. We didn't have enough money. Enrique helped me in so many ways at home and with the children. I didn't know how I could manage. I couldn't sleep. The doctor gave me sleeping pills. I didn't want to take drugs, but he said my anxiety was too much. He said that I needed a little help for a few days so I would have the strength to take care of the funeral. The medicine did help me, but I stopped taking it after a week or two.

We had an open casket at Enrique's funeral. Before the funeral I talked with my children about if we should send their dad's body to Mexico or keep him here. I knew Enrique didn't want to be buried because he said he wanted his ashes thrown in the mountains. The children didn't want their dad to be cremated. I explained that if we buried him, his body would change to ashes anyway. I told them about how fruit decomposes and that the human body decomposes, too. We talked about having their dad's ashes at home with us all the time instead of having him in a cemetery. We decided that we didn't want to throw his ashes in the mountains. We would keep him with us.

Three months after my husband's suicide I went to a Catholic retreat for three days. The purpose of this retreat was to find out who you really are and what you want in life. I think that was when I started to live again. I think I felt born again. That retreat helped me because I learned that everything can have a good side. I had to find a reason to go on without Enrique, and my children became my reason. I decided I would devote myself to my children in a way I had not ever really done before.

Enrique used to tell me I was too busy for the children. I worked because I like to work, not because we had to have the money. The money I made helped, but he made enough to support us. But I was always working, or shopping or going to the beauty parlor. He told me some day I would be sorry because my children would not be close to me like I wanted. He was right. I was too busy, but after he died I dedicated myself to them. I don't think I can ever find someone to love like I loved Enrique. He was the best person in my life, but when I lost him, I found my children.

I was so worried about them. They were fighting more. They were doing all right in school, but I worried their father's death would hurt them in the future. I really worried that maybe they might kill themselves some day if they didn't get help. I still worry about that. They had counseling at school, but my older daughter—she was nine—would cry and didn't feel comfortable there. My six-year-old didn't understand her dad had really died. Sometimes she would say he died and then ask when he was going to pick her up from school. She cried a lot and was afraid of many things. My son got more aggressive at school and said negative things to his friends. He was also having trouble learning English at that time. He was always upset. I felt so worried and more sad than ever.

Four months after Enrique's death I took the children to a support group for children who had somebody die in their family. They were shy about going but interested, too. My son wouldn't go in the room at first, but they finally talked him into it. I guess my children didn't talk much that first meeting. We met with the counselor after the group, and the children told me that her mother had killed herself when she was young. They felt a little better, knowing this had happened to someone else, and that they weren't the only children whose parent committed suicide. They learned to talk about their father's death and even learned to say the word suicide. I couldn't say it, but they could.

During the time the children went to the group I heard them talk more about their feelings. They said they were angry their dad had left them. They also did some very nice art projects with the other children in that group. Those projects seemed to help them with their feelings and also to remember the good things about their dad. They were in an art show for children who had lost a loved one. Some of their art was displayed at the County Court Building. That made us all proud. I don't want them to feel ashamed. Enrique's death wasn't their fault. I think the support group and those people who led the group helped us a lot. We learned there are wonderful people who care about us.

My older children went to that group for about nine months. My youngest daughter stayed longer. She went back a year or two later when she started having trouble with friends and was confused about how to fit in at school. We still keep in touch with the leader of the support group. Each year the children sing in a children's choir at a community memorial service where the names of people who died are read aloud. One year Caroline read some of the names. Her list ended with her father's name. I was so proud of her standing up there in front of so many people. I remember when she used to be so shy.

A few months ago she turned fifteen. We had a traditional Mexican *Quinceañera* for her. This is a party to honor her because she is now a young woman. Her brother was her escort and they danced together. Her sister and I were also on the stage to give her the tiara. She talked about her father. She told everyone that even though he died, she still felt he was part of her life. I was so proud of her and all my children. We worked hard to make this a special day for her. I wish Enrique could have been there. I know he would have been proud, too.

I try to raise my children with clear, strong rules. They don't always do what I say or want them to do, but I trust them. Sometimes they don't listen to me, but when things go wrong or they realize what I said was true, they come back to me and we talk. I never expect them to be perfect. Maybe sometimes I expect a lot. Now that they are teenagers, we disagree more. This is difficult, but I love them. They are good children—kind, and they care about me, each other and other people. My son recently did yard work for a neighbor. He saved the money to get me some perfume that I once put on myself at the mall. I didn't even know that he noticed or found out the name of the perfume.

Of course, I worry about them, like any parent—probably more because of what they have gone through. I try to keep them busy, in karate and football and other activities. I think this is good. It doesn't give them much time to get in trouble. Of course, getting a good education is very important. I am always after them to get good grades and do well. My older daughter wants to have a boyfriend now, but I tell her she needs to get better grades first. I want my children to go to college and be able to support themselves in the world.

I believe Enrique's death has brought my children and me closer, but I miss him so much. I still feel sad and sometimes when I hear music that we both loved, I remember being with him. Some days I cry, but I don't cry as much as I did when it first happened. Sometimes I feel angry with Enrique and think in my mind, "Why did you have to go? You didn't think about all the responsibility I would have. You are happy where you are, but look at me. Life here is very hard sometimes, and I worry about the children. I'm mad that you aren't here to help us."

Sometimes I still can't believe Enrique killed himself, even though it has been six years. I still question why this happened. I think maybe he was frustrated that he had to work so much. Sometimes I think he was sad because of the abuse he suffered when he was a child. Maybe he just felt alone. I don't know. Usually when we talk about the reason for Enrique's suicide we end up with the same thing—we don't know.

I used to think I would never have another relationship, but I surprised myself by falling in love a few months ago. I don't know what will happen with this new relationship, but I feel happier now. I have started exercising and dressing up more. I didn't care so much before. I felt a little guilty in the beginning that I was interested in another man, but the priest told me I deserve to be happy. I guess I do.

CHAPTER FOURTEEN

A Divorced/Separated Partner's Perspective

"Sometimes I feel angry,
mostly about being a single parent,
and not having the family life I envisioned."
—ELLEN

If you are a divorced or separated parent, you have experienced the pain and anxiety that comes when two people realize they can no longer be together. You have had to face the loss of previous hopes and expectations for the future. You have probably become acquainted with the world of custody negotiations, financial dilemmas and running a household on your own.

Underneath it all, there has been your deep concern about the impact of your divorce or separation on your children. Coping with the pain of a family breakup is heartrending. But with your former partner's suicide, you are now faced with helping your children adjust to a new trauma. Not only are you solely responsible for your children's care, but the burden of explaining and helping your children cope now falls on your shoulders as well.

You will also experience your own grief. Perhaps you thought reconciliation was possible, but had resigned yourself to being a single parent for now. Maybe you had been divorced for years or had begun life with a new partner, yet you continued to be concerned about your former partner's decline. In all likelihood, you have had to deal with his or her mental illness, alcoholism or substance abuse.

While many of your concerns will be similar to those who were still with their spouse at the time of the suicide (see previous chapter), you also face emotional and logistical challenges unique to divorce or separation.

Blame and Exclusion

As a divorced or separated spouse, you may find yourself without the support married surviving partners receive. Your grief may be minimized, ignored, even questioned. This lack of support is termed "disenfranchised grief."[1]

Many divorced or separated spouses also report they are blamed for the suicide and sometimes excluded from mourning opportunities. Your former partner's family may feel that if the divorce or separation hadn't occurred, he might have weathered his depressive storm. They may hold you responsible for creating an environment that led him to take his life. As discussed in the previous chapter, blaming you may be their way of dealing with their anguish. Even if you feel guilty yourself, you must be careful not to accept blame. Your former partner's suicide was not your fault.

Theresa recalls her anger towards her ex-husband's family when they ignored her and her nine-year-old daughter at the funeral. "I knew they were angry at me because of the divorce, but they punished my daughter, too. We were ignored at the service and not invited to be a part of the procession or speak at the funeral. That antagonism lasted for five years after his death. Only recently have we begun to repair our relationship. My in-laws missed seeing my daughter grow up. She lost out on having her grandparents at a time when she needed them."

The "Feelings Roller Coaster"

Your grief may include feeling shock, disbelief, sadness, confusion and guilt. You are likely to cycle rapidly from anguish to anger as you realize your former partner has followed through with what you perceive as the ultimate betrayal—abandoning your children.

"I knew she had problems," reports Daniel, a policeman and the father of two young children. "She was severely depressed, and we had been separated for about a year because of her erratic behavior. She was living in her own apartment, but we were trying to work things out. Her suicide devastated me. Even though I try and understand the nightmare she was going through, I can't. I feel incredibly sad about her death, but I have to admit I am also angry with her for giving up. Our children are suffering so much."

Mental illness is often a factor in the breakup of a marriage. Becky, who left her husband after eighteen years of marriage and four children, recalls, "I married Doug when I was young, just twenty-two. I didn't understand then that he suffered from depression, alcoholism, anxiety and panic attacks. I had to grow up quickly as I learned to live with his illness. Even though I wanted to try and help him feel better, I realized that I couldn't change him, and I had to accept him for who he was. This was difficult for me. I went from being a bubbly, outgoing person to being quiet and withdrawn. Eventually, I had to leave him, even though I was fearful about how I was going to manage four kids on my own."

A year after they separated, Doug ended his life. Now, six years later, Becky reflects, "I believe it's important to keep his memory alive, not as someone perfect, but as a real person, someone special who loved each one of our children. This is hard for me sometimes. I have remarried and am blessed with a wonderful partner. We have had a son together and have a good life. I am back to being myself again. I wish I didn't have to talk about Doug ever again because it's uncomfortable for me. We were in the middle of divorce proceedings and I didn't feel the same way about him as the kids did. But I know I need to talk and remember him because they need it. I want to be as truthful and loving as I can about who he was and what his challenges were. He loved his children very much, but mentally he simply wasn't able to cope. I hope they will understand this more as they mature. I continue to worry about them, given Doug's family history of depression. Their emotional health is always in the back of my mind. I don't want them to feel suicide is an option. I want them to know they can always talk to me about anything, and we will find a way to work with any feelings they have trouble managing."

Trudy, who was never married to the father of her two young children, felt her life improved after she and the children left him. "Nick suffered from depression and struggled with alcohol. He had trouble keeping a job and became addicted to methamphetamines.

He tried to get his life together, but he couldn't stay clean. His visits became sporadic and seemed to occur when he needed money. When he died from an overdose of drugs three years after we split up, I was really sad. I was in a new relationship with a good man who loved the kids and me, but I still cared for Nick. I always wanted the best for him."

Trudy struggled with what to say to her children, aged five and eight. "Even though they didn't see Nick that often and they had bonded with my new boyfriend, Nick was still their father. I had always been upfront with my kids about his drug problem, but I worried about saying the right thing. Even though he left a note, at first I told them he had died as a result of the drugs. Later, after talking with a therapist, I told them about suicide and what it meant. I explained that the drugs changed the way their father thought, creating confusion in his mind and a sense of hopelessness. I was so sad about Nick's death, really sad. To be honest, I would also have to say that I felt a sense of relief, too. At least his suffering was over."

*   *   *   *   *

It will take time to sort out your feelings about your former partner's suicide. You may be surprised by their intensity. Even former partners who have been divorced for years may discover they are deeply impacted. Regardless of the circumstances of your divorce or separation, you have the right to seek support and comfort for yourself as well as for your children.

Rosemary, a teacher whose former husband took his life, comments: "Hearing from my daughter that her father had killed himself was a terrible blow. Frank, her father, and I had been previously married for over twenty years and had two children together. We'd been divorced almost that long, each of us remarrying. Although Frank and I had made up and talked occasionally, I had no idea how depressed he must have been. My first emotion was shock followed by anger for what this would do to our children and their children. This was followed by a wave of grief as I remembered all the promising days of our life together as young people. I am very happy in my second marriage and my husband was extremely understanding of my grief, but I still felt somehow disloyal to be mourning the man I had been married to previously. I was relieved to be able to get to a group and talk about this grief, which had seemed somehow to be out of place."

*   *   *   *   *

In the following story Ellen, a petite, energetic mother of two children (Matthew, aged thirteen, and Emily, eleven), describes her journey since the suicide of her husband six years ago.

ELLEN'S STORY

"I'm sad about all the things we will never have together as a family, sad and sometimes, mad."

When I married my husband Jeff, he was a fun, attentive man who was a hard worker. We had so many plans for the future. We both had good jobs and managed to save enough money to move to a smaller, more family-oriented community to raise our children. We bought a house and began to fix it up. We had planned to start our own business and were taking real estate classes when Jeff began to change. He became disillusioned with our business venture and developed an obsession with the stock market. Before I knew it he had lost all our savings, and we were in debt. He got another job that required him to do a lot of traveling. He wasn't around much and when he was, he secluded himself. I felt like I was raising the kids alone. Our marriage was in trouble, but he refused to see a therapist.

He eventually changed jobs again, twice, which necessitated him moving to other states and living apart from us. He became increasingly isolated, unhappy and paranoid. He had been such a responsible man, highly respected at the firm where we had both worked. He had so many skills, but he seemed to be deteriorating emotionally. I was completely baffled when he began to talk about his suspicions of co-workers, how they were plotting against him, that sort of thing. When I look back on this time I realize that he must have been suffering from a mental illness, but it wasn't obvious to me then. He kept sending paychecks, and I kept hoping things would get better.

Then the paychecks stopped, and I discovered he had quit his job. He called me and insisted I file for divorce. He wasn't making any sense and I refused, so he drove clear across the country to talk with me in person about filing. He didn't want to have a long-distance relationship, but he couldn't seem to manage being with us either. He loved the kids very much, but didn't want contact with us. It was so confusing.

I insisted that he continue phone contact with them. They needed to hear his voice, but his calls were sporadic. He did come back for Emily's fifth birthday, and the children enjoyed the visit because he spent all his time playing with them. I remember getting mad at him for interrupting our routine and keeping them out late. Having him stay with us was hard for me, since he was there as a "guest" and not as my husband and partner. That was the last time the kids saw or spoke to him.

Three months later he was dead. During that time he had made a number of calls to me late at night. He was paranoid and upset, but he refused to get help. I never imagined he would do something as drastic as killing himself.

When I learned of his suicide I was shocked. I couldn't believe this was happening to our family. Because the kids were at a sleepover, I had a little time to prepare before telling them. I called Matthew's therapist, who had been a real support for Matthew around his father's absence, and I set up a time for him to meet with us. Together we told Matthew and Emily what had happened. Matthew wanted to know how his dad had died. He kept asking questions until he heard enough details. Emily didn't really understand completely. I told them that their daddy did not know how to solve his problems or ask for help. I explained that he thought killing himself was the only answer, but that I believed no problem is so bad that we can't solve it with some help.

I have always been open with my children about my feelings. I wanted them to know it was O.K. to be sad and angry and to talk about whatever feelings they had. We talked about the roller coaster effect of feeling fine one minute and then how, suddenly, a wave of sadness can descend. I shared with them that this happened to me, too.

I wanted them to know that I would always be there for them, and that we could give and get hugs whenever we needed them.

For a few months after Jeff died we would take turns saying "Daddy thoughts" before bedtime. I don't know that Emily remembered that much about him, as she was only four when he left us. Sometimes she would say, "I want Daddy" when she was mad at me and things weren't going her way. I finally told her that it hurt my feelings when she said that because I *was* there and he wasn't. We talked about how I could help her feel better, and she said I just needed to keep saying, "He's not here." I guess she needed that gentle reminder. I think the "idea" of not having a dad is what makes her sad. I remember when she was younger she would place a picture of him alongside her boom box on the chair next to her bed. She liked to listen to music before she fell asleep, and she seemed to want him near. Now that she is eleven she doesn't talk much about him, but she still has his picture on her dresser.

During the first six months following Jeff's death, I had terrible insomnia. Matt had trouble sleeping, too. Many nights he would wander into my room, crying about missing his dad. We would talk about Jeff for a while, and that would soothe him. He was also very angry, and most of that anger was directed at me. Fortunately, his therapist helped him learn other ways to deal with his anger, and to redirect it elsewhere. I was angry, too, mostly about being a single parent, and not having the family life I envisioned. I felt upset with Jeff for not giving us a chance to make our marriage work. I just wish he could have gotten some help for himself.

Shortly after Jeff's death, the kids joined a children's bereavement support group. Emily was reluctant to talk in the group, but I think it was a comfort for her just to be there. She loved working on the craft activities and bringing home projects about her memories. Matthew was more reluctant to go, but seemed to enjoy himself once he got there. I think this group was very beneficial for both of them because they learned that other kids also had loved ones die. I was in a women's group at the time, and that helped me work through my sadness and anger.

I think it's important that kids have a place, a support group or counseling, where they can share their feelings, but they need to process the death in their own way and not be forced to talk. As parents, I also believe we need to be real with our kids and let them see us grieve. We need to answer their questions as honestly as we can, giving them enough information, without editorializing or providing excessive details.

It's been six years since Jeff died. The first year was so hard—trying to accept what had happened and go on from day to day. Sometimes I couldn't believe that I was a single mom, truly on my own with two young children who were totally dependent on me. I needed to do my own grieving, but I also had to take care of them.

I wanted them to have good feelings about their dad and remember him. On the first anniversary of his death we wrote messages on helium balloons, shared memories, then released the balloons "up to heaven." We watched the balloons until all we could see were tiny specks in the sky, and that's when we decided their daddy reached down and got them. It was very touching for me and meaningful for the kids. I have told them that their daddy is now our "guardian angel," and he will watch over us, protect us and be proud of all the things we do.

Life does go on. We used to look at pictures and watch videos of them with their dad, but that doesn't happen as often anymore. I still want to acknowledge their dad on special days, but the old rituals don't seem to have relevance for the kids now. I hope they will think of something new, but I know I have to let them make those decisions. They are both almost teenagers now with more independent ideas. In a way this new stage of development is hard for me—another letting go.

Sometimes people ask me if I am interested in marrying again, and I just have to say that I'm not ready. After being out of the dating scene for so long, it's scary thinking about trying to meet someone. I guess sometimes I feel lonely, but most of the time I am O.K. with being on my own. Dating would also require me to be away from the kids at night, and I feel we need to be together then since they are at school all day long. I guess that because I am so involved with them and all their activities right now, I don't really feel I have the time or the energy to be involved in a relationship. Maybe that will change when they are in high school.

For now I want to focus on them. Sometimes they will comment on something they are learning or have accomplished and wish that their dad could know about it. Those are the times that make me the saddest. I think about all the things he's missing, and all that they will never have together. Sometimes I still feel angry, but mostly I just feel sad. For the first three or four years after Jeff died, I was very angry. I saw his death as senseless, unnecessary and selfish. I was upset that he had deprived our children of a father. It was especially troubling for me when Matthew would express envy and sadness upon seeing other families with dads. The day I told them that their dad had died, he asked me, "Does that mean we will be getting a new dad now?" His father had been gone for so long, and he really wanted a dad. Fortunately, he has many males in his life—his "Big Brother," his karate teacher, his therapist, and an older gentleman who is our "adopted grandpa," but it's not the same.

Now I realize that Jeff probably had a mental illness. When Jeff was twelve, his father died after drinking himself into a coma. The death certificate read, "Suicide, no will to live." The family never talked about it. Recently his brother took his life as well, and his sister started therapy after she came close to attempting suicide herself. That is scary. Something has to be going on here genetically. I know I have to be aware of how my children deal with their feelings. I want them to know they may be at risk for mental illness, and we have begun to talk about this. I want them to know there are many ways to get help if the need arises.

We are all finding our way through this experience and making a new life for ourselves. I volunteer as a clerical assistant at the hospice where the kids attended their grief support group. I also help out in their classrooms. They are involved in lots of activities—Emily plays the guitar and piano and loves to draw. Matthew is an artist, too, and also a video game whiz. They are smart and talented. I can't wait to see how they turn out as adults. Already I see Jeff in both of them, especially his sense of humor in Matt and Emily's musical talents.

Jeff's suicide was terribly traumatic for us, but we have grown closer as a family. As the kids get older, we will continue to talk more about the deeper issues of why he left and did what he did. We will probably never have all the answers, but I want them to know I am here for them—for whatever questions they have or challenges they face. We are still a family, and I am proud of them.

I need to move real slow right now.
The world got torqued at a different angle when you jumped.
The moment you let your weight go into the wind
when you felt the force of gravity pulling your body down
the moment your decision was final
the earth twisted around on itself
shifting time to a new shape I can't quite get used to.

My body has a different odor now.
My sweat and the taste in my mouth have become sour.
The sheets smell of it when I wake up in the middle of the night
Limbs cold as stone, heart pounding
Ears throbbing with a moan.
I rub myself awake,
come back, I call on my spirit, come back home.
I'll sit in the warmth of a bath, shivering from this chill that won't go away
and think of you.

Some friends think nothing has changed.
They speak to me at a rambling pace with smiles and laughter.
Their faces look familiar but I can't follow the language
and the gestures seem foreign,
masks ready to crack into a pile of dust at their feet.

Some friends try to make the whole thing go away.
Bear hugs tight enough to squeeze out my breath
and I guess they hope to squeeze out the pain as well.
Frowns and concerns projected at me larger than life
Probing eyes and probing questions, are you really all right?

Some friends sit with me in silence,
lighting the shrine and sending the smoke of incense up in your name.
Some place a hand on my back where the ache to be touched is most tender
and just smile with their eyes closed as they hold me.

I try for comfort when I can.
A down wrap around my shoulders, the crackling of a fire
and the soft sounds of closeness passing between friends
These are the things of sanity for me
These are the moments I try to elongate to cope with the hole in my heart
these are the ways of healing for me.
Because you've given me no choice,
I need to move real slow right now.

—Sharon Lukert

CHAPTER FIFTEEN

Taking Care of Yourself

"Good self care doesn't mean you are feeling
sorry for yourself or being selfish;
rather it means you are creating conditions
that allow you to heal."
—Alan D. Wolfelt, Ph.D.
Center for Loss and Life Transition

One of the best ways of helping your child cope with the trauma of her parent's death is to take care of yourself. This may seem impossible right now, but taking care of your body and doing your own grief work is essential to your well-being. It will ultimately impact your child in a positive way, even if it means occasional separation from her as you gather your strength.

There are times when grief is so overwhelming that a surviving parent is physically and emotionally spent, unable to be available for his or her child. If you are in this situation, try not to feel guilty. Know that it's important to allow yourself time alone to mourn. Both of you will benefit from you taking care of yourself.

Be gentle with yourself. Remember that there is no right or wrong way to grieve, just as there is no set rhythm or timeline. Allow yourself time to focus on your loss, but also recognize that you and your children will need breaks from your painful feelings as well. Try not to make any major decisions right now. Give yourself permission and time to tend your own needs.

Asking for Help

Although you may feel alone in your grief, you will discover there are others who understand and are ready to support you. Seek out trusted friends and family members. This may be a very small circle in the beginning. You may not know what to say at first, but most survivors find that when they acknowledge the suicide and ask for help, their family and friends are anxious to be there for them. You may not know what you need initially, but you are likely to discover that tasks or chores that once seemed simple may now feel impossible to manage. Don't be afraid to let your friends know when you are feeling overwhelmed and need a listening ear or someone to pick up the kids from soccer practice.

Becky, whose estranged husband took his life, remembers how her friends were there to support her. "I was completely overwhelmed following Doug's death, but my friends really carried me through. One friend left her job and moved in with me for two weeks. She helped with the kids and researched resources. She told me about support groups at our local hospice which I managed to get the kids into, although my thirteen-year-old would never go. Another friend helped me apply for Social Security for the kids. She also found a way I could get financial help for the kids' dental needs. Without my friends' assistance, I wouldn't have known such services existed."

Joan, who was pregnant when her husband of ten months ended his life, relates, "One of the things that helped me hang on to what small amount of sanity I did have at the time was the fact that my mom dropped everything and moved in with me. She even slept with me every night for a while. I was forty years old, but it still made a world of difference."

You are also going to encounter people who want to support you, but don't know what to say or how to be around you. They worry they will say the wrong thing or make you sad, so they act as if nothing has happened. Others, less sensitive or inappropriately inquisitive, will ask intrusive questions, or they may be quick to state their opinions about what you should have done, how you should think, or what you should feel. You may feel angry or wounded by their lack of support or insensitive comments, wondering how anyone could label your partner as "cowardly" or insist on knowing the details of his death. Try to remember that most of these people are not trying to deliberately hurt you or make you feel guilty. They are operating from a place of fear, and often, from fear, come judgments.

You do not have to take care of these people. It is not your job to make them feel comfortable in your presence. If you choose to comment, you may want to tell them you understand they are upset, but their remarks are hurtful. You can also let them know that you don't want to talk right now. You will learn to avoid some people and seek solace in others who are open to listening and accompanying you as you grieve.

Staying Connected

Maintaining contact with others in the days and months after your loved one's suicide is important, though it may be difficult. You may have times when you feel unable to get out of bed, much less talk to anyone. Try to stay connected with others who care about you. Communicating by telephone or email can sometimes help on those days when leaving the house feels unbearable. Rely on your answering machine to screen telephone calls, but consider talking to those family members or friends whom you can count on for support.

Some survivors find comfort from spiritual or religious communities, seeking out trusted members of the clergy or others who may have had experience with grief. You may appreciate a visit at home from those who are able to offer a loving, non-judgmental ear. Don't worry about whether your home is tidy or not. Visitors who love you and want to support you won't care.

Going Back to Work

While most people who are grieving a partner's suicide need some time off work, you may find you have no choice and must go back out of financial necessity. Perhaps you also believe that work will help you through this time by distracting you or keeping you connected to supportive friends. Work can be comforting for some survivors, but try to be realistic about what you can manage. Ask for a more flexible schedule or a way to work from home if possible.

Taking Care of Your Body

You are undoubtedly noticing that your body feels strange. You may feel like it is operating independently of you, or that you aren't really in it, but watching yourself from afar. You may not feel like eating—or you may feel like you can't stop eating. You may have absolutely no energy, or you may find yourself experiencing excessive, uncomfortable bursts of it at odd hours, along with a need to busy yourself with tasks or chores. You may discover that your short-term memory is gone, and you may wonder if you will ever have the presence of mind to be able to take care of things again. You are likely to feel anxiety in the form of heart palpitations, sweats, or body aches. Numbness may set in as you exhaust yourself from tears, and that lump in your throat may make it difficult to swallow. You may experience headaches, stomachaches, or feel like you have the flu. This is not your imagination—this is grief.

Grief can also frighten you with its intensity. Some days you may feel totally out of control, unable to stop crying. Other days you may find yourself operating on automatic pilot, appearing organized and in control on the surface, while feeling completely disconnected inside.

Your children need you to take care of yourself. They need you to find constructive ways to express your feelings. This will make them feel more secure, and it will model for them that expressing feelings is a necessary part of recovery. Holding back tears or words of anger or distress can create discomfort and illness. If you notice new or unusual physical symptoms, talk to your family doctor. This is not a time to ignore your body, even though you may feel like nothing really matters and that no one can help you. Following are three areas where some emphasis can help sustain you for the difficult road ahead.

Sleep—Be aware of your body's continual need for rest. You may discover that you long for sleep, but are unable to relax enough to rest, or that you are plagued with bad dreams. Sleep deprivation will make it difficult to manage your life and your family. It may be necessary to visit your physician for medication to help you sleep, or to temporarily manage your anxiety. Do not judge yourself for needing extra help. Many survivors find medication eases the initial grieving period. Without sleep you can't take care of yourself or your children.

Food—You may not feel like cooking for a long time, but nutritious foods are essential for your well-being and for the health of your family. You might consider asking a friend to organize other friends to help with meals. Your friends will probably find their own comfort in providing nutritional sustenance for your family. However, you may be inundated with substantial quantities of food, and unable to store large amounts. Your "food manager" friend can help by making a long-term calendar, coordinating food choices to avoid ten lasagnas, and even accepting the food for you if you don't feel like visitors. She can also package the contributions in smaller amounts, keep track of who has made food for you, and coordinate the return of dishes or containers. Don't be shy about allowing friends to help you in this way. They want to "do something." Why not allow them to nurture you and your children at this time? You can always freeze food contributions within the capabilities of your freezer, or dispose of or give away those items your children won't eat.

Exercise—Because your body may be in a kind of shock, you may find it hard to move, preferring to sleep or remain sedentary indoors. Unfortunately, sleep or being in a prone position for long periods does very little to stimulate endorphins, those natural opiates or "euphorics" that reduce our perception of pain under certain stressful conditions. Activating those endorphins can help your body feel better and be healthier. With even a small amount of physical exertion, you can increase your heart and breath rate, and maybe even sweat a little. By remembering to drink lots of water, you can help cleanse your body of toxins. This may sound impossible right now, or it may be a low priority, but eventually you will benefit greatly by finding a way to incorporate exercise into your day. You might consider exercising to TV or joining a gym. Walking with a friend may provide you with the structure you need. Exercise can help move blocked energy, elevate your mood, and provide a sense of accomplishment. It can also enable you to be in nature and to connect with others. It is important, however, to avoid unrealistic goals and expectations. If you don't have the energy just yet, be kind to yourself and let yourself off the hook. If the kids are in school and you would rather stay in bed and watch the soaps for now, do it. At some point you will be able to move again—and it will do you a world of good.

Alcohol and Drugs

The trauma of suicide leaves a surviving partner vulnerable to developing a reliance on alcohol or recreational drugs. Even though mood-altering substances may afford you a measure of temporary relief, over-indulging will simply postpone and deepen the inevitable pain that accompanies such a loss. Developing an addiction problem will only make your recovery more difficult, so exercise great care if you do use alcohol or recreational drugs during the grieving process.

Expressing Grief Your Way

Many survivors find comfort by writing, painting or listening to music. Creating poetry, keeping a journal or writing letters to your loved one may help you vent or clarify your feelings. If you find you don't have the words you need, you might draw images to represent how you are feeling or what you are thinking. Some survivors find it helpful to write to God or whatever spiritual source or presence they believe in, asking for guidance and support. Others report that using clay or making collages helps them channel their grief.

You may wonder when you will ever have the time or inclination to take care of yourself while also tending to the needs of your children.

You may be feeling too much guilt to think you deserve time for yourself. Remember again: *You did not cause your loved one's suicide.* You couldn't be with him 24/7. You could not control his emotional state. Your task now is to do the best you can to take care of yourself and your children.

Going to the Cemetery

Some survivors like going to the cemetery to visit or care for their loved one's grave, while others find it too painful. My friend Julia, whose husband took his life, said she couldn't go to the cemetery. It was simply too upsetting. She felt she *should* visit his grave, that it was the "proper" thing to do, but she found upon reaching the cemetery parking lot that she couldn't get out of her car. Another woman, Carol, told me that visiting her partner's grave was comforting for her. She would take her journal and sit on a nearby bench, allowing her tears to come as she wrote letters to him. She felt this time away from her responsibilities allowed her to focus on her feelings rather than be distracted by the many tasks at home.

It's up to you to decide if a cemetery visit is helpful for you. If you feel comfortable visiting the cemetery, you may want to invite your children to accompany you on occasion. Don't be surprised, however, if they don't want to go. Many children are uneasy about going to a graveyard, and they may worry about seeing you cry. You can let them know that you would like their company (if indeed you would), but that it is also O.K. for them not to go.

Support Groups and Psychotherapy

Support groups are an excellent way to meet others who are also coping with the anguish of a loved one's suicide. Although you may think you can't bear to listen to someone else's suffering, talking with others who understand your loss will make you feel less alone. You can probably find a support group through your local hospital, community center, church, hospice, or on the Internet. Ask your physician or therapist if they know of a "Survivors of Suicide" support group in your area— or consider starting one. These groups are not for people who have attempted suicide and survived, but for people like you who are coping with the aftermath of a loved one's suicide. Many support groups are offered free or for a nominal charge. (See Chapter Twelve – *Support Groups: Solace and Safety* for more information.)

You may also find that the group experience doesn't fit for you or that the chemistry of a particular group doesn't feel right. Sometimes the timing is off or you don't feel safe with the leadership. If this happens, honor your feelings. Support groups work for a lot of people, but they aren't for everyone.

You may prefer a one-to-one experience, feeling that you are too vulnerable to face a group, or that your particular experience sets you apart from others. Perhaps you want to consult a professional because you have concerns about your children and are looking for guidance. You may have times when you have suicidal thoughts yourself. *Know that having suicidal thoughts doesn't mean you will act on them, but if you do find yourself having such thoughts, it is imperative that you talk to someone about them.* A skilled therapist can provide perspective and support as you learn coping skills. If you don't have the energy to research therapists, check with your doctor for a referral, or ask a friend to do the research for you. One important consideration is to find a therapist with bereavement experience who is knowledgeable about how depression and mental illness factor into suicide.

Finally, be kind to yourself and know that at some point you *are* going to be ready to go on with your life. Even though things will never be the same, you will find your way through your grief. When you eventually discover that you are beginning to have good days and even enjoying life again, remember that this doesn't mean you didn't love your partner or that you are betraying him. It simply means that you are beginning to heal.

CHAPTER SIXTEEN

Complicated Suicides—Complicated Mourning

"It seemed like everyone was calling:
good friends, people I hardly knew and people who felt
the public deserved more information.
I couldn't answer the phone. I couldn't leave the house.
I could barely get out of bed."
—HELEN, WIFE OF A POLICE OFFICER WHO CARRIED OUT SUICIDE

All suicides are complicated, given the psychological hardships they bestow on survivors and the social stigma surrounding the act. But some are further complicated by the nature of the person's relationships, or the way the suicide happens, or because the person may have been a public figure. Sometimes the suicide occurs in a public setting and thus generates considerable media attention. All of these issues can complicate the mourning process.

Blue Suicide

Blue suicide, or "suicide by cop," is when a person purposely puts himself in a position to be shot by a police officer. Often the suicidal person brandishes a weapon or charges an officer in a threatening way, eliciting a defensive response that may cost the person his life. In most such situations, the person has a history of mental illness that may include drug or alcohol problems.

Blue suicides are often front-page news, adding to a family's grief and shame. Such was the case when a thirty-one-year-old mother in my community called 911 to report an armed female captor was holding her hostage in her home. When police broke down the door they discovered a woman wielding a knife and a gun. She aimed the gun at the officers and did not yield to their demands to release the weapon. One officer fired, wounding the woman. It was only when she fell that they discovered the gun was plastic and that she had made the distress call herself. When they asked her why, she replied, "I wanted you to kill me." She died several hours later.

The subsequent police investigation revealed she had made several prior suicide attempts. She had a history of methamphetamine, alcohol, and prescription drug abuse. She had also told a friend about a newspaper story detailing how the police had shot a bicyclist who had fired at them. In a sad irony, she said if she were going to get herself killed, she would use a toy gun because she didn't allow guns in her house. Later, police officers found a note on her front door telling her nine-year-old son not to come into the house because "the exterminators are coming." He had gone to a neighbor's home.

I worked with a youngster who experienced a similar trauma. Justin's mother worked full-time. His dad, who suffered from mental illness and was unable to hold a job, was five-year-old Justin's primary caretaker. He walked Justin to and from kindergarten every day. Justin considered his dad his favorite playmate, especially when his dad made animal noises or carried him around piggyback. They liked to play with Justin's toys and watch police shows together. One day his dad brought home two squirt guns, much to his son's delight. They played cops and robbers, running all over the house and hiding from each other. Justin's dad decided he wanted the guns to look more like the police guns on TV, so he painted them a metallic gray. Tragically, he took his now realistic-looking gun to a nearby grocery store and attempted to rob a cashier. When the police responded to a silent alarm, Justin's dad cried out, "I've got a gun; shoot me or I'll shoot you." The police, not knowing the gun was a toy, shot and killed him.

I saw Justin shortly after his father's death. His mother was worried that maybe he was demonstrating some of the same mental confusion as his dad. Justin was bewildered about why the police, who were supposed to be the "good guys," had shot his dad. I reassured them that this was indeed a confusing death for everyone, but especially for a five-year-old. We talked with Justin about how his dad had been confused between "real" and "pretend" because his brain wasn't working right. In the weeks that followed, Justin needed to tell his story many times about how the police shot his daddy. Sometimes he told it as if he himself had been there. He described the blood and how the ambulance came and took his daddy away. His mother would remind him that he hadn't been there when his dad died. Sometimes Justin would nod and say, "Oh, yeah. I was at Grandma's." Other times he insisted he had been there.

I saw Justin in a support group setting and referred him to an individual play therapist who specialized in children's trauma. Justin spent many sessions with his therapist, acting out the robbery scene in the sand tray. At first he placed a character representing himself in the scene, but eventually that character stayed on the shelf. Justin's mother plans to see that he continues working with his therapist. She hopes that as he matures he will develop a better understanding of his father's illness and death. She wants to be aware of any behaviors that may indicate Justin is predisposed to mental illness. She feels she didn't take his father's behavior seriously enough, and wants to make sure Justin gets help if he needs it.

Gay Parents

Suicide survivors are often stigmatized, their grief "disenfranchised," while traditional social supports for grieving are withheld. The situation can be even more difficult for gays, who, despite increasing cultural visibility, continue to be marginalized both socially and legally across much of the country. Many gay or lesbian partners are not included in funeral preparations, and if they are not the birth parents, they may be denied access to children they helped raise.

Fifty-eight-year-old Susan, a former teacher whose partner, Jeanie, took her life thirty years ago, recounts her experience: "Jeanie and I had been together for three years and shared parenting responsibilities for her six-year-old daughter, Anna. Anna was with her father during the week, but we had her most weekends. Jeanie felt sad that Anna wasn't with us more, but there wasn't much support then for being a lesbian mother. Jeannie's ex wasn't happy about our relationship, and although Jeannie's mother was supportive, her father disapproved. After Jeanie's death, he even ended up demanding that I return items that Jeanie had given me.

"When Jeanie killed herself, Anna was snatched from my life. I tried to keep in touch with her, but her father refused to let me see her. I grieved for both Jeanie and Anna for years. In looking for other relationships, I was always attracted to women with children. I love children. I was a teacher for many years, but I never got to finish parenting Anna, and I missed her.

"Five years ago, when Anna was in her early thirties, I got a call from Jeanie's sister. Anna had contacted her expressing a desire to talk with me about her mother and our life together. Of course, I agreed to meet with her. She came riding up on a motorcycle, this petite little woman, barely five feet tall, looking just like Jeanie. Right away she asked me if I had a tattoo, recalling that her mother and I had matching tattoos. When I showed mine to her, she showed me one she had done, in remembrance of her mother. She wanted to know everything about Jeanie, even the hard stuff, so I told her about her mom and our life together. I also told Anna stories about what she was like as a little girl, before her mother died. She showed very little emotion until I gave her a brown leather jacket that had belonged to Jeanie. Her eyes got teary as she tried it on. It never fit me, but I had kept it all those years. I just hadn't been able to part with it. I finally knew why."

Media Pressures

Sometimes suicide becomes a media event due to dramatic details or the death of a prominent person. When this happens, surviving family members are subjected to additional pressures and pain. Having the private details of a loved one's life discussed on television or the specifics of his death splashed on the front page of the local newspaper creates tremendous strain, greatly complicating mourning. A real person has died, someone who was loved and cherished in very personal terms, but survivors often are forced to delay their grief as they deal with what becomes a public spectacle rather than private tragedy.

"I fell apart every time I heard the phone ring," says fifty-two-year-old Helen, whose husband, Jim, a prominent law enforcement officer, ended his life. "It seemed like everyone was calling: good friends, people I hardly knew and people who felt the public deserved more information. I couldn't answer the phone. I couldn't leave the house. I could barely get out of bed. My kids were in shock. My sister made a message for the answering machine, and we went to my parents' home in another state for two weeks. We had to get away."

Helen's three teenagers were keenly aware of the looks they received from others when they returned to school. The news about their dad quickly spread throughout the school, and kids they hardly knew came up to them, offering condolences. Others looked away or stopped talking when they approached. After several weeks the talking and whispering stopped, but they always felt that they were no longer kids with normal lives, but "those kids whose dad committed suicide."

Chicago area anchorwoman Joan Esposito, whose husband took his life ten months into their marriage, recalls how devastated she was. "He ended his life two days after we discovered we were pregnant with our first, very-much-wanted child. Within days of his death I was the subject of a local call-in radio show. Two disc jockeys who had made their reputations by being shocking asked their viewers to call in and vote on whether I should have an abortion or not. This was terribly upsetting for me. You have to be pretty thick-skinned as a TV reporter. You learn to ignore the gossip, but the rumors these guys started took on a life of their own. Because I was a well-known public figure, out of respect for me the local TV stations didn't run the story of Bryan's suicide. I did hear later, however, that one station had planned to send a TV crew and truck to film our beach house in Michigan where Bryan had ended his life. My media friends got wind of this plan, called the station and begged and pleaded for the story to be pulled. It never ran, but I still don't really know if the station manager graciously ceded to the pressure or if the TV crew just got lost."

Survivors also report that in addition to the unwanted publicity and intrusion into their private lives, many media accounts do not do justice to their loved one. Ianthe Brautigan's father, Richard Brautigan, was an author whose work is identified with the sixties counterculture and continues to be popular with college students. She writes in *You Can't Catch Death—A Daughter's Memoir*, "...everything that was written about him right after he died portrayed him incorrectly. Either friends wrote with old vendettas cutting sharply through their words, or journalists wrote without care or concern for who he was; their job was to write salacious stuff that would sell. I did not recognize the dignified, brilliant, hysterically funny, and sometimes difficult man who was my father in anything that they wrote."

Such experiences can delay mourning. Negotiating the minefield of grief after a suicide is exhausting and confusing. Survivors may feel grateful that their loved one's accomplishments or character are remembered with respect, yet also feel victimized by the incessant conjecture or the non-stop replay of intimate details. Some report that having a spokesperson to run interference with the outside can help, but they are still unable to completely escape insensitive comments and intrusive questions.

Ultimately, time and the next crisis or "newsworthy" event will shift the focus, but the impact of not having the opportunity to grieve privately adds another layer of grief and pain to an already devastating situation.

Finding the Body

Most children who lose a parent to suicide do not discover the body, but sadly, some do. This is a profoundly traumatic experience, necessitating immediate crisis support.

If your child witnessed his parent's death or saw the body right after the suicide, he is likely to have a difficult time erasing the image from his mind. Normal reactions to suicide (denial, guilt, anger, a sense of responsibility, fear, horror, helplessness, bad dreams, low self-esteem) may be magnified. He may become increasingly aggressive, agitated, or even talk about suicide himself. This response is indicative of post-traumatic stress disorder (PTSD).

The symptoms of PTSD may last from several months to many years. Because a child's feelings of security have been seriously compromised, early intervention is essential. Family, friends, and school personnel must work together to help re-establish the child's sense of safety. A child who experiences such a trauma must also be evaluated by a mental health professional. A treatment plan should be set up that includes specific therapies designed to decrease traumatic images while also providing bereavement support.

Dara, now thirty-two, was thirteen when her mother hung herself. She recalls, "I still remember what it was like when I came into the house and found her that day. There was a note on the door that said, 'Don't let Dara in the house,' and I knew. I knew when we drove down the driveway and all the blinds were down. I saw the note but my father had me come in the house anyway because he needed my help. He thought there was a slim chance she was still alive, but she was dead. I ran to the neighbor's, and I remember crying, 'Oh my God, I can't believe it—I don't have a mom anymore; I don't have a mom anymore.'"

Although Dara's family didn't talk about the suicide amongst themselves, her father did get her into therapy at the urging of a family friend who was a social worker. "Just talking about things helped me feel that I wasn't dreaming, and that something absolutely horrible did happen, even though everyone around me was content to pretend that it didn't. I realize now that I was depressed most of my teenage years and into my twenties. But it wasn't until I had a very stressful job as an on-air news reporter that I began feeling really overwhelmed. I seemed to be crying all the time. I finally saw a psychiatrist who remarked that I hadn't really gotten angry at my mother. I had been so bent on feeling bad for her that I forgot how much she messed up my life. After getting angry at her, it was easier to forgive her for what she did."

Sometimes children who find a parent's body are so overwhelmed by the visual sight that they are unable to comprehend what has happened. Such is the case for five-year-old Julie, who, along with her seven-year-old sister, Elizabeth, discovered their mother's body. Their mom had died by hanging, but due to gravitational pull, her body had settled to the floor and her feet were on the ground. The notion of suicide is hard enough to understand, but Julie has had a difficult time comprehending suicide by hanging. She says, "Mommy *wasn't* hanging. There was no string. Her feet were on the floor." For now Julie says her mom died by "brain sickness." And that is also true. She knows the word suicide, and sometimes says her mom "had suicide." Eventually she will understand more about what she saw. She and her sister are seeing a psychotherapist. They are both experiencing unrelenting night terrors and deep anxiety. They have also begun to talk about the experience that Julie says, "broke my heart."

Julie and Elizabeth will need continued therapy to help them cope with their mother's death and to feel safe again. Their dad, Daniel, is working hard with all the professionals involved in his daughters' care. He meets regularly with their therapist to learn ways to deal with behavior issues that have emerged since the suicide. The therapist has helped him implement comforting and predictable routines. He is also in frequent contact with the girls' teachers as Julie and Elizabeth navigate school friendships and classroom assignments. He has enrolled the girls in a children's grief support group as well. He knows they will need support for the long haul.

Daniel is also struggling with his own feelings. "My wife's death has been so traumatic," he says. "I have had a lot of support from my family and my wife's sister, but sometimes I feel like I just want to move away from here. But we have been advised to stay a year rather than have everything change even more. Their therapists, teachers, and the principal at their school have been great. I was open with everyone right from the beginning, and that seems to have helped. Things are getting better. For the first few weeks they didn't want me out of their sight and were terrified to go to sleep. Things have settled down somewhat, but sometimes I am so exhausted. I am devoted to my girls, but it is hard trying to do all that is necessary to take care of them and help them deal with everything that has happened. I feel angry with my wife for putting us all in this position. I know she couldn't help being ill, but her death has hurt our children and me more than I can describe."

CHAPTER SEVENTEEN

When More Help Is Needed:
Depression and Bipolar Illness in Children

"Depressive illness and bipolar disorder are genetic disorders
strongly associated with suicide. But these genes are not deterministic.
There are things you can do, and the most important one
is to recognize clinical depression and to seek help."
—Dr. J. Raymond DePaulo Jr.
Johns Hopkins Hospital

While I hope this book has been a helpful resource for readers, it is not meant to take the place of psychiatric or medical interventions, psychotherapy, or support groups. Because suicide is a very traumatic occurrence, I believe that most children and teens of a parent who has taken his or her life benefit from having a check-up with their family doctor, seeing a psychotherapist, and possibly attending a support group. Survivors, children as well as adults, need a place to share their pain and confusion with others who understand.

If you are the surviving parent, you may feel too overwhelmed to determine who can help you professionally. Ask your doctor for a referral to an experienced grief counselor who is knowledgeable about bereavement issues around suicide, or request that a trusted friend or family member research resources for you. Your children need to be supported as they cope with the inevitable emotional trauma that follows a suicide. Even if they say they are fine or resist seeing someone, make an appointment anyway, if not in the weeks following the death, then soon thereafter. You need to send the message that you believe it is important to talk about the death and come together as a family. The suicide death of a parent will, without question, dramatically impact your child's life. You have two tasks: attending to your own grieving and making sure your children receive support as well.

Mental Illness in Children

The factors that contribute to suicide are varied and complex, but we are learning that in most cases mental illness plays a significant role. A person who takes his or her life may not have had a diagnosed mental illness, but the likelihood is great that he or she suffered from a mood disorder. You may be wondering if the illness that contributed to the suicide will find its way into the lives of your children as well.

Because genetics can play a part in determining who may eventually suffer from mood disorders, it is important to learn all you can about these illnesses. While there is no specific "suicide gene" that we know of, genetics research does tell us that children who have a parent with a mood disorder may also be predisposed to mental illness and thus more at risk for suicide than children who do not. The most common mood disorders are major depression and bipolar disorder.

Depression

Depression, also called "major depressive disorder" or "clinical depression," is a serious health problem that can affect people of all ages, including children and adolescents. As discussed earlier, depression is more than having a bad day, feeling down or having "the blues." It is a form of mental illness that affects the way one thinks, feels, and behaves. Depression is different than those normal feelings of grief that a child may experience following the death of someone special. It isn't something children or teens can simply "snap out of" on their own. Depression is characterized by a persistent feeling of irritability or sadness. People suffering from depression lose the ability to experience pleasure in activities that once made them happy. They may have sleep problems, changes in appetite, difficulty concentrating, and a marked lowering of self-esteem. Depression is an illness that, if left untreated, can lead to a host of other problems that may include substance abuse, promiscuity, school problems, social isolation, and suicide.

The National Institute of Mental Health (NIMH) estimates that up to 2.5 percent of children (some as young as four) and 8.3 percent of adolescents in the U.S. have symptoms of depression.[1] Research indicates that the onset of depression is occurring earlier in life today than it has in previous decades, when many doctors believed depression was strictly an adult disease.[2] While we recognize that genetics can play a part in determining who will suffer from depression, we don't know whether there are more depressed young people today or simply an increased awareness of the problem.

Scientific studies on the teenage brain are yielding clues that indicate teenagers may be more vulnerable to mood disorders due to changes in brain structure during adolescence. Other researchers believe the stress of higher divorce rates as well as increased social and academic pressures are contributing to the problem.[3] Increasing numbers of families are also coping with poverty, homelessness, drug addiction, sexual abuse, and other traumatic circumstances that can trigger depression.

Many children who are depressed do not get the help they need. Part of this is due to continued stigmatization around mental illness, inadequate mental health resources, and a lack of education and information about how mental illness impacts young people.

Recognizing depression in children and teens is difficult. Parents and other adults may view rebellious, moody, or irritable children, particularly teens, as simply "going through a phase" that they will eventually outgrow. Since such behavior is often viewed as the norm for teens, unless a child is overtly disruptive or violent, he or she may fall through the cracks. Teens can mask depression so well that even their friends and close family members may not recognize they are suffering from anything more than the ordinary ups and downs of being a teenager.

Such was the case with fourteen-year-old Marissa, a pretty 4.0 student and cross-country team member whose mother became concerned when she observed her daughter becoming aloof, distant, and lethargic. When she asked Marissa about how she was feeling, Marissa told her mom she was simply tired from all her schoolwork and experiencing normal teenage angst. "I noticed she seemed to be having trouble getting to sleep at night and would sometimes end up on the couch after we had all gone to bed. I asked her if she was feeling depressed and she said, 'No, Mommy, I'm not depressed, just tired.

I'll be fine—don't worry—this is just a teenage thing.'" Several days later Marissa left school after her first class, took a taxi to the Golden Gate Bridge and jumped, stunning her parents, her friends, and her community.

In hindsight, her mother now feels she missed the signs, but Marissa masked her depression well. "No one, not even her best friend, knew that Marissa was cutting herself, because she covered the cuts on her wrist with lots of bracelets. Her journal was full of comments about hating herself and seeing herself as fat, but she was five-foot-two and weighed only one-hundred-eight pounds. We had all experienced 9/11 three months before Marissa died, and she was disillusioned with our country, very disturbed by the terrorist attacks, and how the world seemed to be getting more violent. Here was my beautiful, sensitive daughter, who was kind to her little sister, successful in school, a girl with a bright future who said she wanted to go to college in New York and study psychology and journalism. She had lots of friends and enjoyed competing on the cross-country team. I picked her up from school every day after classes or practice, and we often took runs together at the park near our home. We didn't argue, had lots of talks, and got along well. I thought we were close. I never, ever, ever thought my daughter would end her life. I never thought this could happen in a family like ours that was so loving and supportive."

Marissa's mother says she wishes she had read her daughter's journal and checked her backpack. She also wishes she had been more computer savvy so she could have reviewed what Marissa was doing on the computer. She discovered after her daughter's death that Marissa had made many visits to websites that gave specific instructions to readers on how to kill themselves. "I was raised to respect a person's privacy," she says, "but I wish I had paid more attention to my early inklings that something might be wrong. I had no idea she was so troubled—no one did."

Marissa's parents had divorced when she was five, but they remained relatively friendly. Her mother had remarried and Marissa had a three-year-old half-sister she adored. Both her mother and father have struggled with depression themselves, and her mother, a recovering alcoholic who stopped drinking four years before Marissa was born, learned after

Marissa's death that depression and alcoholism have plagued her family for generations. "I knew our family had issues with alcohol, and so did my ex-husband's family. So we were focused on educating Marissa about the dangers of alcoholism, but we didn't know much about our family history insofar as mental illness. After Marissa died I learned that my great-grandfather took his life and my grandmother had what they termed in those days, a 'nervous breakdown.' My brothers struggled with depression and one of them died of alcoholism two months before Marissa ended her life. I remember saying at the time, 'Well, he is in heaven now and he's feeling peace at last. I am so glad he isn't suffering anymore and he is surrounded by God's love.' I think now that Marissa may have heard those words as a way out, an opportunity to end her own internal suffering, suffering I was unaware of, but that is how it can be with depression. You don't always know, because not everyone shows obvious signs."

Marissa's mother has become proactive in the field of suicide prevention since her daughter's death. Although she describes herself as an introvert, she now speaks to high school and college students about depression. She identifies herself as a "suicide survivor," someone who has had a loved one die by suicide. As a survivor she has also worked on a film, narrated by actress Mariel Hemingway, whose grandfather, novelist Ernest Hemingway, and sister, actress Margaux Hemingway, also died by suicide. The film is designed to help elementary school teachers identify youngsters who may be demonstrating early signs of depression.

She is also watching Marissa's little sister very carefully. "I am determined to educate my younger daughter, my family, and myself about mental illness, what to look for and how to help her, should the need arise," she says. "My little girl is nearly six now and seems fine, confident, happy and easygoing, but that could change. I will always be open to the possibility that she might have to deal with mental illness, too. I'm not going to obsess about this to the point I can't experience joy, but I am going to be vigilant. She is my joy now."

If depression runs in your family or if you are beginning to think it might, you will want to learn all you can about mood disorders and how they are manifested. While depression in youth is not uncommon, *most* children do not suffer from mood disorders. But according to Dr. J. John Mann, chief of the department of neuroscience at Columbia University and chair of the American Foundation for Suicide Prevention's Scientific Council, "The closer your connection to a depressed family member—a depressed father rather than a depressed uncle, for example—the greater an individual's likelihood of suffering depression."[4]

With that in mind, you will want to be mindful of the possibility that your child may have a genetic predisposition to depression or bipolar illness if there is any such history of mood disorders in your family. It is important to remember these conditions are treatable, especially if diagnosed early. Educate yourself and your child early on about the symptoms of depression. You may want to say something to your child like Kay Redfield Jamison, author of *Night Falls Fast*, suggests: "Depression is a common illness and it might happen to you or it might happen to one of your friends. The odds are it won't, but if it does, this is what it feels like and these are the symptoms. If you ever find at any time that you or any of your friends feel so terrible that any one of you think of ending your life or doing something to hurt yourself, I want you to tell me because there are lots of things we can do to make you feel better."[5]

Dr. J. Raymond DePaulo Jr., psychiatrist-in-chief at the Johns Hopkins Hospital, offers this: "Depressive illness and bipolar disorder are genetic disorders strongly associated with suicide. If you look at people who have died by suicide, the majority of them have those illnesses. But these genes are not deterministic. There are things you can do, and the most important one is to recognize clinical depression and to seek help."[6]

Depression Warning Signs

The behavior of depressed children and teenagers may differ from the behavior of depressed adults. According to the American Psychiatric Association Diagnostic and Statistical Manual of Mental Disorders— DSM IV, symptoms of major depressive disorder common to adults, children and adolescents include:[7]

- Persistent sad and irritable mood
- Loss of interest in activities once enjoyed
- Significant change in appetite and/or body weight
- Difficulty sleeping, or over-sleeping
- Physical signs of agitation, or excessive lethargy and loss of energy
- Difficulty concentrating
- Feelings of worthlessness or inappropriate guilt
- Recurrent thoughts of death or suicide

The way symptoms are expressed in children and teens varies with the developmental level of the individual. Signs that may be associated with depression found more often in children and adolescents than in adults include:[8]

- Frequent vague, non-specific physical complaints such as headaches, muscle aches, stomach problems or tiredness
- Frequent absences from school or poor performance in school
- Talk of or efforts to run away from home
- Difficulty maintaining relationships
- Outbursts of shouting, complaining, unexplained or increased irritability, anger, hostility or crying
- Chronic boredom
- Lack of interest in playing with friends
- Self destructive behaviors—alcohol or substance abuse, unprotected sex, self mutilation
- Social isolation, poor communication
- Morbid or unusually intense interest in death or suicide
- Extreme sensitivity to rejection or failure
- Reckless behavior
- Eating disorders (predominantly in girls) and specifically binge-eating, bulimia or bulimarexia (a combination of bulimia and anorexia where girls binge-eat, purge, starve.)

The presence of one or even several of these symptoms doesn't necessarily mean your child is clinically depressed. However, if one or more of these signs persist, a professional evaluation by a mental health professional who specializes in assessing children and adolescents is recommended.

Bipolar Disorder

Bipolar disorder is a serious but treatable illness also known as manic-depressive illness. Once regarded as strictly an adult disorder, bipolar disorder can appear in children and adolescents, and is more likely to affect children whose parent or grandparent has had the illness. It is a disorder that arises from malfunctions in the brain circuitry controlling the swings and cycles of emotion, and is characterized by unusual shifts in mood, energy, thinking, and behavior. The normal highs of pleasure, joy, and contentment and the normal lows of sadness, grief, and disappointment become exaggerated and prolonged. Symptoms may be present in infancy or early childhood or may suddenly emerge in adolescence or adulthood.[9]

Because there have not been epidemiological studies on bipolar illness in children, we do not know how common the disorder is, but it apparently affects an estimated one to two percent of adults worldwide. It is suspected that a significant number of children who have been diagnosed with attention-deficit disorder with hyperactivity (ADHD), attention deficit disorder (ADD) or a conduct disorder (CD) may have early-onset bipolar disorder instead of, or along with, those disorders.[10]

According to several studies, a significant proportion of the 3.4 million children and adolescents with depression in the U.S. may actually be experiencing the early onset of bipolar disorder, but have not yet experienced the manic phase of the illness. The National Institute of Mental Health (NIMH) states that twenty to forty percent of adolescents with major depression develop bipolar disorder within five years of the onset of depression. They also state that the existing evidence indicates that bipolar disorder beginning in childhood or early adolescence may be a different, possibly more severe form of the illness than is older adolescent and adult-onset bipolar disorder.

The symptoms of bipolar illness in children and teens differ from those experienced by adults. In the manic phase, for example, young people tend to be more irritable and prone to destructive outbursts, rather than to the euphoria or elation adults often describe. In the depressed phase, children and teens tend to experience those characteristics mentioned in the previous discussion of depression symptoms. According to Dr. Demitri Papolos, research director of the Juvenile Bipolar Research Foundation and co-author of *The Bipolar Child*, many children with the illness are ultra-rapid cyclers, moving back and forth between mood states several times a day.[11]

There is no standard test for bipolar disorder, but the following checklist, adapted from *The Bipolar Child*, may help you recognize warning signs. If your child has demonstrated twenty or more of these behaviors, health professionals recommend you have her evaluated by a psychiatrist or psychologist with experience in bipolar illness, particularly if her deceased parent suffered or may have suffered from the disorder.

1. Is excessively distressed when separated from family
2. Exhibits excessive anxiety or worry
3. Has difficulty arising in the a.m.
4. Is hyperactive and excitable in the p.m.
5. Sleeps fitfully or has difficulty getting to sleep
6. Has night terrors or frequently wakes in the middle of the night
7. Is unable to concentrate at school
8. Has poor handwriting
9. Has difficulty organizing tasks
10. Has difficulty making transitions
11. Complains of being bored
12. Has many ideas at once
13. Is very intuitive or very creative
14. Is easily distracted by extraneous stimuli
15. Has periods of excessive, rapid speech
16. Is willful and refuses to be subordinated
17. Displays periods of extreme hyperactivity

18. Displays abrupt, rapid mood swings
19. Has irritable mood states
20. Has elated or silly, giddy mood states
21. Has exaggerated ideas about self or abilities
22. Exhibits inappropriate sexual behavior
23. Feels easily criticized or rejected
24. Has decreased initiative
25. Has periods of low energy or withdraws or isolates self
26. Has periods of self-doubt and poor self-esteem
27. Is intolerant of delays
28. Relentlessly pursues own needs
29. Argues with adults or bosses others
30. Defies or refuses to comply with rules
31. Blames others for his or her mistakes
32. Is easily angered when people set limits
33. Lies to avoid consequences of actions
34. Has protracted, explosive temper tantrums or rages
35. Has destroyed property intentionally
36. Curses viciously in anger
37. Makes moderated threats against others or self
38. Has made clear threats of suicide
39. Is fascinated with blood and gore
40. Has seen or heard hallucinations

There is limited data on the treatment of bipolar illness in children, although studies are underway. Treatment so far is based mainly on experiences with adults. Early diagnosis and treatment are essential, as the consequences of not identifying the illness can be severe. Bipolar illness can worsen as a child matures, as each recurrent episode seems to increase the likelihood of developing more complicated symptoms and contributing to the possibility of substance abuse in adolescence.

Bipolar kids are often creative and tend to be verbally skilled, but school can be a problem because the illness makes it difficult for them to think, plan, and solve problems. Symptoms of the disorder often become more apparent when children enter third grade, and the academic demands of school become more pronounced. They may experience increased frustration and a loss in self-esteem as they face tasks they are unable to manage.

Once puberty sets in and hormones take over, teens who may have appeared asymptomatic before may show signs of the disorder.

A further notable consideration is that some children and teens suffer increased depression during the fall and winter months, experiencing symptoms that may subside during the spring and summer. To the casual observer this phenomenon seems to suggest a relationship with beginning the school year and additional stress, but it may in fact be more related to signs of Seasonal Affective Disorder (SAD). As seasons change, there is a shift in our "biological internal clocks" or circadian rhythm, due partly to changes in sunlight patterns. This can cause our biological clocks to be "out of step" with our daily schedules. The most difficult months for SAD sufferers are January and February, and young people and women are at higher risk.[12]

Early Intervention

Depression and bipolar illness are treatable, and most children who receive proper, timely intervention can be helped. Early diagnosis and appropriate treatment are essential. A thorough diagnostic evaluation may include a physical examination, lab work, psychological testing, and interviews with you and your child. Because as a parent you know your child best, sharing your own observations and feelings is important. Trust your instincts. Even though you may be feeling uncertain about your judgment or what you are observing, if you feel something is amiss, it very well may be.

Comprehensive treatment for depression often includes both individual and family therapy. For example, cognitive behavioral therapy and interpersonal psychotherapy are forms of individual therapy shown to be effective in treating depression. Treatment may also include interventions involving the home or school environment as well as the use of medication. Many professionals suggest trying psychotherapy first before considering medication, unless a young person is overtly suicidal or at risk of harming himself or others.

Because a biological dysfunction is clearly indicated in bipolar illness, medication combined with psychotherapy is the preferred mode of treatment. Finding the right medication can be challenging, and often several combinations must be explored to find the right medicine and the appropriate dosage. This can be frustrating. It requires patience and persistence, no small feat when having to also cope with the aftermath of a co-parent's suicide.

Kathy, who describes herself as an "eternal optimist," is the mother of two children with bipolar disorder, ages eleven and fourteen, whose father also suffered from the disorder and took his life eleven years ago. She states, "This genetic curse has been very challenging for all of us. It has been incredibly stressful, but the good news is we learned early on what we are up against and have been able to get treatment. Neither of my children is as devastated by the facts of the disorder as they might be if they were not so educated, or if it happened later in their teens or early adulthood. Along with psychotherapy and taking medicine, I constantly remind them that they do have a great degree of control by understanding the disorder and what triggers their stress, as well as learning to make positive choices and not giving in to impulses."

Besides the prudent use of medication and psychotherapy, parents and children need to work together to build resilience by maintaining a healthy lifestyle that includes exercise, familiar routines and rituals, a reasonable and consistent bedtime, good nutrition, and rest. Hobbies, sports, or developing other talents also contribute to building self-esteem, an important building block for increased mental health.

The importance of working with a qualified mental health professional experienced in the treatment of mood disorders in children and adolescents cannot be overstated. For help, parents may want to ask their primary care physician for a referral. Another option is to contact the American Academy of Child and Adolescent Psychiatry. This organization has many regional resources for doctors and therapists who specialize in diagnosing and treating depression and bipolar illness in children and teenagers.

Medication

Most parents are naturally reluctant to treat their children's psychological illnesses with medication. You are likely to have concerns about the effectiveness of various drugs, as well as questions about the long-term effects. We do not yet know whether developing brains respond differently than adult brains to pharmacological treatment, or how medication used with young people will impact the need for medication as an adult.

With these concerns in mind, a conservative approach to medication for youngsters makes sense. This may mean trying other treatments first and educating yourself about the known benefits of using medications versus the risk of *not* treating a disorder with medications. However, there seems to be considerable compelling evidence that SSRI (selective serotonin reuptake inhibitor) anti-depressants generally reduce suicide risk, and that failing to adequately treat children or teens at risk for suicide or severe depression may have severe consequences. Many physicians who work with psychological illnesses recommend that the more serious a condition is, the more strongly a trial with medication be considered.[13]

In 2004 we heard much from the media about the possibility that some depressed patients taking anti-depressants might actually be at increased risk for suicide. This information was based on data from controlled clinical research trials that showed increased suicidal thinking and behaviors in some patients. However, no actual suicides were reported in any study—only increases in suicidal ideation.[14]

According to Dr. J. John Mann, chair of American Foundation for Suicide Prevention's Scientific Council, several studies indicate "those areas of the U.S. that have the highest prescription rates of SSRIs, both in adults and children, have had the biggest falls in suicide rates."[15]

Nevertheless, as a result of the media attention, the U.S. Food and Drug Administration conducted public hearings in September 2004 to address the controversy. At that time, they decided to direct manufacturers of antidepressant medications to revise the labeling on their products to include a "black-box" warning that notifies health care providers and consumers about an increased risk of suicidal thoughts and behaviors in youth being treated with these medications.

While a number of clinicians are concerned that such labeling might decrease the use of these medications in young people who might benefit, the positive side of the FDA ruling is that it requires regular contact between the patient and physician. Hopefully, this will result in better monitoring of medication prescribed to children and adolescents.

It is important to note that prescribing medication is not an exact science. It often requires experimentation with different medications and dosages. Parents must work closely with the prescribing child psychiatrist. Properly prescribed medication can make a huge difference in a child's mental health, but parents need to be carefully educated about possible adverse effects. Don't be afraid to ask questions or voice concerns. A good psychiatrist counts on your observations as he or she formulates a treatment plan.

It is important to be particularly attentive because many people do not realize that a negative reaction (e.g. increased jumpiness or irritability, talking faster, staying up later at night, and having more trouble awakening) could mean a child diagnosed with depression may in truth be suffering from bipolar disorder and experiencing hypomania. This is sometimes induced by using an antidepressant without a mood stabilizer. Your feedback as a parent or caregiver is essential, since you, your child, and all those who support your family need to work as a team to help your child learn to manage his or her disorder.

There is no one-size-fits-all approach to coping with psychological illnesses. Psychotherapy and appropriately prescribed medication can help those who suffer from these illnesses by stabilizing their moods and helping them learn what triggers stress. This can result in a renewed ability to make positive choices. As a parent, a pro-active attitude, awareness, education, and treatment are your best tools in situations where your child's susceptibility to suicide may be greater than normal. Do your own research and talk with others who are also dealing with these issues. Check out local university-affiliated medical centers and learn about organizations or legislation that may assist you. For more information, check the resource list at the back of this book.

Children with a parent who may have suffered from a brain illness prior to ending his or her life also need reassurance and reminders that they are unique individuals with a different genetic make-up and a different set of life experiences than their deceased parent. No one is "fated" to die by suicide. More treatment options are available than ever before, and studies are underway to determine additional resources for health.

Eleven-year-old McLain, who has been diagnosed with bipolar disorder, says, "All I know is that I feel better since I started on the medicine. I used to be so sad and worried. I'm not so much anymore. My mom knows a lot about suicide and my illness. She trusts my doctor. They watch me to see how I am doing with my medication. My mom and I talk a lot about how I am feeling. Sometimes I get frustrated. I wish I didn't have this illness, but I know I have a choice about how I deal with it. I could be ashamed and feel sorry for myself, but I don't. I have learned not to be ashamed about the suicides in our family and the illnesses that caused them. My mom has taught me that choosing to be open and honest is the best way to help myself."

* * * * * *

Kathy, a mom who lives in Atlanta, Georgia, shares her story. I first heard of Kathy and her children, Parker and McLain, now fourteen and eleven, from Dara Berger, who featured them in her 2003 documentary, "A Secret Best Not Kept." Even though the impact of her husband Marty's suicide eleven years ago continues to reverberate in the lives of Kathy and her children, she is a positive force as a mom, as an educator, and as a suicide prevention activist. Kathy and her children have been involved nationally with SPAN (Suicide Prevention Action Network). They have lobbied for more money for suicide prevention and research on depression and mental illness. Both Parker and McLain have done public speaking for SPAN and are contending with their own illnesses.

KATHY'S STORY

"I have learned to be very direct with my kids about their illnesses."

My husband Marty suffered from bipolar disorder, an illness that went undiagnosed for many years—probably due to the fact that he self-medicated with alcohol. When he got depressed he would often talk about suicide. His depression became so bad that he was unable to do everyday, ordinary tasks. He described himself as feeling paralyzed.

Marty finally agreed to see a psychiatrist. Unfortunately, he was misdiagnosed as suffering from depression rather than bipolar illness, and was treated with an anti-depressant that didn't seem to work initially. Finally, after about three months he suddenly seemed "over" his depression, and we thought the antidepressant was a "miracle" drug. I realize now that he suffered from bipolar II, which differs from "classic" bipolar disorder. Both forms have full-blown depressions. However, those who suffer from bipolar II do not reach the psychotic heights of true mania. They experience what experts call "hypomania," a period of elevated, expansive mood and increased energy. Eventually his psychiatrist prescribed lithium after Marty "crashed" a few months later, but he never told us that he suspected Marty was bipolar.

By this time I was pregnant with our second child, and Marty was back in the depths of depression. Because he didn't tolerate the lithium and suffered from severe gastrointestinal upsets, we ended up getting him an appointment with a different psychiatrist who prescribed another antidepressant that Marty's siblings were taking. His brother and sister were supposedly stable, but in retrospect, I don't really think they were. Both of them made subsequent suicide attempts.

I didn't really understand about depression or bipolar illness then, but I know now that depression and other mood disorders can run in families and may go undiagnosed for generations. Marty's first experience with suicide came when he was nine and his father took his own life. Marty shared with me his memories of discovering his mother and sisters crying in the family kitchen early one Sunday morning. They warned him not to go outside, but, of course, being a curious little boy, he couldn't resist. What a trauma it must have been for him to see his father sprawled on the porch, dead of a self-inflicted gunshot wound. Tragically, his family never had any counseling or talked much about the suicide; they just buried him and went on.

Five years before Marty completed suicide, his sister shot herself. No one in the family talked much about her suicide either, but Betty's death triggered a major depression for Marty and his older siblings. They were all so susceptible. They all viewed suicide as a way out of their despair.

When Marty died we had been married seven years and I was six months pregnant with my daughter, McLain. My son, Parker, was two years old. I knew Marty was feeling tremendous pressure from his job in the weeks before his death. He made several comments about suicide and was drinking heavily. I had asked him several times to stop drinking, knowing that alcohol interfered with his medication, and we also had discussed hospitalization. He promised me he would go for treatment, but he never did. I felt angry, but mostly I was afraid.

The day before he took his life, he drove from our home in Georgia to Tennessee, where he called me to let me know he was there buying beer because Georgia law prohibits the purchase of alcohol on Sunday. I felt uneasy about his absence, and while he was gone, I searched his study. I found an empty gun box, but I didn't tell him I knew about the gun until the following night when I realized he was planning to kill himself.

We had a major confrontation that Monday evening. He hadn't showered or shaved all weekend…his hair was askew. He looked so disheveled, but he went upstairs and put on his suit. I told him I didn't want to have this baby without him, but he didn't respond to my talking, crying, and pleading. He just stared right through me, didn't say a word and went down to our garage in the basement where he proceeded to drink and smoke cigarettes. I was very worried, but I didn't know what to do, so I did nothing. He had made threats and attempts before that had failed, and I held onto the hope that he would not do the unthinkable. Exhausted and frightened, I went to sleep.

I remember hearing a shot that night, just one, but I didn't think much about it, as our neighbor is a policeman and often engaged in target practice. Looking back, I realize I was probably so terrified about

Marty's behavior that I went into some sort of denial. When I woke up in the morning and Marty wasn't there, I was scared and worried, because in the past, he had always come to bed eventually. I got up to take care of Parker, who needed to be fed. It was then I noticed Marty's car was still in the garage. I searched the house and our yard and when I couldn't find him, I called my parents.

My parents, who lived nearby, came right over. They called the police who found Marty's body deep in the woods behind our home in a sleeping bag. I guess it was obvious to them that since Marty had left a suicide note on his desk and had been seeing a psychiatrist (information I had reported in the initial interview before they began their search), that I wasn't involved with his death. So I wasn't treated as a suspect. I am grateful for that, as the routine grilling many spouses are often subjected to around their partner's death further traumatizes them. In the years since Marty's death, however, I have learned that many police organizations are training officers to respond to suicides more compassionately or at least bring someone with them who is trained to assist survivors.

I was stunned by Marty's death. I remember feeling like I was one step outside my body. Periodically I would realize that the most horrifying thing, my worst nightmare, had come true, *and* I was still functioning. I was taking care of all kinds of business on autopilot. It was like some other force was responsible for my ability to function. I'd call it my inner strength, my auxiliary power, my reserves being called to action. I was aware of knowing that I must do certain things even though I didn't really want to or feel like I could—like eating. I knew I had a baby inside me who needed me to take care of my body, her body, and that my two-year-old needed me to be the mommy he knew, not the grief-stricken, catatonic shell of the person I felt like inside. The numbness lasted until after the funeral. After that I'd go in and out of that state for many weeks, but I was always highly functional. No one but me knew that I was operating on battery power. Most everyone commented, "You are doing so well. How are you doing it?"

McLain's birth was a definitive moment of my grief. It was an equal mix of the best and worst experience I have ever had. I had a scheduled C-section, which was a blessing. My mother and sister were in the delivery room with me while my dad took care of Parker. My sister videotaped McLain's birth. The moment the doctor pulled her out, I felt Marty leave me. In my mind, I felt like he was, in some way, still alive while she was still in utero. The minute she took her first breath, in my mind he was gone. There is no "reality" in any of those thoughts, but it was my reality at the time. I let him go on that day, and I let go of a lot of grief at that moment. I had a new life, a new baby girl—a new beginning that I never asked for or wanted. I knew there was no other choice but to survive and thrive. I had an important endeavor ahead of me, and I had no idea at that time how wonderful and daunting it would be.

I cried every day for the first six months after Marty's death, although the intensity of my grief lessened with each passing week. I noted the first day I made it all day without crying. It was a huge milestone.

For many years, the most difficult days were my kids' birthdays, Marty's birthday, our wedding anniversary, and Christmas. On those days it was difficult fighting the urge to lament what he was missing and how much he would have loved seeing his beautiful children reach all those wonderful milestones we look forward to as parents. I wanted to be as completely happy as a parent should be on these usually happy days, but it was hard to do. I learned to push those laments out of mind with years of practice. They are fleeting thoughts now on those days, but they still make their appearance.

After many years, I have come to terms with the reality of our family's dynamic. We are a mom and two kids and I have not remarried. Maybe I will someday—I don't know. I really have no desire to get married, but I would like a partner. Early on it was difficult for me not to feel cheated on the children's behalf, but because they were young, they didn't understand what they were missing. Now, I accept the reality of our situation and rarely feel cheated, but since they are older, they are very aware of feeling deprived and sometimes express anger about this.

About two years after Marty's death, I got involved with SPAN (Suicide Prevention Action Network) because I knew I could make a difference. Most survivors of suicide are too grief-stricken or ashamed, or just want to put the suicide in the past and not talk about it, but I knew I could. I also knew I wanted to do the opposite of what Marty's family did after his dad's suicide, as their lack of action/attention obviously had impacted their entire family. I was determined not to have history repeat itself.

I read everything I could on bipolar illness and suicide and made as many professional contacts as I could. It was like I was arming myself for a great battle that seemed highly likely to occur in the future. I figured that even if I didn't need this ammunition for my family, I might be helpful to someone else. My first step was starting a survivors-of-suicide support group in my area because I had a driving desire to help others make it through what I experienced. The move into advocacy was the next obvious step. Also, I felt that my example, being outspoken and unashamed and wearing my response to this experience as my badge of courage, would be a positive thing for me to model.

I have great inner strength and good mental health. My parents are my main support system. They have been incredibly supportive and have helped our family emotionally and financially. It is hard to imagine what life would be like without them, especially when I realized my children were also struggling with mood disorders.

Even with all I learned about bipolar illness, which, relative to the general public, is a lot, it was still very difficult to identify the disorder in my children. They may have demonstrated symptoms earlier, but it wasn't until McLain was about eight and in the third grade and Parker was eleven, a sixth-grader, that I recognized problems. It seemed the two of them started having trouble at about the same time, but McLain was making the biggest fuss, so she ended up getting the most attention.

McLain has always been a very loving, physically demonstrative child, emotionally sensitive and highly intuitive. Her feelings are easily hurt, and at eight years old, she hadn't developed emotional resilience. After being bullied by a girl who was supposedly her friend, she *refused*, and I mean refused, to go to school. The bully moved a few weeks later, thankfully, but things didn't improve all that much—and then got a lot worse. She began having extreme temper tantrums, would hit me and throw things. At one point there were seventeen holes in the walls of our home, places she had damaged. She couldn't seem to stop, would say she didn't care if she was hurting anyone because she could only think about how much she was hurting.

Around the same time, I went to a mental health forum that featured Mike Wallace, William Styron and Art Buchwald. I got there because in the process of looking for help with SPAN Georgia activities, I had been communicating with Tom Johnson, the former head of CNN who was helping moderate the panel. He invited me to attend. Dr. Charles Nemeroff, who is Tom Johnson's doc and whom he credits with the successful treatment of his depression, was on the panel, and he had copies of his recent book, *The Peace of Mind Prescription*. I bought a copy and started to read it casually as part of my own education and work with SPAN. One evening I was reading a section about spotting bipolar illness in children and teens. As I read the case history by a woman regarding her ten-year-old daughter's behavior, I was astonished. I could have been the author. I was able to contact Dr. Nemeroff and get a referral to a local psychiatrist who deals with children and bipolar illness.

Finding a really good psychiatrist is so important. I can't stress that enough. Professional help can be very expensive, but not every doctor knows how to identify bipolar illness or depression in children, since the symptoms manifest differently. It seems that people are so in awe of doctors, blinded in some cases by the "god-like persona" we attach to them, that many fail to recognize that doctors don't always have all the answers or may not be up to date on the current information about specific illnesses unless they specialize in treating that disorder.

I have learned to put little faith in letting doctors do all the diagnosing. You have to be an advocate for your children, so I do the research myself and arrive at meetings as well-informed as I can be. I have learned that it is important to ask a lot of questions. Start with your child's school counselor to see what resources are available. Check the Internet and take a crash course on mood disorders in children. The website www.bpkids.org is a good resource.

I have also learned that because of the state of health care in this country, many families don't get the help they need unless someone is willing to be the "squeaky wheel." My HMO didn't help, as every appointment was six weeks apart and I didn't feel the doctor I saw was meeting the needs of our family. So I researched alternatives. I bought a health care policy that was minimal coverage with a low premium, because I fully expected to pay for most of McLain's treatment on my own. I wanted the best possible doctor for her, and I was willing to pay for it even if I couldn't afford it.

I used a pharmacy in Canada to get better prices on medications. At two hundred dollars an hour for the doctor and several hundred dollars a month for medications, it didn't take long for me to look for alternative methods to cover these high expenses. Our family is middle-income, so I didn't think we would qualify, but I discovered we were eligible for PeachCare in Georgia, which is Medicaid with a fancy name. This funding provides financial help for psychiatric services and medications. It covers all the kids' health care needs, which is a great help! Each state has something different, so you have to be persistent.

At first I was completely devastated when McLain was diagnosed as bipolar, but I have discovered this illness is more manageable than many others like leukemia or diabetes. We have had to try different medications to find a combination that worked for her.

The mood stabilizer she was on initially seemed to be working fairly well, but it made her sleepy in class and she also experienced weight gain, so we changed to another medication. The medications she now takes help with her anxiety and mood, with no apparent side effects. She has always had intense separation anxiety, but this has eased up with the medication, too.

She is feeling much better and doing fairly well, but we still struggle. Sometimes she seems to have an irrepressible agenda. She holds on to a concept, need, want or whatever like a pit bull. I have learned to ignore her when she gets this way, but often this precedes a meltdown. It doesn't seem to matter how calmly I say no, she persists endlessly. Next to the violence, it's the most upsetting to me.

I think because early on she overwhelmed me with the violent rages, I gave in to her in some ways. There really is no rationalizing with a completely irrational child. The normal parenting strategies are useless, and before I understood her illness, I felt like an impotent parent. I was really hard on myself and felt even worse when the people

I confided in as a way to get help, assumed poor parenting was causing her horrifying behavior. I missed having that very important parenting partner—her dad. I had no way to gauge my parenting, as no one else was there during those outbursts to see what was happening and help me evaluate. I kept those first meltdowns a secret for several months, but they continued to escalate to the point where I was forced to seek my parents' help. I think the secrecy and shame I experienced must be a lot like what spousal abuse victims report.

Parker was diagnosed bipolar as well, about a year after McLain. He has always been confident and articulate, and although I didn't recognize his illness initially, I never closed my mind to the possibility that he, too, might be diagnosed. It took us a while to figure out that he was also showing signs of having a mood disorder. McLain would fly into rages, hit me, and Parker would attack her. I really think his depression was triggered by his frustration and anger at McLain's rages, because he always felt he needed to protect me. He became increasingly irritable and non-communicative, behaviors that are often labeled as part of puberty, but coupled with his reactions to McLain's rages, I became concerned that his behavior was more than a hormonal reaction or a response to her outbursts. He was truly unhappy and seemed to be unable to express his anguish in a way that worked for him.

Medication has really made the difference in both kids. I wish I could say that the psychologist helped, but I honestly think that in our case psychotherapy did very little. Since Parker's antidepressant and mood stabilizer have been adjusted, he has been as normal as can be. He had a lot going for him before his diagnosis, and now that he's stable, he's a joy to have around. He's still a teenager and sometimes doesn't use the best judgment, but so far life is pretty good for him. His grades are back up and he's looking forward to high school. We communicate very well and very openly. I am so grateful for that.

I have learned to be very direct with my kids about their illnesses. McLain still has temper tantrums, but when she starts down that road, I remind her that although there may be a reason for her behavior, she still has to behave appropriately. I tell her that she has options—she can go to her room or stomp on the deck outside, but she can't throw things. I tell her she can't control what is going on in her brain, but she can control her response. I don't forbid her to have rages; I just forbid her to hurt herself or anyone else.

My kids have always heard me talk about their dad's suicide. I don't hide it from them. I remember one little boy in Parker's first-grade class who came up to me and asked me how Parker's dad had died. I stumbled a bit, but before I had a chance to think up an appropriate response, Parker, who was sitting nearby, said matter-of-factly, "He shot himself." The kids hate that their dad died by suicide, but they can talk about it. They feel no shame at all. The only perspective they have ever had is that their dad had an illness and it caused his death—no different from other kids who may have had a parent die from a car accident or another type of illness.

As far as what I say to other people, well, I don't tell everybody, but I am fairly open. I usually say he suffered from bipolar disorder and it caused him to take his life. After you say it a number of times, it isn't as hard anymore. I see this as my chance to educate others, but you don't have to tell everyone. Sometimes complete silence is the best way to respond to inappropriate questions.

Once in a while, however, there are people who are rude and persistent, who don't get the hint when you don't give details about the death. I remember the "Welcome Wagon" lady who came over when we moved into our new house. She was intrusive and overly inquisitive, and I finally told her, "He blew his brains out when I was six months pregnant." She left pretty quickly.

I am an optimist by nature, and I believe people underestimate their ability to turn things around. I am trying to model positive attitudes and behaviors. We still have difficult days, even with medication, but things are so much better. Knowledge is power, so I do my best to keep informed about current research and treatment. I realize medication is likely to be a lifelong commitment for my kids, but I am committed to keeping informed about alternative treatments as well.

My main job is caring for my kids, and that is the hardest job in the universe—and the most important one. I have also found meaning by being available to other survivors. My community is small, but I have been open about our situation, and people find their way to me. The kids and I have all done volunteer work for Suicide Prevention

Action Network as well as public speaking and lobbying for legislative reform around suicide prevention, education and treatment. I am very proud of my children. They are bright, loving, kind, and willing to share what we are going through as a way to help others.

This has not been an easy journey, and I have learned that it is important to take care of myself. I am also very lucky to have such wonderful support from my parents. I believe in living life fully, and part of living for me is being creative. I do mosaic art, taking pieces of broken china, glass, stones, shells as well as castoffs like costume jewelry, old coins, trinkets, etc., to create indoor and outdoor sculpture. Mosaic is a metaphor for life, an art form that takes pieces of the past and gives them new significance…it's a transformative process, creating new life, beauty, and purpose into a unique piece of art.

My life continues to be a transforming experience as well. I try to demonstrate and emphasize to my children my belief that it is through caring, sharing, and working together that we can expect the best of life, even though we have experienced terrible losses. I subscribe to a quote I once heard stated by former Surgeon General Dr. David Satcher: "Life is full of golden opportunities carefully disguised as impossible situations." I am a mom who has to deal with all those doubts, insecurities, and worries that all moms experience, but I also believe that life, even with all its difficulties, is always worth living!

CHAPTER EIGHTEEN

Grieving and Growing Over Time: The Wonder of Human Resilence

"Despite the passage of four decades,
I still wonder what he felt and thought, how he could
have left his children, why he would trade the
possibilities of the future for such a bleak certainty."
—ERICA GOODE, JOURNALIST
NEW YORK TIMES, 2003

In my work with children over the past thirty years I have learned an important truth. Children are warriors. They are more resilient than most adults believe. If given love, guidance, respect, and encouragement to be who they truly are, they are capable of bouncing back from great trauma and adversity.

That being said, no child "gets over" the death of a parent. We are forever changed by this profound loss. The suicide of a parent is deeply disturbing, creating both short- and long-term concerns. How any given child fares over time and into adulthood depends on a complex mix of personality, chemistry, the nature of her social relationships, and subsequent life experience.

The study of suicide has been mostly confined to those who end their lives, rather than those left behind. This is changing, however, as researchers begin to study survivors, though there are not as yet any long-term studies on child survivors. We don't know for sure what subtle imprints will be left by a parent's sudden exit. We do know that surviving children suffer more feelings of anxiety, anger and shame than children whose parent has died from other causes. They also have more difficulty accepting the death and more behavioral problems in the two years after the suicide.[1] But no one seems to know what the longer-term issues will be as children age. Realistic conclusions are difficult to draw because of limitations in both study design and in tracking children long-term.

Grieving Over Time

Children continue to grieve as they enter each new developmental stage. A toddler whose mother died may feel sad or confused the first time she makes gifts for Mother's Day in pre-school and realizes she doesn't have a mother like her classmates do. A teen graduating from high school is likely to be reminded of a parent's absence as he sees other kids posing for pictures with *both* parents at graduation ceremonies. Even when he becomes an adult, a survivor will continue to experience moments when he longs for the missing parent to share his joys or help him cope with challenges.

Seventeen-year-old Crystal relates how Father's Day continues to impact her every year. Her father took his life when she was nine, and her mother remarried three years later. Crystal now has two younger stepbrothers. "I always feel sad on Father's Day," she says. "My step-dad is pretty cool most of the time, but I just feel sad *my* dad isn't here. I guess I will probably always feel that way. I never thought he wouldn't be here to walk me down the aisle when I got married."

James, who was a self-described "wild teenager" when his father died, says his biggest regret is that his dad never got to see him become successful. "In my thirties when I finally turned the corner in my business, I experienced an unexpected sadness. I thought I would feel jubilant, but instead I found myself grieving again for my dad who had been dead for nearly twenty years. The depth of my feelings surprised me."

For me, becoming a parent myself brought me incredible joy as well as a deep yearning for my mother. I wanted to share the happiness I felt, but I also wanted her support, since being a new mom sometimes felt overwhelming. I wanted to know how she felt about my birth and if she breast-fed me or worried when she cut my fingernails for the first time. And when I felt uneasy about my son's crying or when giving him his first bath, I longed for her wisdom and experience.

For some who were unable to grieve following the death, intensely painful feelings can occur years later.

Actress and activist Jane Fonda's mother is believed to have suffered from post-partum depression and was eventually diagnosed with bipolar disorder. She killed herself when Jane was twelve. In her book, *My Life So Far*, Fonda recounts her experience: "When I was in my forties and the tears for Mother did finally come—unexpectedly and for no apparent reason—they were unstoppable. They came from so deep within me that I feared I wouldn't survive them, that my heart would crack open, and like Humpty-Dumpty, I'd never be able to be put back together again."

Encountering those "sneaker waves," or grief bursts that come without warning, can be disconcerting. As a Northern Californian who hikes along our wild, rugged coastline, I know that large waves can sweep up on the beach and carry off the unwary. Not long ago, I was browsing a store's book section and came across a volume on mother-daughter relationships. Just the picture on the cover of a teen and her mother, heads together, smiling as if they shared a special secret, was enough to bring tears to my eyes. I had not expected to have a mini meltdown at Costco. But such is the way of grief—even after all these years.

Reaching the Age of a Deceased Parent

When I turned thirty-seven, the age when my mother took her life, I remember feeling a sense of profound sadness that she had been unable to live beyond this time in her life. I found myself feeling more determined than ever to live my life fully.

Many other adults, however, report anxiety as they approach the age when their parent carried out suicide. Some worry that they have inherited suicidal tendencies and are destined to repeat the pattern. Vaughn, now in her sixties, recalls, "I was deeply depressed for several years in my thirties. I developed a phobia that I would die at thirty-six, like my father had. I remember locking up all the knives and staying away from balconies, fearful that I would have no control over my impulses. I couldn't talk about my depression. I felt so isolated and worried that I would be stigmatized if anyone knew—and I was terrified that maybe I would end up like him."

Karen, who was twelve when her mother died, was unaware of any trepidation about reaching the age her mother had been when she took her life. Because her mother was an alcoholic and abusive, Karen remembers feeling relieved following her death, although she recalls, "I couldn't say the word 'mother' for years—my lips would quiver. We never talked about her or got any counseling; we just moved from the area and went on with our lives. I see now that I buried my feelings, but I actually did well at everything after she died. I got married at twenty and became a successful realtor. I thought I was happy. Then, when I turned thirty-six, the same age my mother was when she died, I found myself on my bed in a fetal position, crying, 'I want my mom.' I was shocked at the intensity of my feelings. I thought I was fine and then here came this tremendous pain and longing. My family had always seen me as strong, together, and upbeat. This episode scared my husband. He didn't understand how I could be in such anguish and physically ill because of something that had occurred so many years ago. I was frightened, too. I wondered if, because there was craziness in my family, I would also go crazy. Fortunately, I knew I needed help, and I made sure I got it. The next few years were rough, but I believe I was born with a certain resilience. I do bounce back. I am stronger now, more compassionate, someone with scar tissue, but healing. I have learned to set boundaries and have deeper insights into life. I am more awake. I just wish I had gotten help as a child. I was so wounded by my mother's abuse and the circumstances of her death. A survivor needs to have therapy or some sort of group work/sharing experience to deal with the legacy of suicide, the guilt, sorrow and anger—and all those questions."

The Roots of Resilience

Researchers who study resilience say it is a complex process that can be as unpredictable as the weather. It seems to be a mix of body chemistry, individual personality, family and community support, and adopting a realistic view of the world—the good as well as the bad.

The research also indicates that resilient children tend to have at least average intelligence, with personalities that draw people toward them. These are the kids who were born with or have developed traits that make people like them. They are often described as cooperative and friendly. How this happens is, of course, one of those unanswerable nature vs. nurture questions. Are resilient kids born this way, or do they develop resilience as they try out behaviors and attitudes that garner them positive reinforcement from others?

Most research supports a combination of the two. According to a study done by Werner and Smith[2] that examined high-risk children from birth to adulthood, resilient children displayed the following characteristics:

- Affectionate and good-natured
- Good reading and reasoning skills
- Positive self-esteem

They were also able to develop an "internal locus of control," defined as a strong belief that they could control their fate by their own actions.

So, how does this happen for children who must cope with the suicide of a parent, an event that is clearly out of their control? Are there ways to help foster resilience in children?

Many experts believe that the most important factor in determining resilience is the strength of parental bonds. When that bond is disrupted by suicide, how a surviving parent copes is probably the most important factor in determining how a child will fare.

If you are a surviving parent, it is critical for both you and your children's sake that you do the work of mourning, which means exploring, expressing and learning to manage your own grief. Maintaining a strong connection with your children is also essential.

This means realistically assessing who your child *is* rather than whom you may want him to be. Take into account your child's personality, temperament, individual strengths and interests. What does he like to do? What makes him happy? Is he shy or more outgoing? Seeing your child as he is will help you structure his environment in ways that build self-esteem and promote physical, mental and emotional health.

While we can't necessarily teach resilience, there are some concrete things we can do to help a bereaved child (or any child) grow up healthier and happier. Suggestions include:

Encourage your child to develop a hobby or hone a talent. Kids who develop a skill that sets them apart from others often derive strength from the process. It can be anything—playing a sport or a musical instrument, becoming a good chess player or creative cook, or learning to ride a horse. The possibilities are endless.

Support your child in finding a champion or mentor. Every child needs positive relationships with other adults in addition to his parent—people who wholeheartedly believe in him. These champions might include a grandparent, teacher, coach, a friend's parent, a neighbor, youth group leader—any respected older person who can add to the child's web of emotional support. This extra attention often makes the difference for children who might otherwise fall through the cracks.

Help your child learn to problem-solve and develop a positive attitude. Some things are clearly out of a child's control. A parent's suicide is number one on that list. However, it is important to acknowledge that life is not just a question of luck. Your child can learn skills that will help her to stay safe and handle difficult situations. This requires her learning to look within and recognize what she can control. She can learn to evaluate her choices, take responsibility for how she expresses her feelings, and become aware of how she chooses to look at what happens to her.

Teach your child to ask for help. Let him know there are good people in the world who want to help him. Encourage him to be his own recruiter. This means helping him become aware of what behaviors and attitudes draw people to him in a positive way—smiling, being engaging and friendly rather than sullen or argumentative. Help him learn that if someone lets him down, he can find another who will not disappoint him. You must also be willing to model help-seeking behavior yourself.

Encourage your child to help others. Resilience studies indicate that children who are required to help others are more likely to rebound from adversity. Helping others can be as simple as raking leaves for an elderly neighbor or participating in a service project at school. Being of service to someone else allows a child to feel good about himself and more connected to others. Recognizing that other people also face challenges may help him put his own struggles into perspective.

All children need predictable routines and a clear set of behavioral expectations. Sometimes surviving parents and other concerned adults are inclined to let go of limits or expectations following the death of a parent. They become reluctant to push or discipline a grieving child. While some flexibility is necessary, being a passive parent or accepting all behaviors indiscriminately will ultimately make life more difficult for you and your child.

"After my husband died," reports Sylvia, "I could barely take care of myself. It seemed like my children were fighting constantly, and I couldn't manage them very well. That had always been my husband's job. My nine-year-old son immersed himself in video games and began to isolate himself. I tried to have conversations with him, but it was easier to let him go off to his room and play his games. At least he wasn't fighting with his sister. I noticed when he would get home from school he was very tired, but I just thought he was grieving. I didn't discover until his teacher asked me about his fatigue level that he was waking up in the middle of the night and playing video games for hours. I had to take the TV out of his room and take charge of his games. I didn't want to monitor his free time, but he couldn't handle it. Fortunately, my dad helped out by coming over after school several times a week to play baseball or ride bikes with the kids. My son joined

Cub Scouts and both kids now go to Homework Club twice a week. I still probably let them watch too much TV, but things are better."

So, let's talk about television. According to the American Academy of Child and Adolescent Psychiatry, children in the United States watch an average of three to four hours of television a day. Unfortunately, many of today's TV shows revolve around themes of sexuality, race and gender stereotypes, drug/alcohol abuse, and violence. The American Medical Association and other organizations have conducted numerous studies that show a correlation between extensive TV viewing and childhood obesity, early onset of sexual activity, increased alcohol and tobacco use, and increased aggression, delinquency and violence.

While some developmentally appropriate programs can enhance a child's education and creativity, too much time spent watching TV also takes away from important activities such as reading, schoolwork, playing, exercise, family interaction and social development. The American Academy of Pediatrics recommends that youngsters under age two not watch any television, that older children watch no more than two hours daily of "quality" programming, and that televisions be kept out of children's bedrooms.

Children who are coping with the death of a loved one are particularly vulnerable. They need contact with real people and the opportunity to develop communication skills. While alone-time and opportunities to distract themselves are important, they may also need limits around time spent with technology—computers and video games as well as TV viewing.

Search for Meaning

How we manage to pick up the pieces and move forward in our lives after a loved one's suicide is a challenge that we will face over many years. We hope not only to survive and rebuild our lives, but to again feel joy and purpose.

Many survivors become seekers, looking for ways to live meaningful lives. Although not everyone is able to transcend the impact of a loved one's suicide, many develop increased compassion and an awareness of how precious life is. They often celebrate life by becoming involved in meaningful work.

"I was six when my mother took her life," says Dan, a forty-three-year-old high school guidance counselor and the father of three sons, "and twenty-three when my sister did the same. I have taken the trauma of my own life and have turned it into something meaningful. With therapy, I realized I had gifts to share and a capacity to relate to young people who are struggling. It has taken a lot of hard work to deal with the legacy of suicide, but I was determined to break though my initial stoicism and emotional deadness. I am deeply committed to my wife and children as well as my students. I guess you could say I am a 'wounded healer,' but that makes me able to reach out to others in a way that brings me great joy."

Discovering what it means to be alive, what makes life meaningful, is a process we engage in over time. Many survivors discover the suicide of their loved one precipitates a new direction.

Sarah, referred to briefly in Chapter Eleven, is now a hospice chaplain in her fifties. She remembers when her partner took his life. "Ron suffered from alcoholism and depression. I cared deeply for him, but our relationship was troubled. We couldn't seem to go forward, and I broke things off with him. He ended up jumping off the Golden Gate Bridge. I was devastated and my children were distraught. They were in their late teens at the time, and although Ron was not their father, he was a father figure for them. I felt terribly guilty and had a very difficult time maintaining in my job as a nurse. I had been a Buddhist for many years, and during that year after his death, I decided I wanted to focus on my Buddhist practice. I eventually took the vows to become a nun, and I lived in a Buddhist abbey for three years. During this time I experienced my grief at a very deep level. When I was ready to be out in the world again, I decided to become a chaplain. I work with people of all faiths who are facing the end of life. My life feels purposeful even though I still feel sad and sometimes guilty about Ron's suicide. I know I have to experience all my feelings and not push them away."

Dara Berger was thirteen when her mom died. She remembers how hard it was "being the little girl on the block whose mother hung herself." She recalls: "No one would talk about what had happened, but

I knew some day I would—it just took me eighteen years until I found my venue." Dara directed and produced a documentary film, "A Secret Best Not Kept." The film is a journey of healing, learning and hope. It documents Dara's personal story and the story of others who have lost loved ones to suicide. "I had no idea how much doing the film would change my life. I met so many wonderful and loving people, many of whom I continue to have a relationship with today. Until I met them, I never understood how many people had suffered the same way as I did. I am just so glad that something so wonderful came out of that pain, something that could potentially help others."

Many survivors find meaning by joining organizations that promote awareness and raise money for suicide prevention. Others devote energy towards advocating for better resources on behalf of those with mental illnesses. And some, like Doreen Cammarata, write books. Doreen's children's book, *Someone I Love Died by Suicide*, was written in honor of her mother, who died when Doreen was nearly seventeen. "My mom was so spectacular—she lit up a room and was always so compassionate and loving, the kind of person everyone wanted to be around. Her depression began around my sixteenth birthday. Shortly after I turned seventeen she took her life. Before her death I was an insecure, scattered adolescent, but I grew up overnight. Fortunately for me, I had a wonderful high school counselor who, from day one, created a safe haven for me. She permitted me to grieve, and she educated my teachers about what I needed. She empowered me to take my experience and change my life. I became a high school counselor for at-risk youth, too, and eventually a grief and bereavement specialist. Now, as a partner to my husband and the mother of three active little boys, I am truly celebrating what it means to be alive."

Caroline, whose story was detailed in Chapter Four, and her sister now volunteer with me as helpers in my children's support group. Their brother is a "big brother" to a little boy whose mother died suddenly. Watching them each choose to be a positive force in the lives of other grieving children is truly heartwarming. They are transforming their experience into growth, creating meaning out of a traumatic event that turned their lives upside down.

Mark, whose mother took her life when he was eight, is a former East

Coast corporate attorney whose search for meaning led him to work in the non-profit sector. Now in his fifties, he directs an organization that aids homeless and mentally ill people. "The last time I saw my mother," he recalls, "she was stretched out on the living room floor with a Bible in her hand. I thought she was sleeping so I didn't wake her up before I went to bed. My dad, a brilliant rocket scientist who led aerospace design teams, told my five-year-old sister and me the next morning that she was dead and that there was 'no use crying over spilt milk.' This event, and my father's subsequent marriage to a woman who was the proverbial "wicked stepmother," disrupted my world. My stepmother also killed herself fifteen years into their marriage. Prior to her death, however, they both developed serious drinking problems. My father was eventually hospitalized for severe depression and treated with electroshock therapy that changed him forever. I will never forget visiting him in the hospital and seeing this incredibly brilliant man who someone might think was a stumblebum by the way he looked. But I now look at my mother's death, my father's mental illness and the alcoholism of those who raised me as my preparation. I have had enough pain in my background to be able to connect with the people I serve, people who are challenged by mental illness, homelessness or the inability to maintain a job.

"When I look back on those years, I feel sorry for that young boy who was overweight, unloved, and unlovable in his own eyes. I felt so very alone. I learned first-hand the hard lesson that at any time our lives can be turned topsy-turvy, and people can leave us at any minute. But I have also learned that when someone goes through something as hard as the suicide of a parent, it can result in the development of character and wisdom that isn't gotten through easier means.

"I feel happy in my own life now. I have been married nearly thirty years and have a deeply loving relationship with my wife and children. I am who I want to be—strong, empowered, and useful in my life."

Redefining Closure

I am frequently asked by other adults, "How will these poor kids ever make it after such difficult experiences? Do they ever get over it? Do they ever have *closure?*"

I have to admit—I don't like the word "closure." It's a tidy word without much meaning when connected to the loss of someone as fundamental to a child's identity as a parent. Closure is defined as "a finish; end; conclusion." It's as if there is an expectation that grief has a proper, predictable course—a beginning, middle and end. But we don't really "get over" our grief when a parent dies. With support, we eventually move through it so it no longer defines who we are. But the grief remains as a part of us. It ebbs over time, but it doesn't end.

Your child is likely to discover her own reservoir of feelings as she matures. She will learn that her parent's death will indeed shape her, but that the experience will, in time, become only one part of who she is. Her life story can continue to enlarge, rather than be constricted by this one tragic event. Rather than aspire for "closure," we can hope for the courage to come to terms with this great loss.

*   *   *   *   *

In the following story, sixty-seven-year-old Vaughn, the mother of four children and four grandchildren, who now works as a hospice nurse, describes her journey since her father took his life when she was nine years old.

VAUGHN'S STORY

"No one ever talked to me about my anger."

My dad, married and the father of two daughters, was a full colonel by the age of thirty-six. Our lives revolved around the military. I remember that day in 1944 when we took him to the disembarking station at Ft. Smith in Arkansas. I was wearing a green dress with white smocking and brown oxford shoes with green socks. It was not yet daybreak. I was seven years old and my dad was going to "The War." It would be two years before I would see him again.

My dad had always been very idealistic about war, reading every textbook available and listening to stories from his uncle who had been in the Civil War. He grew up dreaming about going to West Point. Military strategy was his expertise. He knew about every battle that was ever fought. But the reality of war turned out to be very different than his textbook understanding.

My mother, six-year-old sister and I were with the first group of families who crossed the Atlantic on military transport ships to be reunited with American servicemen following the occupation. I was so excited, knowing I would finally get to see my dad at last. I had missed him so much, remembering how we used to write in the sand together and how I always felt so safe with him. He was a southern gentleman from Tennessee, an only child with a big extended family who wrote daily to my mother and grandmother. He wrote my sister and I often as well, illustrating his messages with little bunnies, scenes from the countryside and other drawings designed to delight little girls.

He was a tall man, six-foot-three, who had a bit of a limp due to an arthritic heel. I'll never forget arriving at the train station in Germany and seeing a tall, lanky shadow in the distance, silhouetted by the bright station lights. I was so elated to see that long-limbed figure in the light, moving steadily towards us, his familiar gait confirming his identity. To me he was the father I had remembered, lifting me in the air, delighted by my presence. I didn't know then that the war had changed him.

We were together as a family in Germany for only six weeks before he took his life. During the time he had been away from us, he had been part of the constabulary that cleared out the camps at Buchenwald, and a member of the military team trying the Nazis, sitting in on the Nuremberg Trials. Prior to his war experience he had always seemed like a fairly calm man to me, mild-mannered and sweet. As a child, I didn't realize he was depressed and had developed a drinking problem. He had suffered in those years away from us.

We lived in an occupied German neighborhood with other officer families. One night my parents attended a party. My father became unhappy with how the MC of the event, a junior officer, was conducting the festivities. My father was drinking, and he became belligerent. He stepped onto the stage and hit the junior officer, an offense that was an automatic court martial in those days. General Patton had slapped a soldier some months earlier, and although he hadn't been court-martialed, his action had set in motion a statute prohibiting physical violence towards lower ranking officers. My father knew this.

His friends stepped in and took him and my mother home. My sister and I were in our bedroom with our two little puppies. We could hear our parents arguing. My mother was saying, "How could you do this? How could you behave this way?" I heard the door slam as she shouted, "Oh, just go to bed!!" She locked him in the room, fearing that he might wander around the house drunk, and frighten us. She came into our room with food for the puppies. As we were watching the puppies eat, we heard a crash. I thought a lamp had been knocked over.

I remember the look of panic on her face. She ran out of our room. Then I heard her screaming hysterically that he had "cut his throat." She doesn't remember saying this, but I heard her clearly. My whole body felt hot, a heat that registered in my nine-year-old mind as the house being on fire. I jumped out of the window and began yelling for the MPs, those wonderful men who had befriended us since our arrival. My sister just started jumping on the bed in our room and screaming.

My mother was running down the street crying out that my father was bleeding. Our good friends were arriving home from the party about this time, and they came to our aid. My sister and I were whisked away to the neighbor's house and never saw the ambulance come. We were told our dad had slipped and fallen, but we would be able to see him in the morning. I remember feeling excited about going to the hospital to visit him. We were told our mother was at a neighbor's house, so my sister and I settled into bed with our family friend's grandma. All three of us slept in the same bed that night, my sister and I each clutching our little dachshund puppies. I remember hearing those puppies playing. In the morning I discovered that they had had a tug of war under the bed and chewed up our friends' shoes while we slept.

The next day our dear friend Bill, who became like an uncle to us, came to walk us over to his house. As we walked past the gardens, holding hands, he said, "I want to tell you something while we are in

God's sunshine. God created a perfect world, but in that world there is sometimes sadness." I listened carefully, never thinking his words would relate to me. When he told us he couldn't take us to the hospital because our father had died during the night, I turned cold. I couldn't believe this could ever happen to me. We were military children. We knew people had died in the war, but we never thought death would come into our world.

I was stunned. I wanted to be with my mother, but in those days the doctors believed in sedation as a way to cope with grief. She was home, but we weren't allowed to see her. We were told she needed to sleep. She could not comfort us for weeks.

We went upstairs to where Uncle Bill's children were drawing pictures, and my sister started to draw. Uncle Bill stayed for a few minutes and then left, thinking we were O.K. I went out on the balcony and cried. I guess someone told Uncle Bill I was crying, because he came back out on the balcony and held me. That was the last time I remember crying with anyone there to comfort me. After that I cried alone.

Three weeks later my mother got a job with the military, and we were assigned to live in a compound of apartments. People tried to be kind to us, as everyone knew what had happened. My sister was able to receive their kindness, but not me.

I was very angry.

I wouldn't let anyone hug me or touch me. I abused my puppy. I would drop him on the ground. As soon as he yelped, I would pick him up and comfort him. I felt guilty and ashamed of my behavior. I knew people were trying to be nice, but I was so angry. No one ever talked to me about my anger.

We had a very sweet live-in governess who was a displaced person from Estonia. She was nineteen, very kind and playful. Sometimes I would play with her, but most of the time I acted out. She would have to drag me to the bus stop for school. I would kick and claw the whole way.

My mother got the brunt of my anger. One night she came to tuck me in as I was falling asleep. I was convinced that she was trying to smother me, and I fought her. She cried, trying to explain that she was just there to tuck me in, but I was furious with her. I was never angry with my father for dying. I blamed her. I felt her behavior the night he died had been too frantic, too hysterical. I was convinced that if only she had been calmer, more present, maybe she could have saved his life.

I was angry, but I also began to take care of her emotionally. She cried at night and would often fall asleep in her chair. I would check on her in the early hours of the morning, often guiding her to bed and getting her settled. But we remained distant. If only we had been able to cry together instead of grieving alone, so isolated from one another. Before this time I had seen her as a safe harbor, but I became overwhelmed by her continued neediness. I was angry that even though she could be responsible and loving, she was more often self-involved and unable to comfort me. She had come from a difficult background herself, was a wounded and abused child before that chapter with my father, but I still wish we had been able to connect in a different way. She is eighty-nine-years-old now and lives near me in an assisted living facility. It seems I have always been her caregiver, although now it's appropriate. I wanted her to take care of me back then, but we just couldn't seem to connect.

We never talked about my father's suicide. He had a military memorial service in Germany, a ritual that involved his empty boots being placed backwards on a horse. I didn't get to be involved in the funeral, because the adults felt children should be protected from the grim reality of death. They also believed children didn't really feel that deeply, but, of course, we did. We got the message that we weren't supposed to have feelings, so I hid mine.

I survived by creating fantasies to comfort myself. My favorite fantasy was that my father's roommate had died and the hospital had mixed up their IDs. I decided that my father was alive, but had amnesia. I would wander around the German village and imagine I would see him in the distance, walking towards me. In my fantasy I would approach him and ask him if he knew who I was, watch the initial confusion on his face, and then see a look of joy come over him as he recognized me. We would hug and live happily ever after.

I also loved those old Saturday matinees, the ones where the Cavalry would come and rescue everyone. Since I was a military child, I identified with the Cavalry heroes. I often created families in my daydreams, families with strong fathers, fathers who were always protective, fathers with solutions for everything, who took good care of me. In my real life I attached myself to friends who had strong relationships with their fathers, mostly other military families. My "Uncle Bill" was one of those kind fathers who included me in his family's activities.

I held on to my fantasies for a long time. My teachers would often tell me to "get my head out of the clouds," and they would mark on my report card, "Vaughn is a bright student, but she could do much better if she wasn't always daydreaming." I am grateful for my rich imagination and the ability to lose myself in daydreams. That helped me survive when my sadness got too overwhelming.

I remember the day the fantasy ended. We stayed in Germany after my father's death, but when I was seventeen, I went for a visit to my grandmother's home in Tennessee. She took me to the cemetery to see my father's grave. As I stood there, I felt a stillness come over me. I knew then that he was really dead.

My mother remarried five years after my father died. Lou was a good man, a special services officer who was playful and a tease, a protective male, but not really the fatherly sort. He was more like a big brother. My brother was born when I was fourteen, but Lou and my mom divorced ten years later. I was an adult by then, married with children of my own. I had transferred my need for a father figure to my husband, but he wasn't up for the job either. Our relationship ended in divorce.

Because I was never able to work with my grief as a child, any time I had a loss, my grief would come back full force. I experienced separation anxiety with anyone I loved. I would find myself feeling anxiety and deep sadness with every boy who broke up with me. I eventually suffered panic attacks in my second marriage, when I was in my late twenties.

Because of my own experience with loss, I was determined, to the point of obsession, to be there for my children. When the panic attacks began happening, I was very frightened. This, of course, exacerbated the anxiety, as fear of fear is the core symptom of the disorder. My family physician told me I had no physical problems. Not knowing how to help me, he referred me to a specialist who said my only hope for recovery was electroshock therapy. I spent thirty days in a hospital and endured fifteen sessions of this so-called treatment, a punishing experience that left me in a profound depression.

I know now that this course of "treatment" was wrong for me and unnecessary, but I had been raised to believe in authority figures. I wanted someone to tell me what to do. I didn't trust myself. My deep depression lasted for several years. I developed a phobia that I would die at thirty-six, like my father had.

Eventually I went to the library and researched anxiety and depression. I discovered Norman Vincent Peale. His book on the power of positive thinking began to turn me around. I found a gestalt therapist who helped me learn that my fear was simply a part of me, rather than an alien force to fear. I began to see that my anxiety and depression were signals, indicating that I needed to explore my inner world. When I felt anxious I learned that I needed to look at what was not working in my life, like my marriage. I began to ask myself who I was or wanted to be beyond being a mother. And in time, I began to work on my grief.

Therapy helped me get to know myself. That has been one of the gifts of grief. At sixty-seven, I can say that I have finally found some peace. As I look back on my life I see I have been working on learning to accept who I am in each moment. I am contentedly single, and I have a loving family who lives nearby. I have a wonderful job as a hospice nurse, caring for people at the end of their lives. I feel like I make a difference. I have been able to draw on my life experience, which enables me to feel that I am living a meaningful life. I have opportunities to grow. Death is no longer a mysterious or frightening concern.

I have learned that healing is the wrong word for resolving grief. We don't really heal totally, but our sadness becomes tolerable. If I could change anything about my childhood grieving experience, I would have had us grieve as a family. I yearned to be embraced and comforted by my mother. Isolation was all I knew. Because children don't know much beyond what they are experiencing in the moment, it wouldn't have been in my repertoire to say what I needed.

But I am comforted now. For many years I tried to consciously let go of my father. I would visualize him drifting off to heaven, but at the last minute I would grab his arms and pull him back to me. Ten years ago I had a significant dream. I had always had many dreams about him, sometimes at night, sometimes in daydreams. In those dreams, I was always a child. In this dream I was an adult, my current age, and he was that young man I remembered as a child. We hugged and he got on the plane and he flew away. Finally, I felt peace inside.

"Loss is our legacy. Insight is our gift. Memory is our guide."
—Hope Edelman, *Motherless Daughters*

The suicide of a loved one shakes our very foundation. Although a definitive answer to the "why" question is likely to elude us, we have learned that suicide seems to be the result of a confluence of events, most of which share mental illness as the backdrop. It is tempting to cite suicide as an "understandable" response to the pressures of life— relationship problems, shame, financial instability, legal troubles. But we know that everyone faces setbacks or hardships in life. For most people, however, these stresses do not trigger a suicidal response. Our basic instinct to survive does not permit us to end our lives, however deep our temporary despair.

Researchers have concluded that acute psychiatric illness is the single most common and dangerous trigger for suicide. When combined with basic life stressors or other factors (substance or alcohol abuse, impulsive personality, social isolation, family history of mental illness or violence, sexual abuse, access to firearms, or exposure to the suicidal behavior of others), the chance of suicide is greatly increased.

You may never learn why your loved one ended his or her life, but this death is like no other. It is not a gentle leaving in the night. You are left behind to cope with intense pain and a sense of betrayal. As Mary Pat McMahon, chair of the American Foundation for Suicide Prevention's Survivor Council, said at the end of the 2005 National Survivor Day Conference, "This is a journey. We become different people. We may look the same, but our priorities and interests change. Sometimes our friendships and relationships change."

What will not change is your love for your children and your deep commitment to seeing them through this trauma.

Children who lose a parent need two conditions to continue to flourish. They must have a stable, surviving parent (or another loving caregiver) to meet their physical and emotional needs, and they must have the opportunity and encouragement to express their feelings.

You may not feel very stable right now, but you will discover as you do the work of mourning that you can, as Therese Rando describes in her book, *How to Go on Living When Someone You Love Dies*, learn to "accommodate" your grief. While you may be steeped in acute pain now, you will eventually begin to socially and emotionally re-enter into everyday life.

Mourning is very hard work. It requires not only time, energy and determination, but also a softening of the emotional armor we instinctively put on to manage the intense pain that it involves. Mourning asks us to allow that pain and—particularly after a suicide—accept the reality of our circumstance, even as everything inside us wants to insist that it can't be true.

Because your loved one died by suicide, you must also realistically assess any history of mental illness in your family. It is imperative that you become educated about the symptoms and available treatment for these illnesses, both for your own sake and for your children, who may be at risk themselves. Be prepared to discuss these issues openly with your children, so you can change patterns that may exist in your family.

Knowledge is power. Helping your children become educated about brain disorders enhances their ability to monitor their own emotional states, and to reach out for help if they become depressed or begin to rely on alcohol or drugs to deal with their pain.

Suicide is devastating, but the brain disorders that contribute to suicide are treatable. It is our attitudes around these illnesses that must change. It wasn't that long ago that cancer was an illness that evoked secrecy and whispers. More recently, HIV/AIDS has come "out of the closet." But mental illness continues to be stigmatized. We haven't yet fully shifted our thinking to acknowledge that the brain, just like the heart or lungs, can become diseased.

The good news is that scientists and researchers are hard at work trying to learn more about illnesses that impact the brain and destroy lives. Significant gains are being made to develop medicines and treatment strategies to fight these illnesses. Sadly, our loved ones, many of whom may have suffered from brain illnesses, diagnosed or undiagnosed, did not get the help they needed. But there is hope for those who suffer now, and for the next generation.

I share deeply in that hope.

I have had the honor over the years of listening to many stories of love and loss from children who speak simply and often with great clarity. When words are inadequate or do not come easily, many express themselves through drawing or writing poetry. Although their stories often make me sad, I have learned that these are not children to be pitied. Instead, they are children who, with the support of caring adults, may be able to transform their experiences and become remarkable human beings.

As I mentioned earlier, I believe children are warriors. I count myself among them.

Several years ago during a teen grief support group I was leading, I participated in a writing exercise with the kids. We drew "angel cards"—each tiny card illustrated with a captivating angel and a word like love, discipline, communication, gratitude. I drew "forgiveness."

When it was my turn, I shared what I had written:

"For a long time after my mother died, I thought I was somehow to blame, that maybe she had gone away because I had done something bad. At four years old, I didn't understand what dying was about. And then when I was older and discovered that she died by killing herself, I was stunned. I was angry. I was hurt. How could a mother leave her children? I vowed never to do that to my children, believing such an act was unforgivable.

"Now, many years later, I understand she was frightened and feeling intense physical and emotional pain. She felt alone, without hope. I don't know why. I probably never will. But now I feel compassion. I grieve for her in those moments before she took her life. My anger is gone. I forgive her—and I forgive myself for not being enough to make her want to stay."

The American Academy of Child and Adolescent Psychiatry

3615 Wisconsin Ave., N.W.,
Washington, D.C. 20016-3007
202-966-7300
www.aacap.org
A non-profit membership based organization of child and adolescent psychiatrists and other interested physicians. Its website has a "Facts for Families" feature that provides up-to-date information on issues that affect children, teenagers, and their families. Does not provide individual consultations or referrals to specific child/adolescent psychiatrists.

American Association of Suicidology (AAS)

4201 Connecticut Ave., N.W., Suite 408
Washington, D.C. 20008
202-237-2280
www.suicidology.org
A not-for-profit organization that promotes research, public awareness programs, public education, and training for professionals and volunteers with the goal of understanding and preventing suicide. Sponsors an annual "Healing After Suicide" conference for survivors.

American Foundation for Suicide Prevention (AFSP)

120 Wall St., 22nd Floor
New York, N.Y. 10005
888-333-AFSP
www.afsp.org
A not-for-profit organization dedicated to funding research, developing prevention initiatives and offering educational programs and conferences for survivors, mental health professionals, physicians and the public. Has a user-friendly website that provides information and education about suicide and mental illness. Also sponsors an annual National Survivors of Suicide Day conference every November and conducts community walks throughout the U.S. to support survivors and raise money to fund research.

American Psychiatric Association
1000 Wilson Blvd.
Suite 1825
Arlington, VA 22209
888-357-7924
www.psych.org
Resource for referrals to psychiatrists.

American Psychological Association (APA)
750 First Street, NE
Washington, D.C. 20002-4242
800-964-2000
www.apa.org
Resource for referrals to psychologists.

Child and Adolescent Bipolar Foundation
1000 Skokie Blvd., Suite 425
Wilmette, IL 60091
847-256-8525
www.bpkids.org
Educates families, professionals, and the public about pediatric bipolar disorder; connects families with resources and support; advocates for and empowers affected families; and supports research on pediatric bipolar disorder and its cure. Excellent, easy-to-navigate website.

The Compassionate Friends
P.O. Box 3696
Oak Brook, IL 60522-3696
630-990-0010
www.compassionatefriends.org
For all parents and siblings who have experienced the death of a child, brother, or sister. Sponsors support groups, newsletters, and on-line support groups throughout the country, as well as an annual national conference for bereaved families.

Depression and Bipolar Support Alliance (DBSA)
730 N. Franklin Street, Suite 501
Chicago, Illinois 60610-7224
800-826-3632
www.dbsalliance.org
A not-for-profit organization committed to fostering an understanding about the impact and management of depression and bipolar disorder. Distributes information packets free of charge to anyone and maintains a toll-free information and referral line.

The Dougy Center
The National Center for Grieving Children & Families
P.O. Box 86852
Portland, OR 97286
503-775-5683
www.dougy.org
Publishes extensive resources for helping children and teens who are grieving the death of a parent, sibling, or friend, including, "After Suicide: A Workbook for Grieving Kids."

Healing Hearts Press
P.O. Box 1843
Sebastopol, CA 95473
www.HealingHeartsPress.com
Website with books, links and other resources for survivors.

The Hopeline Network (The Kristin Brooks Hope Center)
P.O. Box 151293
Alexandria, VA 22315-1293
202-669-8500
www.hopeline.com
HOTLINE: 1-800-SUICIDE (784-2433)
Non-profit organization dedicated to suicide prevention, intervention and healing by providing a single point of entry to community-based crisis services. Also focuses on bringing national attention and

access to services for postpartum depression and other women's mood disorders. Promotes education and advocacy through formal research and evaluation of crisis line services, and by championing the need for national funding for community-based suicide prevention crisis services.

Lifekeeper Foundation
3740 Crestcliff Ct.
Tucker, Ga. 30084
678-937-9297
www.lifekeeper.org
Promotes suicide awareness, education, and prevention through art forms such as Lifekeeper Jewelry, Poetry, and the Lifekeeper National Memory Quilt Project. Website shares photos of the Quilt Project and tips on making your own quilt and joining it with quilts statewide.

National Alliance for the Mentally Ill (NAMI)
Three Colonial Place
2107 Wilson Blvd., Suite 300
Arlington, VA 22201-3042
800-950-6264
www.nami.org
Grassroots mental health organization dedicated to improving the lives of persons living with serious mental illness and their families.

National Hospice & Palliative Care Organization (NHPCO)
1700 Diagonal Road, Suite 625
Alexandria, Virginia 22314
703-837-1500
www.nhpco.org
Nonprofit membership organization representing hospice and palliative care programs and professionals in the United States committed to improving end of life care and expanding access to hospice care. Each hospice program has a bereavement component and some have suicide survivor support groups.

National Institute of Mental Health (NIMH)
Office of Communications and Public Liaison
6001 Executive Blvd., Room 8184, MSC 9663
Bethesda, Md. 20892-9663
866-615-6464
www.nimh.nih.gov
Federal agency whose mission is to reduce the burden of mental illness and behavioral disorders through research on mind, brain and behavior. Website has lots of valuable information on mental health and a publications list on articles of interest to mental health practitioners, researchers and the public.

National Organization for People of Color Against Suicide (NOPCAS)
4715 Sargent Road, NE
Washington, D.C. 20017
202-549-6039
www.nopcas.com
Provides resources to minority communities: survivor support, suicide prevention and education, including an annual conference.

National Resource Center for Suicide Prevention and Aftercare
The Link Counseling Center
348 B Mt. Vernon Hwy.
Atlanta, GA 30328
404-256-9797
www.thelink.org
Provides suicide-related community education in the areas of prevention, intervention, and aftercare, as well as healing support services for families, youth and those affected by the psychological trauma of suicide. Maintains a national calendar of survivor and prevention programs.

Say It Out Loud Productions
www.sayitoutloud.com
A New York based production company that has produced a feature length documentary, "A Secret Best Not Kept" which explores the many dimensions of depression and suicide. The film features interviews with family members who have lost loved ones to suicide, attempters who have tried to take their own lives and the doctors who are trying to save them. It also focuses on advocacy, changing public policy towards mental illness and improving resources for those in need of help.

Social Security Administration
Office of Public Inquiries
Windsor Park Building
6401 Security Blvd.
Baltimore, MD 21235
800-772-1213
www.ssa.gov

Suicide Awareness Voices of Education
7317 Cahill Rd. Suite 207
Minneapolis, MN 55439
952-946-7998
www.save.org
Grassroots not-for-profit organization that educates about depression and provides resources on suicide and depression, newsletter, and survivor conference.

Suicide Information and Education Centre
Suite 320, 1202 Centre Street S.E.
Calgary, Alberta T2G 5A5 CANADA
403-245-3900
www.suicideinfo.ca
Computer-assisted resource library with extensive collection of materials on suicide, including information kits, pamphlets, literature searches, and clipping services.

Suicide Prevention Action Network (SPAN)
1025 Vermont Ave. NW, Suite 1066
Washington, D.C. 20005
202-449-3600
www.spanusa.org
Community-based advocacy group dedicated to the creation and
implementation of a national suicide prevention strategy. Programs for
survivors include Lifekeeper Memory Quilts (in partnership with the
Lifekeeper Foundation) and memorial day vigils.

Chapter Two • How Could This Happen?
1. American Foundation for Suicide Prevention Fact Sheet
2. Dunne, Edward, John McIntosh and Karen Dunne-Maxim, *Suicide and Its Aftermath: Understanding and Counseling the Survivors.* New York: Norton Press, 1987. p. 38.

Chapter Five • Teen Grief
1. Wallis, Claudia. "What Makes Teens Tick." *Time*, May 10, 2004: 54-65.

Chapter Thirteen • When Your Spouse Carries Out Suicide
1. Adapted from resource material distributed by Sutter VNA & Hospice, Santa Rosa, California.

Chapter Seventeen • When More Help is Needed: Depression and Bipolar Illness In Children
1. NIMH – "Depression in Children and Adolescents." Fact Sheet for Physicians, November 2003. Birmaher B., Ryan N.D., Williamson D.E., et al. Childhood and adolescent depression: a view of the past 10 years. Part I. *Journal of the American Academy of Child and Adolescent Psychiatry*, 1996; 35(11): 1427-39.
2. NIMH – "Depression in Children and Adolescents." Fact Sheet for Physicians, November 2003. Klerman G.L., Weissman M.M., Increasing rates of depression. *Journal of the American Medical Association*, 1989; 261: 2229-35.
3. Wingert, Pat and Barbara Kantrowitz, "Young and Depressed." *Newsweek*, October 7, 2002.
4. Ibid.
5. Jamison, Kay Redfield. *Night Falls Fast.* New York: Vintage Books, 2000. CNN review, December 1, 1999.
6. *Lifesavers*, American Foundation for Suicide Prevention, Winter 2005.
7. American Psychiatric Association. *Diagnostic and Statistical Manual of Mental Disorders, Fourth Edition*—DSM IV, Washington, D.C.: American Psychiatric Press, 1994.

8. Adapted from NIMH – "Depression in Children and Adolescents." Fact Sheet for Physicians, November 2003, and Charney, Dennis S. and Charles B. Nemeroff. *The Peace of Mind Prescription*. New York: Houghton Mifflin Company, 2004. p. 174.
9. Charney, Dennis S. and Charles B. Nemeroff. *The Peace of Mind Prescription*. New York: Houghton Mifflin Company, 2004. p. 180.
10. The Child and Adolescent Bipolar Foundation. "Pediatric Bipolar Disorder Fact Sheet." www.bpkids.org
11. Demitri and Janice Papolos, *The Bipolar Child*. New York: Broadway Books / Random House, 2002. p. 16.
12. National Mental Health Association Fact Sheet. *The Harvard Mental Health Letter*. February 1993.
13. Charney, Dennis S. and Charles B. Nemeroff. *The Peace of Mind Prescription*. New York: Houghton Mifflin Company, 2004. p. 177.
14. Ibid. p. 178.
15. *Lifesavers*, American Foundation for Suicide Prevention, Winter 2005.

Chapter Eighteen • Grieving and Growing Over Time: The Wonder of Human Resilience

1. Cerel, Julie and others. "Suicide-Bereaved Children and Adolescents: II. Parental and Family Functioning." *Journal of the American Academy of Child and Adolescent Psychiatry*, April 2000.
2. Werner, E.E. and R.S. Smith, *Overcoming the Odds: High-Risk Children from Birth to Adulthood*. New York: Cornell University Press, 1992. p. 55-58.

Alvarez, A. *The Savage God*. New York: Random House, 1979.

American Psychiatric Association. *Diagnostic and Statistical Manual of Mental Disorders, Fourth Edition*. Washington, D.C.: American Psychiatric Press, 1994.

Blauner, Susan Rose. *How I Stayed Alive When My Brain Was Trying to Kill Me*. New York: HarperCollins, 2003.

Bolton, Iris, and Curtis Mitchell. *My Son, My Son*. Atlanta: Bolton Press, 1983.

Brautigan, Ianthe. *You Can't Catch Death: A Daughter's Memoir*. New York: St. Martin's Griffin, 2000.

Brown, Sue. "Death Does Not End a Relationship." *The Therapist*. March/April 2005.

Cerel, Julie and Mary Fristad, Elizabeth Weller and Ronald Weller, "Suicide-Bereaved Children and Adolescents: II. Parental and Family Functioning." *Journal of The American Academy of Child and Adolescent Psychiatry*. April 2000.

Charney, Dennis S. and Charles B. Nemeroff. *The Peace of Mind Prescription*. New York: Hougton Mifflin Company, 2004.

Coles, Robert. *The Spiritual Life of Children*. Boston, Massachusetts: Houghton Mifflin Company, 1990.

Deltito, Joseph A. "Do SSRIs Increase the Risk of Completed Suicide in Depressed Children or Adults?" *Mental Health News*. White Plains, NY. Summer 2004.

Didion, Joan. *The Year of Magical Thinking*. New York: Alfred A. Knopf, a division of Random House, 2005.

Doka, Kenneth (editor). *Children Mourning, Mourning Children*. Washington, D.C.: The Hospice Foundation of America, 1995.

_____. *Living with Grief After Sudden Loss*. Washington, D.C.: The Hospice Foundation of America, 1996.

_____. *Living with Grief: Who We Are, How We Grieve*. Washington, D.C.: The Hospice Foundation of America, 1998.

_____. *Living with Grief: Children, Adolescents and Loss*. Washington, D.C.: The Hospice Foundation of America, 2000.

_____. *Disenfranchised Grief*. Lexington, MA: Lexington Books, 1989.

Dougy Center. *When Death Impacts Your School, A Guide for School Administrators*, Portland, Oregon.

_____. *Helping the Grieving Student" A Guide for Teachers*, Portland, Oregon.

Dunne, E.J. and Karen Dunne-Maxim. *Suicide and Its Aftermath*. New York: Norton Press, 1987.

Edelman, Hope. *Motherless Daughters*. New York: Bantam Doubleday Dell Publishing Group, 1994.

Fine, Carla. *No Time to Say Goodbye*. New York: Doubleday (Main Street Books) 1997.

Fitzgerald, Helen. *The Grieving Child*. New York: Simon and Schuster (Fireside Books) 1992.

_____. *The Grieving Teen*. New York: Simon and Schuster (Fireside Books) 2000.

Fonda, Jane. *My Life So Far*. New York: Random House, 2005.

Fry, Virginia Lynn. *Part of Me Died, Too*. New York: Dutton Children's Books, 1995.

Gravelle, Karen and Charles Haskins. *Teenagers Face to Face with Bereavement*. New York: Simon and Schuster (Julian Messner) 1989.

Grollman, Earl A. Suicide: *Prevention, Intervention, Postvention*. Boston: Beacon Press, 1988.

_____. *Talking About Death: A Dialogue Between Parent and Child*. Boston: Beacon Press, 1990.

_____. *Straight Talk about Death for Teenagers*. Boston: Beacon Press, 1993.

Hames, Carolyn C. "Helping Infants and Toddlers When a Family Member Dies." *Journal of Hospice and Palliative Nursing*. Vol. 5, No. 2, April-June, 2003.

Hammer, Signe. *By Her Own Hand*. New York: Soho Press, 1991.

Hample, Stuart and Eric Marshall. *Children's Letters to God*. New York: Workman Publishing, 1991.

Harris, Maxine. *The Loss That Is Forever*. New York: Penguin Books, 1995.

Hewett, J. H. *After Suicide*. Philadelphia: Westminster Press, 1980.

Jamison, Kay Redfield. *Night Falls Fast*. New York: Vintage Books, 2000.

Kluger, Jeffrey and Sora Song, "Young and Bipolar." *Time*, August 11, 2002.

Kremetz, Jill. *How It Feels When a Parent Dies*. New York: Albert Knopf, 1981.

Kroen, Willian C. *Helping Children Cope with the Loss of a Loved One*. Minneapolis: Free Spirit Publishing, 1996.

Kübler-Ross, Elisabeth. *On Death and Dying*. New York: Macmillan, 1970.

Kuehn, Eileen. *After Suicide*. Mankato, Minnesota: Capstone Press, 2001.

Kuklin, Susan. *After a Suicide*. New York: G.P. Putnam's Sons, 1994.

LeShan, Eda. *Learning to Say Good-bye*. New York: Avon Books, 1976.

National Institute of Mental Health. "Depression in Children and Adolescents: A Fact Sheet for Physicians." Bethesda, MD.

Papolos, Demitri and Janice. *The Bipolar Child*. New York: Broadway Books/Random House, 2002.

Parker, Rebecca, and Karen Dunne-Maxim. *Child Survivors of Suicide: A Guidebook for Those Who Care for Them*. Booklet published by the American Foundation for Suicide Prevention, New York, NY.

Pfeffer, Cynthia. "Children Bereaved by the Suicide Death of a Loved-One." *Mental Health News*. New York City Section. Winter 2004.

Rando, Therese A. *How To Go On Living When Someone You Love Dies*. New York: Bantam Books, 1991.

Remen, Rachel Naomi. *Kitchen Table Wisdom*. New York: Riverhead Books, 1996.

Robinson, Rita. *Survivors of Suicide*. Santa Monica: IBS Press, 1989.

Rogers, Fred. *You Are Special: Neighborly Wisdom from Mr. Rogers*. Philadelphia: Running Book Publishers, 2002.

Rubel, Barbara. *But I Didn't Say Goodbye*. Kendall Park, NJ. Griefwork Center, Inc. 1999.

Schuurman, Donna. *Never the Same*. New York: St. Martin's Press, 2003.

Silvermann, Morton M. "SSRIs and Suicidal Behaviors." *Lifesavers*, Vol. 17, No. 1, Winter 2005.

_____."Does Suicidal Behavior Run in Families?" *Lifesavers*, Vol. 16, No. 3, Fall 2004.

Simon, Leslie and Jan Johnson Drantell. *A Music I No Longer Heard*. New York: Simon and Schuster, 1998.

Smolin, Ann, and John Guinan. *Healing After the Suicide of a Loved One*. New York: Simon and Schuster (Fireside Books) 1993.

Styron, William. *Darkness Visible*. New York: Random House, 1990.

Trozzi, Maria. *Talking With Children About Loss*. New York: Penguin Putnam Inc. (The Berkeley Publishing Group) 1999.

Wallis, Claudia. "What Makes Teen Tick." *Time*, May 10, 2004.

Werner, E.E. and R.S. Smith, *Overcoming the Odds: High-Risk Children from Birth to Adulthood*. New York: Cornell University Press, 1992.

Wingert, Pat and Barbara Kantrowitz, Brian Briker, Daren Springen, Ellise Pierce, "Young and Depressed." *Newsweek*, October 7, 2002.

Wolfelt, Alan D. *Healing the Bereaved Child*. Fort Collins: Companion Press, 1996.

_____. *Sarah's Journey*. Fort Collins: Companion Press, 1992.

Worden, J. William. *Children and Grief*. New York: Guilford Press, 1996.

Wrobleski, Adina. *Suicide: Why?* Minneapolis: Afterwords, 1995.

_____. *Suicide: Survivors, A Guide for Those Left Behind*. Minneapolis: Afterwords, 1994.

Wybrow, Peter. *A Mood Apart: Depression, Mania and Other Afflictions of the Self*. New York: HarperCollins, 1997.

Kay Field

M argo Requarth was just under four years old when she lost her mother to suicide. Today, she is the child/teen bereavement services director at Sutter VNA & Hospice in Santa Rosa, CA, where she leads grief support groups, trains volunteer facilitators, and provides crisis intervention to schools and community groups facing bereavement situations. Her nearly thirty-five-year career in the mental health field also includes private practice as a licensed marriage and family therapist and service on the board of directors for the Northern California Chapter of the American Foundation for Suicide Prevention. A graduate of University of California, Santa Barbara and the master's program in clinical psychology at Sonoma State University, she lives in Sebastopol, CA, with her husband, Mike. The couple has two grown sons, Adam and Brian.

40200592R00157

Made in the USA
Middletown, DE
05 February 2017